Our Journey
A Lifetime of Adventure

---

for Jean,
old friend and Wednesday
Walker for all the years.
much love,
Lucy

When I'm on my journey, don't you weep after me
I don't want you to weep after me

Every lonely river must go down to the sea
I don't want you to weep after me

High up on that mountain leave your sorrows down below
I don't want you to weep after me

When the stars are fallin' and the thunder starts to roll
I don't want you to weep after me

Singin' songs of glory, don't you weep after me
I don't want you to weep after me

When I'm on my journey don't you weep after me
I don't want you to weep after me
After me.

~Old Spiritual, sung by The Weavers

Contact the author: lucy@littlebearcreek.co
Cover design: Pat Torpie

All poetry (unless otherwise noted) by Lucy Dougall from The Simple Life,
(c.2014, Lulu), Home and Away, (c. 2011, Third Place Books), Migrations,
(c.2008, iUniverse), and Orkney Days (c.2000, Puget Sound Press).

ISBN 978-1-387-09952-8

Contents

Written for Bill & Lucy
on the occasion of their 50th Wedding Anniversary

Don't Wait

Don't wait for the clear and sunny day, the Chinook wind
For the northern lights on a full moon in August
And all the bills to be paid.
Don't wait for the perfect night's rest, and the one morning
When every joint and muscle flows like smooth silk
And the house is clean.

While others lie in bed sleeping
We will be out climbing the summit, hoisting the mainsail
Hearing the crack of a log as it rolls
on the windy shore.
While others lie in bed dreaming
We will be dancing on tables, drinking wine
And singing the old songs
Jumping from balconies onto the midnight sand.

And when the dawning comes, we will wake up knowing
The party was ours.

~Sorrel North

Foreword
by Lucy

In his final years Bill often used to say, "And to think, I could have missed it." He was, of course, referring to the incredibly fortunate circumstances that led to our partnership and a lifetime of travel and adventure. I felt the same way. Somehow, Bill and I together became more than we ever could have ever imagined before we met. Our mutual love of family, adventure, hiking and travel led to such a rich and unusual life, we both thanked our lucky stars for the grand alignment that brought us together.

This book covers only a small sampling of the many and varied adventures the two of us took over the course of our 62-year marriage. Both of us had the forethought to write up most of our trips shortly after they occurred—and a good thing that was, considering how memory fails!

We spent sabbatical years living in Australia, Chile, Kenya, Nepal and Scotland—entire adventures unto themselves. People often assume that we had exceptional resources that allowed us to take so many trips, but for many of those years, we lived entirely on Bill's schoolteacher salary. We traveled on a shoestring, piecing together equipment for our five children from rummage sales and thrift shops. We took them skiing in the mountains wearing jeans and sweaters, on old wooden skis with lace up boots. We went beach hiking wearing the same gear, with ancient backpacks and plastic tarps for sleeping. We often piled the children into our Carryall for a spontaneous trip down to the Ape Caves or to scramble the vertical mile up to Lake Serene. Bill and I never saw family as an impediment to adventure—we loved the chaos and excitement, and put up with the occasional grumbling of one wet and bedraggled child or another.

As the children grew up and went off on their own adventures, Bill and I branched out and began taking longer, more strenuous hikes. This book is heavy on beach hikes. There was really nothing we loved more than being out on the wilderness beaches of the Pacific Northwest, and the stories here were chosen because of memorable circumstances. But they are only a handful of the hundreds of glorious hikes we were lucky enough to take in the days before everyone discovered camping. Many of our trips abroad were left out, because they were just too long, or didn't warrant an entire story. Some of them linger in my mind as moments in time, and often as colors; like skiing across Iceland by night, when the reflection from glittering ice crystals turned the ice cap a glorious violet. Or watching the Merry Dancers (the northern lights) ripple in green and crimson waves across the winter sky on Orkney Island. I can still see the brilliant turquoise waters of the Caribbean as we sailed through the islands. And when I think about our madcap trip across Spain, I picture Jonathan piloting our great white van, nicknamed Moby Dick.

My life has been a grand and glorious adventure. And to think, if I hadn't met Bill, I could have missed it.

Every lonely river must go down to the sea...

Hikes and Climbs
on the
Olympic Peninsula

In celebration, what to do but pass around
the chocolate and the wine
and start singing?

from Fire of the Gods, **Home and Away**

The Death March
by Bill & Lucy

Bill: This hike has become known as the "Death March," probably because it caught most of the seven participants—also known as The Magnificent Seven—at a time of life when they were closing in on middle age, when comfort and assurance of what is going to happen next becomes a dominating urge. This time in America was the early 1960's. Prosperity was on the rise because of the Eisenhower administration, McCarthyism was all but gone, the Peace Movement was in full flood, and folk singing was becoming a popular enthusiasm. Lucy and I had become caught up, no, swept up, into a nucleus of people full of energy and excitement. The others in this group were Ann and Dave Stadler, Annick and Dave Smith, Bill and Elen Hanson, Dave Nash, Dick Levin, Justine Sires, and maybe some others. Everything was exciting to this group, with energy and motion being the dominating theme. This was expressed by frequent meetings at someone's house, as often as several times a week to eat, argue, discuss, sing, dance, go to movies, and just be together.

Lucy: The idea was conceived one evening at the Stadlers', in late winter of 1961-2. The old gang had gathered, as we did regularly—often several times a week at either our house or the Stadlers'—to sing, dance, eat, play Ping-Pong and get into passionate discussions about everything from Ingmar Bergman to relativity. It was the era of Pete Seeger and all the great peace and protest songs, when hopes were high that the world could be changed for the better. Bill Hanson, Anne Stadler and I met each other on the Peace Section of the American Friends Service Committee and from then on were fast friends, as were our families. It was also the era of the great movie directors. We loved going to movies together and dissecting them endlessly afterwards.

Bill: Often, when a gathering for dinner at someone's house was going to occur, I went directly there after leaving teaching and coaching at the Lakeside School, where I was still a new teacher. This particular Tuesday, the party lasted almost all night at the Stadlers' house in Lake Forest Park. I slept there on the floor, got up, and went back to work, with my teacher work clothes being a little more wrinkled. At one point in this evening, with my specialty position of outdoor activities, I was tying the outdoors and important principles together by talking about William O. Douglas, who at that time was a giant figure in liberal causes. He was also a sort of duffer outdoor enthusiast, but a very important one because he was one of the early preservationists, beating the drums before Rachel Carson's *Silent Spring* opened the floodgates of activism for preserving the environment. His name was a strong stamp of approval for any liberal in those days. I described his leading a publicity trip on one of the Washington wilderness beaches to publicize protecting it against developers. I added that I had always wanted to walk that stretch of beach but had never really had the opportunity to do it (climbing had pre-empted all my attention in recent years).

Lucy: Dave Smith immediately said, "Let's do it next weekend." Five more of us chimed in, making seven all together; David and Annick Smith, Anne Stadler, Bill Hanson, Dave Nash, Bill and me, thereafter known as The Magnificent Seven. We picked the middle segment, from Rialto beach (across the Quileute River from La Push) going north to Lake Ozette. Ruth Kirk's first book, *One Hundred Hikes* had not been published yet, so all we had to go on was Bill's memory of Douglas' description in his book *My Wilderness, the Pacific West*. Bill was the only one who knew about hiking. Some had never camped out, no one had much in the way

4

of equipment, but we were all young and eager and ready for anything

A few of us had Trapper Nelson packs, the original frame pack but made of wood; others had the old back breaking peddler knapsack variety. We wore a rag-tag mix of old clothes, sneakers and hiking boots. Rain pants had not been invented but some had ponchos. No one had a tent so two sheets of plastic were to serve as shelter. I can't remember what sleeping bags we begged or borrowed. For food, we carried cans of spaghetti.

Bill: What we were agreeing to do is considered (even in comfortable, competent, present times) as a major outdoor hike for experienced well-equipped hikers. In addition, it was still winter; about the first weekend in March, 1961. None of us had any sense of the effect of tides. Lucy knew about them because of having spent her youth on the Atlantic shore, but on those wide beaches you could just go higher or lower to avoid waves. As well, her experience was with five-foot tides, not 10 to 12 foot tides (and blocking sea cliffs). In effect, none of us had any concept of what tides might mean on the Pacific wilderness shore.

I contacted a close climbing friend, Dave Collins, and interested him and his wife in ferrying our car from Rialto to Lake Ozette. Friday after work, the seven of us got into our family car, a Plymouth station wagon, with the far rear seat facing backwards, and got ourselves out somewhere close to the beach and slept by the side of the road. The next morning we drove to the end of the road and found Dave and Joanne Collins and their small baby camped in the woods near Rialto Beach.

Lucy: After saying good-bye to the Collins, we hoisted our packs and started along the Rialto shore. Black sand and pebbles ground like rasps under the incoming waves. The sea was awash with logs, thudding against each other, rolling up the steep beach, leaving no safe place to walk. We crawled along giant driftwood logs, hoping they would stay anchored and made mad dashes between them. Bill was about to warn people of the danger of floating logs when a large wave swept an inattentive Bill Hanson off his feet. We saw him on his hands and knees, pack on back like a turtle, clawing his way up to dry land. He retired into the brush to change and emerged triumphantly carrying the first Japanese green glass float. Someone else was left marooned on a rock, water swirling around him. It was *sauve qui peut* from then on.

Bill: After watching Bill Hanson crawling on his hands and knees through the waves, I thought, "the poor guy, he's only 200 feet from our car and he's soaked already." But with a calm he has shown in many awkward situations since then, he stayed cheerful and unruffled. We later found out that we were encountering the highest tides of the season, and it was now full high tide. My reaction to the waves was to stay up in the old driftwood at the top of the beach, and, looking north, I could see the others doing the same. At the very highest tides, the biggest waves wash up into the driftwood logs and actually float them, and this was starting to happen. We were all making great efforts to keep our feet dry, even Bill after he emptied his shoes of water. Working our way slowly along in the driftwood, we finally reached the hole-in-the-wall sea arch. It was mid afternoon by now.

Lucy: The sun came out for our lunch, the beach was beautiful, and we lolled around eating and drinking—there seemed to always be a spot of liquor—still happily oblivious to the impact of the tides. Coming from the east coast or Midwest as we did, we had no idea the Pacific had such a variation (up to 12 feet), nor that there were headlands that you could not get around except at low tide. In any case, we were all grasshoppers at heart, living in the moment, laughing and joking, enjoying ourselves thoroughly. Perhaps we unconsciously thought Bill knew what he was doing, or perhaps we didn't think at all.

Bill: There was no possibility of going through the hole in the wall sea arch because of the high water. Instead we had to climb over the headland. As we scrambled up a sort of path, I looked back down and saw Dave Smith and Ann Stadler between two great logs, a wave rocking the seaward log, with them in-between. I still have this image of Ann having a hand on the log, fending it off as it rocked towards her. With time, the tide gradually went out. After getting off the headland, the beach re-emerged from the waves, and we started making some speed. The beauty of the beaches as they widened raised our spirits. As we rounded the headland leading to the bay before Cape Johnson, spirits were high and photos were taken of us posing and clowning. It was about 5 pm, and we had no idea where we were. I don't remember any maps. So we walked on, now able to be on sandy beaches with no threatening waves and making great progress.

I had heard that there was an old coast guard cabin at a place called Cedar Creek, sort of up on a headland buttress near the creek. So we walked on, and finally reached a prominent stream that indeed was Cedar Creek. But by this time it was now black dark. I proposed to try to find the old cabin, and Bill Hanson produced from the details in his pack a miniature flashlight and offered to accompany me. My feet were still quite dry, and I remember the dwarf flashlight because he shined it away from me as I was rounding the headland and just about to step into a tide pool, which I did. I felt great unhappiness at finally getting a foot wet. Bill went back to the group about this time, and I literally felt my way along the base of the headland and actually crawled on hands and knees up to the top and felt around in the dark for a cabin, but found only brush. I crept across the headland on hands and knees because I wanted to actually be able to feel what was ahead of me in case I came to a cliff.

Lucy: Bill left us on the rocks, telling us firmly to stay put while he went inland and up the headland to scout around for the cabin. After a long wait, he returned to report that the cabin was gone. We scrambled up the slope and searched around until we found a flattish spot for the tarp, after which we hungrily opened the cans of spaghetti. In those days we never had to worry about water. It was everywhere and perfectly pure. We must have built a fire but I don't remember it. I do remember singing and talking and lining up our sleeping bags in a row on the tarp and then laying the other one across to keep off the rain. After all the others fell asleep, a momentary wave of fear swept over me—it was my first night out in the wilderness—but I felt comforted at once, knowing that I was with our little band of friends.

Bill: Ann Stadler actually brought pajamas, which she put on. All I took off were my boots. Spirits were high and lightness was in the air with laughs and little jokes. We all slept well beyond sunrise.

The concept of tides coming in and beaches disappearing had not arrived, so there was no feeling that we should be up and away. Being out there together was by itself a wonderful atmosphere, so we came awake slowly, in good spirits, dressed, and had a lengthy breakfast during which—it being Sunday—hymns and other songs were sung, wine was drunk, and a wonderful feeling of friendship was upon us all. Eventually, late in the morning, we packed up and walked down to the beach, a still moderately wide beach, but one that was being reduced by an in-coming tide, an idea that none of us could yet sense. We walked north happily and casually, feeling carefree, first on the shoreline near the Norwegian Memorial, but then onto the rocky beaches. We finally reached the headland that is the only absolute barrier on this beach hike, at high tide.

Lucy: I remember stopping on a lovely point with a wide beach, clowning around, and playing baseball with the kelp, acting as if we had all the time in the world and then finding ourselves forced inland by the rising tide. This was our first experience in almost impenetrable brush; tough springy salal and huge windfalls resting on other fallen logs about ten feet off the ground. We climbed up onto the logs and tight roped along them, but every now and then somebody would slip and fall off, disappearing completely into a dense thicket of greenery. We stopped periodically to listen for the surf, which we never heard. Progress was unbelievably slow. Anne took a violent dislike to bushwhacking, which has remained with her ever since.

After we finally beat our way out into sight of the shore again, we saw that we were on a steep grassy slope above a cove, the next headland still cut off by thundering waves and high surf. Anne flatly refused to go back inland so we rigged up a little shelter with the plastic—it was raining again—and waited for the tide to recede. Nash provided rye whiskey and I provided chocolate bars so the time passed with much amusement. I remember from that time, and throughout the trip, Dave Smith and Dave Nash's witty repartees, Anne's sudden shrieks of laughter, Bill Hanson's wry comments, and Annick's unquenchable enthusiasm. Bill Dougall was certainly the outdoor leader, all optimism, but thinking ahead rather more than the rest of us. He made frequent sorties down to the beach to check the tide, as the day was progressing rapidly.

Bill: From time to time I dropped down onto the steep gravel and tried to see around either side of the little cove, to find what we had to deal with when the tide did go down enough to move. I would run down as far as I could as the wave drew out, to get a quick look in between the surf. In a storm, waves get farther apart as well as bigger, so I had some leeway. But when the next waves came crashing in over the big rocks in front of the cove, they were substantially higher than my head so I didn't try to cut the time too close. Even though I have now been there several times, I have never since seen waves at that cove anywhere near as big as they were that afternoon, including during major storms. The day was getting on and there was a time pressure to get on with the hike. It was Sunday, and some of us had jobs to get back to Monday morning.

We still had no idea how far we had come and how far we had to go. We knew roughly, vaguely, where we were along the coast, but we had gradually become aware that some distances took a lot more time than others to cover. Revived by songs and rye whisky, the group finally descended into the cove, now almost free of surging waves, and headed north. We waded knee deep through a long trough of water, just seaward from the hundred foot vertical cliff that had forced us down into the cove. This wading took some confidence because there was no assurance there was not a ten or twenty foot deep tide pool somewhere under our feet.

Lucy: We managed to round the point by wading, scrambling on rocks, running between waves and getting wet. On the other side we saw a great red sea of cedar logs. From a distance they looked like pencil shavings. By this time we were getting rather tired, and the sand was coarse gravel that you sank into at each step. At least the tide was going out, leaving us plenty of beach to walk on. Conversation lagged, then stopped entirely as we plodded on into the dusk. Finally Bill spurted on ahead to find the Sand Point trail, the route out to Lake Ozette and the car.

Bill: A quiet realization that daylight was running out seemed to seep through the Magnificent Seven, and tiredness was settling in. When we finally rounded the last headland at Yellowbanks and came out onto Sandpoint Beach, the sun was touching the horizon. We realized that no one actually knew where the trail was that led from the beach through the rain forest to Lake Ozette, and where we hoped that Dave Collins had left our car. Bill Hanson said to me, "You, being the strongest and most experienced, should walk, maybe even rush on ahead, and locate the beginning of the trail." I responded to this flattery (or to being used, I didn't know which) by agreeing, and then was put into the awkward position of finding out that even when I walked as fast as I could, I only very slowly pulled ahead of the group. But I continued, and in the three miles of Sandpoint beach, gained maybe a quarter or half-mile. But the idea was good, because there was still enough light for me to climb over the driftwood and mill around in the woods until I found the trailhead. It was a critical move, because once darkness had become complete there was no possible way to have found the trail. In the early 1960's, the trail to Lake Ozette was not well developed or well visited. It was unusual in March to see anyone on that whole stretch of coastline, even on a weekend.

I left my pack to mark the beginning of the trail, a dumb thing to have done with darkness falling, and went back down the beach to meet the approaching six. I affirmed I had found the trail, and carried someone's pack up to where I had left mine. We formed up, with three miles to go, and started down the trail, feeling somewhat ominous. The brush on either side was well over our heads, and the trail was not straight, but wound back and forth around swampy areas. Not only did the brush close in, it cut off the remaining twilight. Very rapidly the group was reduced to shuffling ahead tentatively, feeling for the path in a probing kind of way, but on the other hand, in a confident optimistic atmosphere. We may have been blundering along through a rainforest and swamp, but we were off the beach with its mysterious and dangerous tides.

Lucy: When we finally turned inland it was pitch dark but we were jubilant, thinking we were within minutes of the end of the trip. Someone reminded us that the trail was three miles long and we soon found out that it was also extremely muddy, swampy and meandering. Bill led the way with his candle, virtually useless at least as far as providing light for anyone else, and Bill Hanson brought up the rear with his feeble penlight. It had occurred to none of the rest of us to bring a flashlight. We shuffled along, Indian file, trying to keep on the single board that was the trail, holding on to the person ahead because we were then in complete darkness. Inevitably, people slipped off the board and landed in the mud on their backs or hands and knees, flailing around to get righted again. Bill Hanson's dime store plastic raincoat was pretty well shredded by salal, branches and rocks—we called it elephant skin because it was gray and crackly—and was more or less finished off on this final stage through the brush. We trudged on and on, the silence only broken by curses or laughter when someone fell. It now seems impossible to believe, but it took us several hours to go the three miles.

Bill: Positions were rotated, so everyone had an opportunity to find the trail, often by missing a turn and falling into the swamp, but always with great good spirits, laughing while lying on his or her back. Here, the ladies carried the spirits and kept the atmosphere light, while the males said serious and important sounding things about the trail and getting out. The candle and penlight gave almost no useful light at all, but they gave great moral support and confidence. In real terms, they allowed us to see most of each other, but never really the trail underfoot or ahead. This was actually of much more value and importance than it sounds. Even though we walked in a line holding on to the back of the person ahead, the lights made it possible to keep the whole group in sight of each other. Without the light, it was always possible for one or more to become separated, to have got off the trail by stopping to tie shoes or shift the pack.

The three-mile trail took about four hours, and for the last hour we began to feel we must be on the wrong trail. But then we started to hear the thumping of the diesel generator at the Lake Ozette resort. There was no electricity to the lake in that time, nor for years after. The thumping got louder and louder, and finally, once we knew we were on the bridge over the Ozette River, we broke into the marching song from *The Bridge Over the River Kwai*.

The feeling was that we had prevailed and had won, and we were pleased to be us.

The car was indeed there, thanks to good friends Dave and Joanne, but it was about 11 pm, and the last ferry that would get us off the peninsula from Kingston was at midnight. Several of us had a workaday job where we were expected at about 8 a.m. the following morning. A few were mothers of children left with weekend babysitters. We loaded into the car, drove to Port Angeles along an endless winding road, and found a motel that was still open. We were always short on money, but did find a single motel room somewhere in Port Angeles for about five dollars total. Five of us went to sleep, doubling in single beds, under the beds, or on the floor, while Anne and Lucy stayed awake all night in a cafe talking and drinking tea so that they would be awake to get us up to drive to Kingston for the first ferry. And so we made the early ferry, got to Edmonds, shifted cars, and went off to jobs or to relieve baby sitters. We should have been worn down, but were bubbling with the excitement that goes with a real adventure.

Lucy: Anne and I went to an all night restaurant, ordered tea and cinnamon buns and stayed up talking, eating and laughing until 5 a.m. when we woke the others, then drove on to Kingston and the ferry home. This trip awakened in us all a taste for beach walking that we have kept and followed ever since. And still, for Bill and me, the best time to go is out of season when the sea is wild and rough, the route unknown, and the trip an adventure.

A thin place cracks open
like a window in the sky
And wild geese cry out overhead
filling you with wild, irrational joy.

from Edges, **Migrations**

Our Cove
by Lucy

There is a tiny beach on the northwestern tip of the Olympic Peninsula—a little cove filled with driftwood—so small that an ordinary hiker might not even remember having passed through. But for Bill and me, and our closest friends, this spot has a magical aura, and is so humble and so private we decided to call it Our Cove. For many years, it became our favorite camping spot on the Olympic Peninsula wilderness beaches.

We discovered Our Cove by chance, having heard through word of mouth about a dramatic headland known as Point of Arches, and a superb stretch of hard sand called Shi Shi Beach just to the north of it. Driving from Port Angeles to the Indian village of Neah Bay was a harrowing experience. The road on the south side of Lake Crescent, which skirts along the very edge of the lake, was narrow and tortuous in the 1960s, used mainly by logging trucks barreling along as fast as they could with their loads of huge logs. There were very few pull-outs in those days, so one had to choose whether to careen at top speed around hairpin turns with a gigantic logging truck in pursuit, or pull onto the side of the road and hope one's car wasn't flung into the lake, to disappear into the icy depths as (we found out later) had become the fate of many vehicles before us.

Bill and I and the Hansons decided to go on an exploratory hiking trip to see what lay south of Point of Arches. The road that gave access to Shi Shi beach passed through the Makah Indian

Reservation at Neah Bay. Beyond that was an old logging road that quickly proved to be virtually undrivable. We spent what seemed like hours pushing and digging to extract our Carryall from one gigantic pothole and mud puddle after another until finally, in defeat, Bill backed the car out. We had noticed on the way in a pink house with a hand-written sign saying *"Parking $3 – leave in envelope under windshield wipers."* Sheepishly, it now being well into the afternoon, we left our car and proceeded down the overgrown logging road for about a mile until an opening appeared.

We found ourselves on the edge of a bluff looking down on the sea far below. There was no trail but Bill felt that shouldn't present an obstacle, as the beach was somewhat visible through the trees. Bill Hanson and I plunged straight down the alarmingly steep bluff, alternately sliding on our behinds and grasping futilely at roots and branches. Elen, being of a more cautious nature was very dubious, and stood at the top of the bluff for a long time contemplating her route. Finally, Bill offered to climb down below her and put his hand under her feet at every step. She talked about that descent for years afterwards.

We walked south on wide and beautiful Shi Shi Beach, heading for Point of Arches, so-named for a spectacular series of sea stacks that stretch out into the ocean. Near the southern end of the beach is a small river, stained dark with tannins, with the unfortunate name of Petroleum Creek. We observed some old hippy cabins, remnants of that brief era, and a carving of a bear chain sawed out of a huge cedar log. It was now late afternoon, about mid-tide, and we were able to round Point of Arches by hopping from one slippery, seaweed covered rock to the next. Over the years we would discover that when the tide was fully out, one could explore the marvelous sea caves at the point, and when the tide was fully in, the headland was virtually impassable. One memorable trip with the Stadlers, we ended up in a shallow cave halfway round the point where we sheltered from the rain, waiting for the tide to go out. I remember that time well because Dave had brought full glass jars of peanut butter and jam and a loaf of bread—rather heavier than our usual camping fare.

14

We continued walking south of Point of Arches, picking our way over stony beaches and wet rocks, ducking through a sea arch and clawing our way along a vertical cliff until we came to a tunnel separated by a ten foot stretch of ocean, creating blow hole. We climbed up to a viewpoint, where we could see fountains of sea and spray shooting up at every surge of the waves. As this spot seemed impassable, we retreated to where we could climb up into the brush and salal and continue walking. Suddenly, we found ourselves looking down into a small cove enclosed by high rocky headlands and almost entirely filled with driftwood. Somehow, in the failing evening light, we knew we had found what we'd been looking for. A little beach to call our own.

The four of us crashed down through salal and underbrush and immediately began looking for a source of water. There were, in fact, two small driblets of fresh water coming through the driftwood at either end. I collected water in billycans in the near-darkness with my flashlight between my teeth, and returned to the campfire balancing on slippery logs, trying not to spill any. After rearranging the driftwood somewhat, we created enough space for a shelter, building a crude framework over which to hang our sheet of plastic. In those days, we had no tents, or really any sort of formal camping gear. We built a fire and then clambered out on the rocks as far as we could to watch the waves come crashing in, each bringing huge logs which landed in heavy thuds on the beach. We gazed in silence for a long while, watching the surging waves and the sun sinking slowly into the dark sea, the sky streaked orange and pink. In that moment, we lay claim to our little beach, our home away from home. Our Cove.

We took many trips out there in the ensuing years with family and friends, visitors from abroad and any new teachers who were game, but never found another soul camping there. One memorable winter expedition, we drove out on a Saturday to Neah Bay with Bill Hanson, Paul Stocklin, Paul Williams and Fred and Tory Campbell. We maneuvered our truck as far along the old logging road as was possible, through the underbrush and across frozen mud puddles. In spite of various members of our party saying they'd be happy to walk the extra mile, Bill insisted the logging road was perfectly passable. The idea of having to pay for parking at the pink house somehow rubbed him the wrong way, and who were we to argue with Bill Dougall?

The wind had been picking up over the course of the day, and by the time we reached Our Cove we were in the midst of a major storm. The seven of us spent a wild night trying to hold the tarp down and build a fire, while threatened by a roiling ocean and relentless gusts of wind. I don't remember getting much, if any, sleep that night, but there was a lot of joking and laughter. The storm had abated somewhat by morning, although a strong gust blew our tarp into the sea where it disappeared under the waves and was never seen again. We had a leisurely breakfast and did some exploring before heading back in the early afternoon. We arrived at our truck and found, much to our deep dismay, that a very large tree had fallen just on the other side, completely blocking our way. Bill Hanson immediately opened the saw blade of his trusty Swiss Army knife and started sawing. The rest of us, realizing the attempt was gallant but obviously hopeless, decided to climb over the log and inspect the rest of the road. We wove through what turned out to be nearly thirty large downed trees. Bill showed not the slightest remorse at having bypassed the pink house and three dollar parking fee, and none of dared point out the stupidity of that decision.

Paul Williams remembered there was a lighthouse or a Coast Guard Station at least three miles back along the road to Neah Bay and he and I volunteered to walk there and ask for help. All of the men had to get back for the Monday workday, and Tory and I did not relish the idea of another night out in the wind. By then it was completely dark, but Paul and I made the distance at high speed and found a ready response consisting of two loggers with giant chainsaws—I have no idea where they came from—who seemed eager for a night's adventure. We rode back with them in their truck and were warmly welcomed by our friends. The loggers had bright searchlights to guide their work and soon dispatched all the trees into manageable pieces clear of the road, releasing us from our prison. Much to our amazement, we arrived back in time for the last ferry from Kingston.

16

My favorite memory of Our Cove was on a clear, beautiful evening, after a peaceful hike along Shi Shi beach under the blazing sun. We stopped at the Blowhole as always, to marvel at the spray of water shooting into the air. When we had finished our comradely supper around a huge bonfire, the night was so brilliant, the stars so vivid, that Bill Dougall, Bill Hanson and I decided to take an evening stroll. We clambered up a small headland and started to climb down the other side when we noticed a cable, almost hidden in the salal, stretching straight uphill. Naturally, we wondered where it was going, and one by one took hold of it and started to scramble up. The cable ended at the furthermost top of a rocky promontory. There, we discovered the remains of an old, crumbling wooden ladder, which continued on up, disappearing into the night sky. Bill Dougall proceeded to begin an ascent, ignoring my cries of alarm, but was talked out of it by his levelheaded friend Bill Hanson. We assumed the ladder must have led up to a lookout, perhaps a remnant of World War Two, when there were indeed towers erected along the coastline.

We immediately christened our ladder the Stairway to the Stars. For years to come, a few of us would always hike up to admire our mysterious ladder. Even in broad daylight it was hard to tell where, or if, the ladder ended. We never did see the top. Slowly, over the ensuing years and storms, the ladder crumbled and disappeared. Bill and I, and our dear friends, were romantics at heart and we liked to name places and thus give them our own history. And that is why my favorite hike to Our Cove, became synonymous with the Blowhole and the Stairway to the Stars. Places and names that, like us, will eventually vanish into history.

Waves roll in and out leaving
their cloud reflections on the sand
leaving a surface that seems solid
but is soft and yielding, taking
but not keeping footprints
in its myriad grains of sand.

from Edges, **Migrations**

Shi Shi Beach
by Peter Berliner

It was a typical Dougall camping trip—meaning that I had no idea what to expect. The entire family except Robbie was going, including Bill and Lucy, Lucy Anne and me, Jill, Jonathan and Sorrel. Lucy Anne and I had gotten married just one year ago. I had only been on one beach hike with the Dougalls—but that was in the summer. I knew we were heading out to the Washington coast, and I guessed that it might involve a whole lot of adventure or punishment, depending on how you looked at it.

It was the day after Christmas, December 26, 1971, and no one seemed in a hurry to go hiking. It was cold out and the skies looked threatening. I was becoming hopeful that level heads would prevail and the trip would be postponed to another day. But I knew it was unlikely. I had already gotten to know Bill well enough to figure out that comfort was low on his list of priorities. As he often said, "If you wait for good weather, you'll never go anywhere." Nevertheless, for whatever reason, he seemed reluctant to push his offspring into action and it was well into the afternoon before we got going.

We piled our packs into the back and on top of the Chevy Carryall, and climbed into its three rows of seats. We drove to Edmonds and took the ferry to Kingston. Then we drove for another hour to Sequim where we stopped at the *Three Crabs* restaurant to feast on crab and oysters. We drove another half hour to Port Angeles and stopped at *Swain's General Store* where we bought plastic tarps, rubber boots for Lucy, several pairs of socks and gloves, and candy bars. By this time it was nearly 8 o'clock. It was dark. It was raining. We were still two hours from the trailhead to Shi Shi Beach.

We drove the winding, interminable road around Lake Crescent and Sorrel, who was in the way back, complained of carsickness but Bill paid no attention. We finally passed through Neah Bay, a small town in the Makah Indian Reservation, and were somewhere in the Olympic rainforest when we ran out of pavement. By this time, most of the passengers were asleep, in various awkward positions. The headlights revealed an old logging road that was awash with mud and snow. Bill guided the Carryall around the deepest, most gigantic mud-puddles I'd ever seen and the car bottomed out repeatedly with ominous crunching, clanking noises. The sound and jarring motion woke everyone up and I saw my own dismal expression reflected in their faces. Finally, Bill stopped the car and said, "Everybody out!"

Bill was concerned the car would get bogged down with all the weight, but he wanted to take it as far as possible anyway down the logging road. The family reluctantly disembarked into the cold and rain. We put on sweaters, rain jackets and boots and started walking in the pitch dark. We skirted around the deep puddles, jumping out of the way as Bill gunned the motor and splashed through them in the empty Carryall. This went on for about a mile until we abandoned the car. Now, everyone donned their packs and the two people who had flashlights—Bill and Lucy—got them out. We walked single file down the treacherous road until it eventually opened out onto a high bluff overlooking the beach. At least, that's what we were told. I couldn't see a thing, and when Bill disappeared over the edge I was certain he had fallen to his death. But the others followed like lemmings, and the next thing I knew I was plunging down a precipitous slope, grabbing onto roots and shrubs to slow my descent. I could hear the ocean roaring, and though it was dark and cold and raining, I was excited that we were finally on shores of the Pacific.

When we stepped out onto Shi-Shi Beach, I assumed we would now begin looking for a campsite. But that was not to be.

20

Instead, we walked another three miles on sand, rocks and gravel to the far end of the beach and Petroleum Creek—a freshwater stream that empties into the Pacific. Everyone was tired and no one spoke much at all. I got the impression that Lucy Anne and her siblings were used to arduous expeditions and knew complaints were futile. It was midnight by the time we reached the creek. It had finally stopped raining and a few stars were visible. Without further ado we began creating a shelter of sorts that would be large enough for all seven of us to sleep under. We dragged in driftwood logs and branches to form the sides (if you could call them that) and spread the plastic tarp across the top. We tied the corners of the tarp to rocks and logs to prevent it from being blown away. Then we unrolled another tarp on the sand underneath. Finally, we unpacked our foam pads and sleeping bags, pulled in our gear, and crawled into our makeshifts beds.

After tossing and turning, and adjusting and readjusting my sleeping bag for hours, it occurred to me that I was not likely to get any sleep. But sometime, late into the night, I drifted off. At some point, it started raining again. The plastic tarp that we had laid over the driftwood logs held and kept me dry. It was just starting to get light when I woke to the sound of a steady rain. Everyone else was either still asleep or feigning sleep, hoping Bill was already up and building a fire. I poked my head out the makeshift entry to the shelter and saw that the tide had come in—so much so that all the driftwood that had cluttered the beach between our shelter and the ocean had been swept away. The waves were practically lapping at the door. I hurriedly pulled out my sleeping bag and backpack and rushed to higher ground, calling out a warning. The others were not so lucky. I watched as a wave swept right through the shelter and heard cries of dismay as the icy Pacific current filled their sleeping bags. A rude awakening, if there ever was one.

Fortunately, Bill did have a fire going. The wet and shivering family appeared one by one, dragging their equally wet belongings behind them. We all huddled around the fire in the rain while Bill boiled water. Then we ate oatmeal, drank hot coffee and waited for the tide to go down. In a little while, we hoisted our packs and began hiking out. Moving again, we quickly warmed—or at least, I did. I paused to take in the setting. Everything around us—the mist, the rain, the rocks and the waves and the sky—was a different shade of gray. White and gray seagulls sailed above us. As the sky lightened, the driftwood cedar logs stood red and orange and yellow against the gravelly sand. When we walked up from the beach and into the woods, everything turned green.

"You see things in bad weather that you wouldn't on a sunny day," Bill remarked cheerfully.

This was only the first of my many adventures with the Dougall's, and my first introduction to Bill's relentless optimism in the face of less than ideal circumstances. My guess is that he would have been disappointed had the weather been fair. His conviction that it was worth it to spend what amounted to 10 hours driving and 6 hours hiking to spend one night on a wilderness beach, was classic Bill Dougall. But truth to tell, on my first winter trip to Shi-Shi Beach and Petroleum Creek, I'm pretty sure that the rest of us would have been far happier to see things in bright sunlight with a clear blue sky overhead. As it was, by the time we reached the Carryall, thoroughly exhausted, we were all soaked to the skin. All except Bill, who was the only one who managed to stay dry the whole time. I still don't know how he managed it.

I held out my hand and said,
"Trust your boots and don't look back."

from The City Girl and the Country Girl, **The Simple Life**

Glug in the Ocean
by Barbara Rona

The entry in my daily calendar for January 12-14, 1967, reads, "Glug in the ocean; beautiful rain forest; to Mosquito Creek." This marks the first time that my then husband, Steve Yarnall, and I participated in a social form Bill and Lucy Dougall invented called a "beach walk." Interestingly, these outings seldom included much beach and certainly very little walking. Rock shelves, slippery cliffs, drenched forests, and roaring rivers aplenty, but not much beach. Stampeding, stumbling, fording, clambering, and plummeting, but very little walking.

Actually, in addition to having minimum beach and minimum walking, this particular winter "beach walk" held lessons that were part of other escapades Steve and I took in the following six years with the Dougalls and such cohorts as Paul Williams, Bill Hanson, and Tory Campbell. That January 12th was a cold stormy day, "No problem," according to Bill Dougall. Our starting point, the Hoh River, had swollen to record heights, thus erasing any path along it, "No problem," and a thick fog enveloped us so that we couldn't see much of either our surroundings or our companions, also "No problem." Lesson #1: It turned out that there were never "problems" on the Dougall escapades—all appearances to the contrary—just "interesting" situations.

Right away, having never worn a pack before, and indeed having never hiked before, I was feeling rather embarrassed that within minutes my pack was already feeling rather heavy and uncomfortable. However, Bill cheerily reassured me that everyone, no matter how long they had hiked, felt this way—indicating, I believe, that pain in particular was "no problem" to this group. Indeed, in all my years traveling with the Dougalls, I don't believe I heard the word "pain" mentioned—though admittedly, in some rather tight spots, we did down a welcome capful of the straight Bacardi rum that filled one of the two water bottles we each carried.

When we had gathered together on some wind-blown rock by the sea, I, being somewhat bookish, rather expected we would be given some preliminary, helpful instructions on how to proceed. But no. Bill, without a word, suddenly bolted from the group, streaking northward along the rocky shore, and entirely disappeared into the fog. Stricken with terror that I would be left behind, I lurched forward into the fog and organized my legs into the fastest running motion I could manage. Within seconds came the "glug in the ocean" part of the trip. Suddenly I was no longer running, but was on my hands and knees, completely submerged in the ocean with a floating log between me and the shore. What I hadn't realized was that ocean waves come in cycles of about seven; so, one wave coming the furthest in had caught me and one coming less far in had allowed me—with hair, skin, clothing, and pack completely drenched—to stand up and blunder ashore. Lesson #2: This was a strictly learn-as-you-go operation.

As I rose from the sea, Bill materialized before me. All smiles, he said, "Dang! I wish I had had my camera." Lesson #3: I could expect no sympathy from Bill or this group; but I could expect an ever-ready attitude that I was just fine, no matter what the circumstances—an attitude that proved to be consistently empowering. I am reminded of the time when Lucy and I—on Nootka Island I believe—were struggling against a driving winter rain and wind so fierce we could lean our full weight into it and be supported. Mud was streaking down our faces. Perhaps fearing the worst—that we might begin feeling sorry for ourselves—Bill, who was behind us, began singing, "*In Your Easter Bonnet....*"

Soaked through, but warm and happy, I hiked forward with the group. Lesson #4: Wool keeps you warm, even when you are wet. Now, of course, other new-fangled materials do too, but due to my initiatory dousing, my deepest gratitude will always be to wool. That experience of baptism by water does bring to mind a baptism by fire we all experienced on the Dougall trip to Cape Scott, where our packs and all our belongings, along with a cedar chip floored boathouse, somehow burnt to the ground. That led to a lovely stay at the Cape Scott lighthouse and a lovely hike out, traveling more lightly than we'd ever imagined possible—but that's another story.

We spent most of our hike in the "beautiful rain forest" mentioned in my calendar entry. What an extraordinary place to which the Dougalls had introduced me—the wilderness—a place that is always exquisitely beautiful. Have you ever heard of anyone ever wanting to change a single detail of it to make it more beautiful; the way a wave is catching the light, or one tree is leaning against another, or a rock is all creased and crinkled? Lesson #5: If you want to leave behind your judgmental mind, join Bill and step across the threshold into the wilderness, or into your wilderness awareness.

By the end of day, we reached Mosquito "Creek," which, of course, was swollen to raging river size. This brings to mind the first canoeing trip we took with the Dougalls, which was definitely to be a beginners trip, but the river, the north fork of the Thompson in Canada, was on that particular day swollen such that Steve and I after shooting around the first bend, pulled over to shore, because waves were piling into the boat; whereupon the Dougalls paddled by in tandem, which looked fine, until I noticed that their whole canoe was submerged with them in it. That adventure ended in Lucy's grabbing a branch and swinging onto shore, and Bill later swimming to shore and then crashing through the underbrush for several miles, chasing their canoe downstream. Again, "no problem," just another day.

The next day, we were to cross Mosquito Creek, which we did by going upstream and then hiking (or inching, as the case may be) across a log—just one of the myriad ways of crossing a river that the intrepid Bill and Paul would in years ahead dream up. Some of these creative ways for crossing a river included leaping from slippery rock to slippery rock, skootching across an aerial log over rapids on the seat of your pants, riding across on an abandoned cable system, wading across in chest-high water holding onto a rope that Bill or Paul had swum across the river, or floating one by one across on a raft constructed on site from stray driftwood with Hanson's aluminum nails, rope, and such. Lesson# #6: The question is never "whether" to press forward but "how?"

Around the campfire that night, as at day's end on so many trips, Bill played his harmonica, his eyes glinting with happiness. He had brought friends together and given them memories—the kind to which, like good metaphors, they could return again and again in the future and mine for meaning. A question remains for me. What is the energy, the tremendous urgency, that takes Bill to the wilderness time after time, often with friends? It reminds me of the tremendous urgency that through the ages has taken certain individuals into spiritual life—and perhaps it is not so dissimilar. The first time I met Bill and Lucy, at a party at Bill and Elen Hanson's on December 17th, 1967, Bill Dougall was agitated because a driver in front of him that day hadn't immediately gone forward when the light turned green. *"He wasn't even awake!"* Bill kept repeating. I thought to myself, *"This man wasn't frustrated just because he was being held up. He was frustrated and bewildered because the other driver wasn't awake to what was around him."*

As I got to know the Dougalls, I learned that Bill's greatest fear is not perishing in some dangerous circumstance. On the contrary, his greatest fear is dying in the Sears parking lot—in the sleepy gray of consciousness pervading such a place. The epitome of spiritual life for many, I have since learned, is, likewise, being fully awake, climbing out of the gray of consciousness into full awareness of and attunement to all levels of reality—the temporal and the timeless, the finite and the infinite—experiencing both at the same time. And where can one do this in modern life?

In our workaday city life, the heavy imprint of the temporal and the finite crowds out the infinite and eternal dimensions. But in the worlds to which Bill flees—his wilderness—the immediacy of the present, finite sensory realm is joined and heightened by the sweep of infinity and eternity suggested by the expanse of sky, ocean, and space, the seeming timelessness of mountains and old growth trees, and the ever-changing flow of rivers. The sure path, more often than not, dissolves into the pathless. I learned this firsthand, in that wondrous wilderness, baptized by the wind and the waves.

Tent in the Sky

One night, we staked our tent
on a high ridge after a long climb.
In darkness we found a site
wind sheltered
by low fragrant pines.

I saw a brimming cauldron,
midnight blue, alive
with a million stars.
The dipper hung up among them
close to Polaris, at rest
after a day of scooping up
the stars and flinging them
wide into the night.

Some overflowed and fell
into distant pockets of the shore
where they became homes,
as welcoming as our yellow tent,
aglow with its single candle.

from **Migrations**

Hiking the Olympics with Lakesiders
by Lucy

Years ago when things were more informal at Lakeside, there was a week during the school year called January Days where teachers offered and students signed up for their preferred activity. Bill always chose an outdoor hike, and I always tagged along because they were sure to be interesting, usually to someplace we had never been.

That particular year Bill decided to cross the Low Divide, a route across the Olympic Mountains, up the Elwah River and down the North Fork of the Quinalt River (46 miles total). Of course the area had been inhabited by Indians for years, but the first such crossing by white men was made by the five man Press Expedition, sponsored by the Seattle newspaper The Press, and led by James Christie. That expedition took six months; from November 1889 to May 1890. They built a boat to tow cargo upriver but because of steep slopes, fallen trees, deep snow and icy water—the worst winter weather ever recorded—they abandoned the boat and walked. It is now an official National Park trail. Bill proposed that we cross the Low Divide in three days. No problem, he said confidently.

Six students and two teachers signed up to go with Bill and me. We started at the end of the Whiskey Bend road and walked in several miles to a small cabin where we had decided to spend the first night. One student left his pack outside on the porch. He had optimistically packed a steak, which was devoured by a bear during the night. The next morning Bill counted to make sure all students were accounted for, but only five were present. We called repeatedly and looked in both directions from the cabin, to no avail. Bill then turned to me and said, "I'll have to go back and see if he somehow decided to return to the cars. But we don't want to cancel the hike so I guess you'll have to be leader." I had neither compass nor map (Bill never carried them) but what to do?

Bill had told me we were to camp the next night at a place called (for some inexplicable reason) Chicago Camp, where there was no shelter. It was the Park's policy to let all the old cabins and shelters rot away so the Olympics would remain pure wilderness. Our smaller group set off on the trail, spreading out somewhat along the way. We hiked all day, over 20 miles, until we reached the spot we believed to be Chicago Camp. At this point, being midwinter, the late afternoon light had failed and it was near dark. Here, we counted students again and found another one missing, the only girl. I thereupon told the two teachers in a commanding tone, to retrace our steps with flashlights and not come back without the girl, even if it took all night.

Chicago Camp was a bleak spot and cold, and naturally it began to pour rain. The remaining students set up their tents and began collecting firewood. I was vastly relieved when the teachers came back quite soon with the girl, who had sensibly sat down in the middle of the trail. The teachers put up their own tent and promptly retired, not emerging until morning. I was so worried that yet another student might go missing, I checked on them repeatedly, admiring the determined ones who kept trying to light a fire. But it was so wet they all resorted to their camp stoves. After everyone was tucked up in their sleeping bags, I lay awake, wondering what on earth had happened to the missing student and all the possible repercussions, considering this was a school sanctioned trip. Had Bill found him? Was the student injured, or worse, wandering around the Olympic Rainforest in a daze? I slept intermittently and fitfully, waking at the slightest noise, straining my ears for the sound of footsteps.

The next morning there was no sign of Bill and the missing student. As well, the temperature had plummeted and it began to snow. We trudged for miles up switchbacks to the saddle called the Low Divide. There was a very welcome (though primitive) shelter there. I told the students to eat something while I went out to find the continuation of the trail down the other side of the pass to the Quinault River. The trail had been obliterated by snow, but after floundering around for a while, I found what appeared to be indentations on the ground that seemed trail-like. Shouldering our packs, our party began hiking downhill, out of the snow and into the rain. We were now on the Quinault river trail, and decided to spend our last night here. By now, the other students and teachers were quite concerned about Bill and the missing student. We had no idea what had happened, and the teachers, especially, were beginning to express deep unease. Because I had been (unwillingly) designated leader, I found myself behaving exactly as Bill would—by assuming a cheerfully optimistic demeanor and reassuring everyone that of course everything was just fine. All the while (unlike Bill) my stomach was churning with anxiety.

A couple of the boys helped me put up our red tent fly and some of the wetter ones slept in it, alongside me. Our dinner had been a dismal affair, huddling in the pouring rain, soaked to the skin. In the morning, we were a rather bedraggled bunch, and everyone was eager to reach our final destination. We set off along the Quinalt River trail, heads bent against the rain, walking fairly rapidly like a horse heading home to the barn. After several miles, a student in the lead suddenly hooted loudly. We all looked up to see another set of hikers coming toward us. They turned out, to our delight and relief, to be Bill, the missing boy and 2 rangers. Bill had made the wise decision to not try and catch up to our group, but rather meet us on the other side. All was well that ended well. But the two teachers who accompanied us did not volunteer for future hikes, having had enough of the great outdoors (they said) to last a lifetime. But there were always new teachers to baptize by rain and cold; ones that had never been on a hike with Bill Dougall.

And so, the next time Bill had a new route he wanted to try out in the Olympic Mountains he invited new teacher, Mo, along with Dick and Dixie. We were to start at the far side of the

Olympics on a regular Friday workday after school. Bill hadn't mentioned to Mo that the car ride would be about five hours, or that he was planning to get in several miles of hiking before camping that first night, all of it in the dark. She remembered long afterward his saying, "To rest is not to conquer". The first part of the trail was very rough and, with only a flashlight, I naturally tripped over a root and fell, hitting my knee sharply on a rock. I knew it would swell up and interfere with the rest of the trip, so as soon as we stopped to camp I grabbed some wet moss and applied it as a compress. When I got into my sleeping bag I put a large, very cold stone against my knee, which did the trick (as well as leaving a huge pile of dirt in my bag). Mo had been cheerful over dinner, remarking that the trail seemed quite easy, even in the dark. In the morning she said she'd slept like a baby.

The next day we walked endlessly uphill. Mo's enthusiasm steadily dampened as the day wore on and it began raining. Bill had pointed out that there were only two options when you hiked in the mountains; either up or down—but when he disappeared far ahead on the trail, we all began to have our doubts. He had mentioned an intersection with a different trail that was to be our turn-around point and where we would camp for the night. As the afternoon waned, Mo asked hesitantly if I thought we would reach the turn-around point before dark, and did I have any idea where Bill was? I shrugged to both questions, having never been this route before. Finally, just before the light failed completely, we reached the trail intersection, and found Bill snoozing, head pillowed on his pack. The rain had stopped and stars appeared in the ink dark sky.

We found a place to pitch our tents, and without even waiting for dinner, Mo fell asleep instantly. The next morning she looked rather the worse for wear, and I refrained from asking whether she'd slept like a baby. Dick and Dixie had been awake early and were ready to get moving, so after a quick breakfast we began the relentless downhill trudge. Most people think that going uphill is harder, but going down a steep trail with a heavy pack is remarkably grueling. And in my case, particularly hard on the joints. My injured knee was beginning to throb quite painfully, but there was really nothing for it but to get back to civilization.

The trail went on and on, down and down, sometimes switchbacks and sometimes not, and it became steadily later and darker. Now, in quite some pain and feeling impatient, I surged ahead with Mo at my heels. She, too, was ready to get home (it being a Sunday night and a school day in the morning). Unfortunately, in my haste and now in complete darkness, I made the mistake of walking right off a switchback until the trail turned into a tangle of brush. Mo followed me, and we spent quite a long time crashing around until we finally got back on the main trail, feeling extremely relieved but somewhat disoriented. We assumed that the others must have passed us by long ago. As we crept our way along in complete darkness, Mo asked if I was sure we were heading the right direction. *"Why?"* I asked impatiently. *"Because,"* she responded, *"I think we're going uphill."*

Just at that moment we saw a light coming toward us. I wondered who on earth could be walking the trail in the dark besides us. In fact, it turned out to be Bill, followed by Dick and Dixie, who in turn wondered why on earth we were heading back *up* the trail. From then on, Mo and I stuck to Bill like glue. Unfortunately Dick and Dixie lagged behind and missed the crucial right hand turn across a little bridge that in a short distance led out to the road. Being rather concerned, I walked back with a flashlight and started calling them and then singing as loudly as I could. They had completely disappeared! It turned out they had walked straight past the turn and found themselves milling around in the bushes. Then they had dropped their flashlights trying to change outworn batteries. Somehow, creeping along in the dark, they found their way back to the bridge and then the road, where we greeted them with relief. But we still had to walk another mile to get to where we had parked the truck. Bill was happy about that, because it meant we'd hiked exactly 50 miles. Like many teachers and students who went on one of Bill Dougall's legendary hikes, Mo said it was one she would never forget. She had learned the hard way that for Bill, to rest is not to conquer.

High on the trail we break out
on an ancient gray moraine, inhale
cold thin air under lowering clouds
that hide the peak. Pitted volcanic
rocks mark the slope like Braille,
silent records of what lies beneath,
reminding us the mountain only sleeps.

from Warnings, **Migrations**

The Dosewallips

(or, How we took a hike with Pete and Lucy Anne and never saw them)
by Lucy Dougall

What turned out to be a very strenuous weekend in the Olympic Mountains started out as a straightforward crossover hike with Lucy Anne, Pete and their friends, as well as few friends of Bill's and mine. We planned to take the Enchanted Valley trail that traverses a pass, heading up the Quinault valley on the west side and down the Dosewallips on the east. It was about 25 miles total. After various discussions over several days, Lucy Anne and Pete's group decided they only wanted to go as far as Anderson Pass— about 10 miles up the east side to the head of the Dosewallips. This would avoid the long drive over to the far side of the Olympics. Bill thereupon devised an alternate, 40 mile route for the rest of us that would begin on the same side of the mountains, cross two passes and loop back by way of Anderson Pass where we would meet them at 10 a.m. for breakfast Sunday morning and all walk out together. Or so we thought.

We planned to begin our hike at the Staircase Ranger Station, where Lucy Anne and Pete would pick up our car and move it around to their starting place so we would not have the car problem on Sunday. Our group consisted of Bill, me, Paul Stocklin and Debby Nicely—i.e. the "hardcore"—several others having fallen by the wayside when they heard the hike was 40 miles long. We drove over to Hood Canal on Friday night after work and slept in a motel as near to the trailhead as possible so as to get started by first light. By some miracle, we actually were on the trail shortly after 7 a.m., walking up the north fork of the Skokomish River

The first nine miles were fairly level; crunching along over the fall leaves, passing through long golden tunnels of vine maple, always enclosed by the towering deep green Douglas fir and cedar trees. Then we started climbing up toward First Divide, the first of the three mountain passes. Since I am slower at going uphill, I gradually dropped behind the others who soon disappeared completely out of sight. In fact, almost everything was out of sight due to thick fog and a steady drizzle. The guidebook referred to "superb views of Mt. Steel and Mt. Stone," neither of which were even remotely visible. I trudged uphill, nibbling blueberries and wondering when I would get to the sharp right bend in the trail that would indicate the final mile to the top of the pass.

Eventually I found myself in a very beautiful meadow covered with heather and blueberry bushes, their brilliant scarlet leaves shining through the dense mist. The trail seemed somewhat faint as it wound over the heather, however it was possible to follow it, which I did, up into another meadow and then steeply down the other side. By this time it was a barely visible track. I assumed that I had now gone over the pass, though it was surprising that there was no sign at the top, which there almost invariably is on any major trail.

At the foot of the slope, the trail vanished entirely. In front of me was a bare and open valley with large snow patches on the opposite side and a shallow creek in front of me. I waded through the water, thinking perhaps it had covered Bill and the others' trail, and kept hoping to suddenly spy the *Home Sweet Home* shelter that was supposed to be a mile below the pass. By this time, the wind was blowing hard and the rain had started in earnest. I stopped to put on several layers of clothing and raingear, got out the map and compass and surveyed the desolate scene. I felt rather nervous at this point. It was clear that I had somehow how missed the sharp turn to the east so I knew I had to go back and find it. Fortunately, I had thought to mark the spot where the trail ended with two sticks crossed on top of a rock. Otherwise, the track was quite undetectable as it was covered by brush. I retraced the faint path up the steep hillside, across the first meadow, then the second, all the while looking for a trail going off at right angles.

Suddenly, and to my intense relief, I stepped right onto the main trail. By then the rain was really pelting down. I was so relieved I nearly ran up and over the 4700-foot pass and down the other side. I heard a welcome "Coooee" from below and shortly found the *Home Sweet Home* shelter, where the others were cozily drinking hot soup. Bill was already sound asleep in his sleeping bag, taking a nap. With more miles to go, after I'd had a cup of soup and woken up Bill, we set right off. Unfortunately we had to drop down 2,000 feet to the Duckabush River and then climb another 2,000 feet up the other side to our destination at Marmot Lakes. We were a bit dubious about camping up there in such bad weather and without a shelter, but decided we had to push on since we had another 20 miles to go the next day. I had already added on several miles to my own journey, due to my detour across the blueberry meadows and the pass beyond.

Later in the afternoon, the weather cleared and we could see the very impressive mountains that were on all sides of us. The slopes were ablaze with fall colors—patches of gold, bronze, copper and crimson. We ran into a ranger, who turned out to be the one I'd spoken to earlier in the week on the phone. He cheered us up by telling us there was, in fact, a shelter at Marmot Lakes. We arrived at close to 6 p.m. and after a very speedy freeze-dried dinner, we were in our sleeping bags. There was no inclination to lounge around chatting as the temperature had dropped to 30 degrees. Bill had not brought nearly enough clothes and I had only my lightweight sleeping bag. We just had not expected winter to arrive so soon. It began to snow about an hour later and it continued to fall through most of the night. The roof leaked badly, and Paul decided to set up his tent outside instead. I contemplated going out to join him, but it just seemed like too much trouble. Instead, I kept shining my flashlight out to see how deep the snow was getting, imagining the trail being obliterated. We were now at 4500 feet, and still had to cross O'Neill Pass at 4900 feet, then continue at 4500 for about seven miles before dropping down again. We knew it would all be under snow.

Dawn finally came. The scene was a winter wonderland, absolutely beautiful. Snow covered everything, but enough indentation was left so the trail could be followed quite easily. The mist rolled in and it began snowing again so we had to wear rain clothes. On the other side of the pass the trail entered an ancient forest, silent and awe inspiring, the huge trees attaining record heights for this altitude. We were now in the Quinault drainage. The guidebook described the view as breathtaking down the Quinault River to Lake Quinault and, if lucky, you could even see the ocean. Naturally we didn't see anything except the trees and the mist. After eight miles, the track we were following intersected the Enchanted Valley trail. It then climbed up to Anderson Pass and down the other side to the shelter where we were to meet LA, Pete and friends for a late breakfast. When we arrived we found a message scrawled in the snow: "We have left."

I couldn't really blame them, as by now it was 1 p.m. Pete had been on enough hikes with us to know that anything might have happened. We might be stranded at Marmot Lakes or snowed in on O'Neil Pass, perhaps not showing up until the next day. So we went into the shelter, nicknamed *Camp Siberia*, and had lunch. The name was appropriate. It was so cold we had to eat with our mittens on, at least those of us who thought to bring them. Bill stoically rubbed his bare hands together and blew on them, then proclaimed this was nothing compared to the Arctic. The 10-mile walk out was quite lovely. It mostly followed the Dosewallips River as it tumbled through a narrow gorge and then fell far below us. We arrived at the car about 5:30. I was very disappointed that we had spent no time whatsoever with Pete and Lucy Anne, being that we'd planned the adventure together. In the failing light of the parking lot, I could just make out another note in the snow, this one made of sticks: "Fun hike. Sorry you weren't there."

Beach Hikes on
Vancouver Island
&
The Queen Charlottes

You would look at a map, see a wild coastline
on an island with no roads or trails
and that was enough to inspire the next trip.
Dropped off by plane in the middle of nowhere—
out of reach for days, with the customary
unknown obstacles—rivers to cross, headlands to climb over,
winter tides and bad weather.

Your inner flame always seemed so strong and bright
that its sparks alone could light the wood and bring us fire,
so even on those cold, wet nights
when the wood refused to catch, I knew
there is indeed a fire of the gods—
a passionate optimism that burnt in you
so fiercely it could fan to flame and
light the inner fire inside us all.

from Fire of the Gods, **Home and Away**

Nootka Island
by Bill

It was a three-day weekend in the middle of February in about 1970, and we were well along in our adventuring up on Vancouver Island. The master plan was one of working our way north on the outside beaches of the island. Nootka Island had the most exposed beaches on this stretch, so we looked on it as the outside of Vancouver Island. We had maps, which were absolutely necessary for information on major obstacles such as rivers and headlands (and which had never proved to be truly informative or predictive on small details). But we still hadn't learned that you never walk north to south, especially in winter, just in case a storm came up. Winter storms always seemed to blow from the southwest and walking into the wind uses up a lot of energy. On the other hand, tactically it was the only way to go, because at the end of the north to south route there was a small settlement and lighthouse called Friendly Cove. This meant we would end up with communications to the real world and a specific place for a floatplane to meet us. It was a gift and bonus to be doing this before the days of cellular telephones, which have the drawback of preventing one from feeling truly dependent on one's own ability and competence.

Paul Williams and Lucy and I scouted around for volunteers and came up with some old fashioned romantics, which is how I now think they might be explained. These were Bill Hanson, Tory Livingston and Barbara Yarnall. Who else but a romantic would take on wilderness beach hiking in the winter on an unknown beach? All of us had a lot of children to deal with, something like twenty-three among the six of us. Winter conditions on an exposed wilderness beach was not all that demanding as an adventure and challenge, compared to the strains of having children in adolescence. In this era of beach hiking, camping equipment was still not very developed (tents, stoves, food, etc.) but the atmosphere of adventure seemed to make up for a lack of information and good equipment. Fortunately, real bush pilots were willing to take a chance, were available, and were not too expensive when divided six ways.

Lucy arranged to have a bush plane meet us in Gold River on a Saturday morning. We planned to have it drop us on a lake we had seen on the map that extended almost to the ocean on the west side of the island. It seemed deep enough for the plane to be able to taxi right up to the lake shore, leaving us with only be a short hike out onto the wilderness beach. We pinned our hopes and plans on the weather over the weekend staying good enough so that the plane would be able to fly in, load us up, and then drop us on Nootka Island. We also had to bank on the weather for our pickup rendezvous at the small settlement with the lighthouse. We knew the weather at this time of year gave us a fifty-fifty chance that it would be too foggy or windy or stormy. In our favor was the fact that these bush pilots needed work in the worst way, and would get there if at all possible—even marginally possible. Also in our favor was the fact that we would be willing to fly with them in uncertain conditions. Maybe it was taking a chance, but lots of things in life at our age involved taking chances. The obvious thing of getting dropped on a wilderness beach where we didn't know what was out there was a risk we'd taken on many previous occasions, and things had always worked out fine.

We left on Friday in the old Chevy Carryall, as early in the afternoon as everyone could get free, and drove via Half-Moon Bay, crossing on the ferry from Vancouver to Nanaimo, Vancouver Island. From there we drove to Campbell River, crossed the island to Gold River, and then spent the night somewhere outside of town. Saturday morning we got down to the dock at the seaport of Gold River and stood there with all our gear. It was a foggy morning, and we waited for what seemed like a very long time, sort of willing the plane to be able to get in. Finally, sometime midmorning, the bush plane appeared suddenly out of the mists and landed. We loaded up our packs and showed the pilot the lake where we wanted to be dropped on Nootka Island. The weather was marginal and we flew relatively low, in and out of wisps of cloud and fog, and over the sea to Nootka. The plane headed north along the inside of the island and then landed on the lake. Fortunately, it was deep enough for the pilot to taxi right up to the west end of the lake shore where it was closest to the ocean beach, a gap of perhaps 200 or 300 feet of brush and trees.

I arranged with the pilot to pick us up at Friendly Cove, the settlement at the south end of the Nootka, on Monday afternoon. The plane left immediately. We were standing on the shore of the lake full of the mutual excitement and energy that goes with the start of any genuine adventure. An adventure is possible when you don't really know what is ahead of you, but where you also have a sense of probably being able to manage what will happen. We were also exploring, since we had no knowledge of the beach or the complications. The weather was not too cold, moderate wind, overcast with a gray and cloudy sky. Each of us performed the last packing and organizing details with our gear and then set off. We went through the brush on a vague trail out onto the beach, and had an immediate sense of, *we're here and we're on our way*. The beach was easy walking on sand and gravel, not much driftwood, long and almost straight, and heading south.

This hike was probably the height of Bill Hanson's adventuring in nature; he was competent, confident, curious, with expensive rubber boots, and a pack full of exotic things that his restless mind had accumulated. Barbara seemed equally confident and willing, free of the tentativeness that she had shown on previous hikes. She seemed to have found out that if you tried things it somehow came out all right, and that discomfort was different from danger. Tory was a Victorian lady traveler in the wilds, ready to give it a go, and be excited by the strange and exotic things she found on these hikes in the wilderness away from her orderly life of the city. Lucy was reveling in the excitement she always felt when in a group, doing something together. The whole atmosphere of this trip was ideal for Lucy—her love of being with a gang of people she felt close to, and sharing an adventure.

Paul and I liked being there and making it up as we went along. Of course, we didn't let it be known we were just making it all up. We both operated in the outdoors on principles and percentages, and mostly, it worked. Paul and I were really similar in how we went about things; we looked for a problem to solve, and in this case, saw nothing but straightforward walking ahead. We both probably wanted some kind of minor complications to come up just to have something to deal with, and pushed on strongly, probably instinctively looking for something to face and figure out, and of course curious about what might be just around the next bend in the beach.

Finally, into the afternoon we came to what on our map looked like it might be a problem; a waterfall maybe 30 to 40 feet high and 40 to 60 feet across at the top, cascading into a pool of unknown depth. But it ran out onto the sand and into the ocean as a wide and shallow stream. Bill Hanson rummaged in his pack full of mysterious things, produced a portable tripod for his camera, and then took a delayed release photo of all six of us, with the waterfall behind us. We were able to wade the stream without even taking boots off. From the map, this stream had looked like the problem of the trip, and our spirits rose with having crossed it. We pressed on and stopped at a point with a Spanish sounding name for dinner and to make camp. The driftwood looked as though high tide reached it and so we made camp a few feet above the beach and in the trees. The ground there was low and flat, with open space for putting up the tarp for a sleeping shelter and for having a campfire. The weather was like it had been all day, indeterminate, not much wind, cloudy, chilly but not cold, with misty rain at times.

Sometime during the night a hard-core storm moved in, with strong winds and rain. High tide came in the middle of the night. Our tent was on a protected shelf in the trees behind the beach, so we had no sense of the storm that was actually blowing out on the open shore. It got light at about 7 a.m. and when we got up and saw the actual beach and breakers, we realized that the light-hearted walking would be over. Paul was responsible for that breakfast, and perhaps it was in the spirit of Bill Hanson for doing the unusual that Paul's breakfast turned out to be pop-tarts. Not popped in this case, not heated either. It was too wet to cook, so our breakfast of pop-tarts was cold, and there was nothing to drink. I thought they were pretty good. The others shrugged their shoulders and ate the pop-tarts, with rain running off the end of their noses. Lucy flatly refused to eat, saying she didn't like that kind of food. I said that was a mistake. In weather like this and walking into the wind, she was sure to have energy problems. I think I actually did bring up the old saw that goes, *If you don't eat breakfast, you will cry before lunch.*

We put on our rain gear and covers on packs, and launched out onto the beach. The footing was easy, a kind of sand and hardpan gravel, but the wind was very strong, and dead against us. Paul and I took turns being in the lead. We lined up everyone single file behind the leader, who was out there in front breaking the wind. After a couple of hours, Lucy said she had to stop and kneel down for a rest, so we all got a break. She was probably regretting by now not having eaten those pop-tarts. I thought she might even be crying, but it could have been rain on her cheeks. The tidal beach here was level and wide, without a lot of surf up onto it. There was a narrow, 10 to 15 foot band of level ground above the tideline, with 8-foot high brush along the edge of the beach. I took a look and it seemed like a way to move forward and be out of the wind. So we all moved up into the brushy, woodsy area where it turned out to be possible to walk, and we moved somewhat faster.

After a while Paul called a halt, and everyone dropped packs and got out something to eat. We sat down on what seemed to be a short log to wait out the eating. After a while I looked down between my legs at the log and noticed a strange shape to the wood. I scraped off some moss, and much to my surprise saw that we were actually sitting on the figurehead of a sailing ship. There wasn't any paint left on it and the wood was rotting away. It looked like a sort of fierce pirate captain with a crooked hat on and a big black mustache and eyebrows. We all marveled at this relic from some old shipwreck and the coincidence of having sat on it, but everyone was interested in getting moving now that they had some food inside.

We stayed in the brush as long as we could, and then had to move back out on the beach. We walked into the storm winds until late afternoon and then came to what showed as a small creek on the map. Now, the runoff from the heavy rain that had been falling all day had turned it into a big creek, more like a river, with rapids and white water. The low tide gave the river an additional downhill run and speed as it poured into the sea. It was a brown, raging torrent. The water ran in a big curve, with us on the inside of the bend. Our side was gravel bar. On the other side was a high, hard sand cliff maybe 6 to 8 feet vertically above the river, with water eroding into it. Paul had brought a quarter-inch line, maybe 50 feet long. I offered to try to get across so we would have a safety line. There was still daylight and we had a long way to go to reach Friendly Cove, where we were due to be picked up the next day. Paul belayed me and I waded out into this wild brown torrent. When I got maybe a third of the way across, the pressure of the water actually pushed me downstream. I stood with my legs apart, sideways to the current, waist deep, and the river literally carried me steadily downstream, my feet bouncing over the stones.

I somehow made my way back and told Paul that there was no way I could get across by swimming, even if we had a longer line, since I hadn't even got to the deepest part where there was actual white water that was eating into the sand bank on the far side. So we backed off, and reported to the others that we would have to spend the night here and hope for a possible crossing tomorrow morning. After looking at that boiling brown water and then watching Paul and me try unsuccessfully to cross it with a rope, the others must have been happy to hear our decision. On the other hand, it left us with a night to pass thinking about having to cross the river in the morning.

Days are short in winter, accentuated by the clouds and rain, and twilight was upon us early. There was an atmosphere of urgency about looking for a place to put up our tarp in order to keep out the wind and rain. We found a wonderfully adaptable place behind and in some high brush and driftwood, and up against some logs. Looking forward to spending the night there, we worked enthusiastically and energetically at rigging the tarp as a shelter for all of us to spread our sleeping bags. The brush cut out the wind. What rain there was came straight down, and was easier to deal with. The tarp was large enough to shelter all of us, and the sand made for soft ground. Meanwhile, Bill Hanson was doggedly working at making a fire. He had a fire location against the flat side of a slightly overhanging log that was five or six feet high. We kidded him about his attempting the impossible, but he organized us into helping by gathering kindling and shaving wood. Remarkably, the kindling caught and stayed lit. Gradually, the fire got substantial enough to survive, and we praised Bill for his diligence and expertise.

Having fire meant we could heat water, cook, and get warm. Everyone helped and all were cheerful. Even with no official setting up of a fire watch schedule, everyone said they would put some wood on the fire if they got up for the call of nature. When Paul offered us more pop tarts, Lucy put her foot down and insisted we eat something she deemed semi-healthy. So we had supper and went off to bed, knowing that tomorrow we would face the unknowns of the flooding river. There was plenty of time for sleeping, given that it was winter and substantially farther north than Seattle. With the heavy clouds, it was dark by five p.m. and would stay dark until about seven a.m., giving us six extra hours of sleeping time. The tension of the coming river crossing, and the discomfort of sleeping on the ground in damp sleeping bags, was canceled out to a great extent by exhaustion from a long day of walking into the storm. It was almost as though the effort of that battle had used up everyone's energy to the point where lying down, even in wet clothing, was a good deal. The night was a succession of sociable meetings of people getting up and putting wood on the fire to keep it burning.

Dawn finally came. We had no option other than to reach Friendly Cove by that afternoon because it was our only way to get off the island. No one knew where we were or where to search for us if we were declared overdue. But there was absolutely no

47

complaining, no looking for sympathy, and no withdrawing from the group in a very complicated situation. Fortunately, the river seemed lower and less violent than it had been the night before. The heavy rain of the previous day had dropped way off as the storm blew itself out. The runoff water from rain in the mountains had already occurred and the crossing looked more manageable.

I put on my pack so it would hold me down by its weight, and tied the rope around my waist. Paul got set to belay me across in case I lost my footing. The water was about waist deep, and the hardest current just at the far side. The current was substantial, a real footing exercise, but significantly less forceful than the afternoon before. Climbing out wasn't difficult onto the sandy bank, even though it was steep. Paul had to wade out into the stream about knee deep or slightly deeper, because the rope was not long enough. I untied and climbed the bank. Paul tied the others in one at a time, and belayed them across. I held on to the rope after the last had crossed and then Paul tied himself in and I belayed him across to the other side. We were starting the day soaked to the waist and Lucy, being the shortest, must have been wet about 6 inches higher than the rest of us. Paul was clearly very chilled from standing continuously in ice-cold water while belaying people. But getting over the river was an emotional lift for all of us. There was great enthusiasm and a sense of accomplishment.

From the map, it looked like we only had about 3 or 4 miles to go to reach Friendly Cove where there was a manned lighthouse, a small settlement, and a sheltered harbor where our floatplane could meet us. Our prospects seemed monumentally improved over the afternoon before. It was drizzling steadily but the driving rain had ended. We were on a long curved sandy cove that ended in a rocky headland that looked impossible to negotiate at water level. The headland was most of the remaining distance to cover, but the map showed that by cutting straight across behind the headland we would save some distance. We explored along the sandy cove looking for any sign of a trail. It seemed very sensible that with a long time settlement (dating from 1793) at Friendly Cove, there would have been hikers out to this beach. We found no sign of a trail. Paul and I got out compasses, and estimating a compass heading from the map, we left the beach and set off for what looked like a 2 or 3 hour crossing.

We spent all the rest of the day making our way through dense and somewhat impenetrable lowland. Crossing a headland usually involves going up through salal or brush and then coming down the other side. Instead, we found endless ponds and swamps that had to be bypassed. To keep traveling in approximately the proposed direction was a major problem, since the route we pursued had no straight stretches in it. The footing was very difficult and required finding logs to cross some of the swamps that couldn't otherwise be bypassed. We were in low trees and brush all the time, so that finding a spot in the distance that would help aim us in the shortest direction was never possible. Finally, we ran out of time and daylight and had to find some sort of bivouac, in the swamps. That was hard to do. We all milled around looking for at least a hill or slope that was not wet or broken up with trees and brush. Someone finally found the side of a mildly sloped mound that was clear of brush and trees, where we could tie the ends of the tarp. Knowing we had missed our rendezvous with the floatplane at Friendly Cove was sort of preying on all our minds, but nobody talked about it. We were pretty tired by then.

After a meager dinner we put a tarp under us as a ground cloth, another tarp on top, and then crawled under and got out our sleeping bags. The three men slept on the outside, and the three women slept in the center under the tarp. It had been another really difficult, long, tiring day. I do remember worrying that we would be at least a day overdue and wondering what this would mean for the floatplane; whether it would come back and if we would be charged for another trip. I thought about what sort of complications being a day late would mean for all of our kids at home, and about the jobs that some of us were not showing up for. But basically, I was just too tired to worry for very long. I went quickly off to sleep, and didn't wake up until morning.

When I woke up, it was just starting to get light. It turned out that all of the others had not slept as soundly or as well as I had. I sat up and said, let's get up and get going. Suddenly everyone seemed to have a restless night to report. I remember seeing

Barbara with a bright cheerful smile on her face, saying something like she thought morning would never get here. Bill Hanson reported a major tactical error in spreading the tarp underneath us in a way that it projected outside the covering tarp, and that rain that landed on the tarp had run down into the shelter and soaked his sleeping bag. The others reported that they were awake all night and were surprised to hear that the night had actually lasted for 13 or 14 hours.

We all packed up and then had something to eat. Paul and I got out the compasses and we headed out again, picking a path through the swamp in the general direction we had to go. The psychological burden was less, because we now knew what it was like. The sleep had given us (or me, at least) some energy to move fairly rapidly in spite of the bad footing, the continual climbing over fallen trees, the pushing through brush, the pulling of feet out of mud where we sank into it, and the circling around ponds. All of a sudden, we could see light through the trees ahead of us. This really lifted our spirits. It could have meant that we had gone way off course and were about to come out over a sea cliff, but we were too beaten down by this swamp travel to consider that it meant anything but something good. And it *was* something good. We abruptly came out of the swamp and trees onto a recently logged area along a stream. At the bottom of the logged area was a gravel beach. It meant we were beyond the headland. According to the map, we had some beach to walk and then could cut across a neck of land on a trail. That would lead us to Friendly Cove.

We had come out toward the top of the logged area and cut across the slash to the rough road by the stream. We followed it down to the beach, turned south and hiked along the steep, gravel-covered shore. The waves rolled up and then drained back down, making the black gravel stones tumble and roll with each wave. It reminded me of a line by Matthew Arnold: *And the waves drew back with a grating roar.* Times were good now, and I could respond to the beauty of the steep black gravel and the now-clear blue skies. The sun was low on the horizon at this time of year, even at midday, and lit up the waves as they rolled in. After the beach, a trail led across a wide grassy field, and on the other side was circular cove with old houses along it. On the right was a rocky neck of land with a lighthouse. We headed for the lighthouse and were welcomed by a surprisingly young couple that was the light housekeepers. They were what in later years would be called *granolas*, into health food and living life in nature. They radioed for the plane, and offered us a glass of soymilk, and told us about all the things you can make with soybeans.

I look back on that trip to Nootka Island as one where a group of us took on a challenge, a set of unknowns, and somehow made it all work. It was a true adventure, because we didn't really know what the outcome would be. But when you're with a group of people who are cheerful and enthusiastic, even surprises like the flooding river are just a set of problems to be worked out. We always had a sense that everything would come out fine in the end, and as usual, it did.

Storm over Nootka Island
by Lucy

Sleeping bag to sleeping bag, we four huddle
in the yellow tent, one thin layer of nylon away
from the storm that rages up the coast. Wind whips
and snaps the tent like a furious dog straining
at his leash. Loud spanking smacks set the tent pole
swaying dizzily at every gust. On either side,
two of us rise up to steady it like Marines on Iwo Jima
holding up the flag. Frayed tent lines flap and shudder.
We wonder if they will hold. Rain pummels down,
turning the ground to rivulets that branch and spread
beneath the tent and lick at our sleeping bags. Under
a flashlight's beam, the dripping tent walls glisten like
polished brass. Sleep comes in fitful snatches.

We rise in the winter dark, rushing to beat the tide,
bolt down hard rolls, forego hot drinks, pack up our

sodden gear now twice as heavy on our backs. Muffled
in warm woolens, rain pants and jackets, we venture onto
the beach, a wide and rocky shelf. Emerging from
the sheltering trees, we are sent reeling by the south
wind's blast full on our faces, freezing conversation,
stabbing icy needles into every crack of clothing.
Instead of walking sociably abreast, we fall back, one
behind the other in single file, heads bent, leaning
hard into the wind. We are engulfed in the wild power
of the storm, in waves thudding and crashing
against the rocks, in fountains of spray and
roiling surf and swirling clouds.

But our goal is far away so we must push on through
the wall of wind. Our boots seem filled with lead.
I stumble as energy drains out with every gust
into the yielding sand. In unspoken agreement
we turn inland to escape the wind-raked shelf,
into the rain forest that stands at the beach's edge,
a different world. Under the dark canopy of ancient
trees, the wind's wild passage is muted and diffused.
Dense with centuries of growth, the forest teems with
vegetable life, spongy moss cocooning every tree and
branch and rock. Wiry, stiff salal like upright bedsprings
bars our way. We wade into squelchy bogs,
claw passages through tangled vines and crawl
over giant nurse logs sprouting trees from random
seeds, a pungent cycle of renewal and decay.

Soaked and exhausted we sink down on a wet log
and search our pockets for restoring food. Sweet
chocolate sends compacted energy in waves. It radiates
to stiffened fingers and dulled minds. Then Bill exclaims,
This is no log we're sitting on, it's a figurehead!

We shine our flashlights on a headless man wielding a sword.
By what strange chance did we alight on this one log
among the untold thousands on Vancouver Island?
Our fingers stroke the rotted crumbling wood, sodden to the core with years
of drenching rains. Long ago
it rode the bow of some barque or brigantine that sailed
the treacherous Drake passage around Cape Horn.

We gaze at the churning ocean, at waves crashing over
sea stacks that stretch like dragons' teeth, and understand
why this coast is called the Graveyard of the Pacific.
Was it the search for furs or just adventure that drove
those men to ride the sea for months on end half way around
the world to this deserted shore? On other hikes we have found
lifeboats, huge green glass floats, bottles with messages, and
the whole stern end of a wooden ship with parts of a coffered
cabin ceiling—some of the wreckage of four centuries of sailing.

We get up from the log, head out to the beach once more
to see what lies around the next point, and the next.

Postscript
by Lucy

Riding back on the ferry from Vancouver Island after a memorable hike with Bill Hanson, Paul Williams, Tory Livingston and the Barbara Yarnall on the southwest coast of Nootka Island, Bill and I picked up a local paper that reported a recent shipwreck north of where we had just hiked. It was a Greek freighter, which had crashed on those fatal reefs, known as the Graveyard of the Pacific, tearing a large hole in her side. We determined to go back up there and check it out. A few weeks later we drove to Gold River and chartered a floatplane to land us in a bay nearer the north side of the island, planning to walk across the narrow neck of land to the ocean side where the wreck had happened.

As usual the plane had to land in the water, requiring us to wade ashore in our green rubber boots. For some unknown reason, Bill Hanson had decided to "go leather", as he put it, and rather plaintively asked Bill to carry him piggyback to dry land. Bill, in his John Wayne voice responded, "That'd be the day!" and left him to make do with his ill choice of footwear. We donned our packs and waded to the beach, which did not look at all promising but rather more like a wall of trees and bushes. Since there was no other choice we headed west, hopefully toward the ocean, crashing through thickets of dense brush, mostly salal. By some miracle we stumbled across an old shack, which we poked in and around and deduced, from evidence I have now forgotten, that it had been a religious retreat of some kind. Bill Hanson, a very determined haunter of rummage sales and junk shops (Bill Dougall's play-barn having been the last resting place for some of his larger gifts to Bill, like an African antelope with a bullet in its side and a 6 by 8 foot Australian flag) suddenly gave a shout of triumph. Near the side of the shack, half-hidden by weeds and mosses was an old pile of bricks. He examined them and found something quite extraordinary—they all had the name "DOUGALL" carved into them!

We were all quite astounded. Here we were on a very small, remote island, and Dougall was hardly a common name. The fact that we had somehow run across this shack and pile of bricks, hidden in the brush, was an exceedingly strange and random coincidence. Bill Hanson made a formal presentation of one brick to Bill Dougall, and we all drank a toast to the discovery. Since weight is always a consideration on a long overnight hike, only three of us were willing to carry a brick home in our packs: Bill, Bill Hanson and me. Since the shack was not habitable, we set up tents and spent the night there. Bill Hanson had been assigned breakfast which he proudly produced, a regrettable choice of canned and cold spicy tamales. I would have preferred cinnamon buns and hot cocoa but BH could never do anything ordinary.

We hoisted our packs and set off again for the ocean. When we reached the beach, we had to hike north for quite a stretch before we saw the wreck. Since we were about three weeks too late, there was only a portion of her bow left stranded on the beach. The rest had washed away and disappeared. Even the bow was huge and impressive and bore the name "TREIS IARCHI." We found out later that the captain of the ship, apparently neither aware nor concerned that this portion of the coast was so littered with sunken ships it had acquired the name, Graveyard of the Pacific. Instead of being on watch, he was down below playing cards with fellow officers. We decided this was a fitting place to have a picnic. While the rest of us ate the more conventional fare of cheese and crackers, Bill Hanson pulled out a can of greasy sardines from his pack and ate the contents with his fingers, licking his chops in delight. His greatest coup however, was finding that most astoundingly appropriate treasure for Bill, the leader of all of our unusual wilderness hikes, the DOUGALL bricks. Their origin remains a mystery to this day.

I wonder if we are not pure enough,
if merely searching for it time after time,
getting lost, benighted, black with mud,
bruised and scratched, worn out
by crawling under and climbing over
fallen trees lacing the steep slope,
drenched like mosses, is not enough.

from Lake Isobel, **Migrations**

The Brooks Peninsula
by Peter Berliner

The Brooks Peninsula is a huge provincial park that juts off the west coast of Vancouver Island. It has been described in one book as, *"...the most desolate, god-forsaken sixty miles of coastline in all of Canada."* But based on our experience, the author was probably just trying to scare tourists away. Perhaps he had only known it in winter, when storms blow in with hurricane force and upwards of 260 inches of rain batters the windswept beaches. I would say that while we did endure three difficult days on the northern side of the Brooks, the southern beaches, where we spent our last two days, were as appealing as those of any resort. For this was an unusual Dougall adventure—one taking place in June, rather than the usual mid-winter expeditions. This had been a deciding factor in my agreeing to go to this "god-forsaken" stretch of coastline. It was the late 1970s and there were five of us on this hike; Bill and Lucy, Paul Williams, Paul Stocklin and myself. Bill referred to us as "The Intrepid Five."

After driving to Canada and halfway across the island, the first real part of our journey began in a town called Gold River, at the end of a dock. That's where we met the pilot Sea-Air Airways had scheduled for us. His name was Mel Doak. I've never seen such a skeptical look as his when Bill outlined our plans for the hike. When it was clear that we weren't going to be discouraged, Mel let on that he had spent considerable time hiking and beachcombing the area himself. Our first stop on the flight to the coast was Tahsis—a tiny town situated at the end of an inlet, at the foot of some pretty steep mountains. We would spend the night there and be flown to the Brooks Peninsula the next day.

We had some time to kill before the next leg of our journey and invited Mel to have coffee with us. He was happy to share his knowledge of the area. "It's really another world over there," he said. "On the north side you might as well be in Africa as anywhere—especially when you get on the meadow. That's a pretty spectacular place. When you get back, I want to talk to you and see what you think of it." Mel then pulled out a map. "When you come around the southern side, which is all pretty good beach, you'll find the cabins. A naturalist who boated in built one last summer. There were some miners living there last I saw." Mel then went on to describe what he called the hippie cabins. "There were three, but one burned down. They're hexagonal, with plastic roofs and nicely made. You'll find them before you reach Peddler's Cove, which is where I'll be meeting you." Paul wanted to know if the people who built the hippie cabins were the ones who had drowned. We had heard about this tragic story some time ago. "The men did," Mel said. "All three of them. We brought the two girls and two babies back a few months ago...in March, I think." Mel seemed matter of fact as he related the story so we didn't press for details.

The next day was sunny. While waiting for the tide to go out, we were given a tour of the town by the mayor. It was mid-afternoon when Mel finally appeared and flew us to the cove that was the beginning of our hike. The first thing we did after disembarking was to lighten our 40-pound packs by having lunch. After eating, we hiked down the beach for a good three hours—long enough to make me feel exhausted, and once again I was cursing myself for agreeing to go on yet one more arduous Bill Dougall adventure. I seemed to have developed a form of amnesia that allowed me to forget how grueling the previous Dougall hike was, and approach the next one with great enthusiasm. But here I was again, crawling under wet fallen logs or thrashing my way through the insidious salal that made our efforts to get over the headlands nearly impossible. I had no choice but to press on.

58

We stopped just as it was beginning to get dark. I was never so tired as that first night, even though we would walk much farther on the days that followed. I slept well and felt revived in the morning. The next day's hiking was quite hard as most of the shoreline was extremely rocky. We walked briskly but carefully over wet boulders, climbed around the steep sides of coves and up over headlands through the salal and mossy trees. At times, we took off our boots and trousers to wade through a creek when there was no other way to cross over. At the end of the day, as the sky darkened, we found ourselves deliberating as to how to get past a tidal inlet walled in by rocks and boulders. Bill ventured over the rocks without his pack but soon came back, thwarted by the tide. Lucy suggested we toss rocks into the water Chinese fashion until we filled the deep spots. We threw in some pretty hefty ones but they quickly disappeared. It all seemed ridiculous and hopeless and I would have preferred to retreat a hundred yards or so and set up the tent. But Lucy's idea served an even better purpose; throwing rocks kept us warm and passed the time until the tide subsided.

While we were waiting, Bill told us about a much more dangerous obstacle he and Lucy had braved on a hike from the Hoh River to Third Beach. There is a headland along the way called Taylor Point, on which very intimidating signs are posted at either side where the trail goes up and over. The signs say: *DANGER. Taylor Point impassible at any time. Persons venturing beyond risk entrapment, serious injury, or death. Last death 9/6/76.* Bill and Lucy had run into a ranger who had told them it wasn't uncommon for hikers to get trapped and even drown on Taylor Point. He had belayed down from the cliffs to rescue people more than once. But naturally, Bill saw it as a challenge. When they reached Taylor Point, the tide was right (or so he hoped) and Bill charged ahead. He and Lucy picked their way across the volcanic stones, which were very slimy with seaweed. The cliffs rose vertically above them. "There really were only a couple of places where you might possibly be able to climb up if the tide came in," Bill related, as he watched me toss yet another stone in the water, "but I wouldn't have wanted to try it."

At this point in the story, Lucy broke in to say that it made her a little nervous when Bill put on his hat and gloves for protection and then told her, in no uncertain terms, "Do not fall in the water!" At this point, they had reached a very bad place; a ten-foot gap where you have to cross on a steep, slanting rock face that has no hand or foot holds. The ocean was deep here, and the rising tide sent waves surging up onto the stone. Somehow, with the usual Dougall luck, they managed to creep across the slippery rock face and avoid being swept into the sea. When they finally rounded the headland, they found four young people sunbathing on the beach. The sunbathers looked surprised and asked Bill if he had Lucy gone around the treacherous Taylor Point. "No," Bill replied, "we were just looking for whales."

By now the tide had receded and we gave up our Chinese rock throwing and picked our way around the headland. I was silently saying prayer of thanks that I hadn't been on the Taylor Point hike, facing a possible drowning. I already found it difficult to keep up with the people in our group—Bill and Lucy and the two Pauls— for the simple reason that they were more experienced and in better shape. It was humbling to be with people twice my age that walked so fast you couldn't stop to spit without falling behind. Their alacrity came mostly from the certain knowledge of exactly how much one has to put out in order to achieve a certain goal. This became very apparent the third and most miserable day, when we were able to cover only about ten miles—all in the pouring rain. After an hour of hiking along the shore, we reached a headland that could not be circumvented even at low tide. It looked more like a mountain, and there was no choice but to go up and over.

For the rest of the day—literally about ten hours—we pushed our way through salal so thick it required us at times to use garden shears to pare back its tangled, springy branches. Bill and Lucy, having done this many times before, had prudently thought to bring the clippers. When we finally reached what we thought was the top, exhausted and soaking wet, we had to walk around and through scrub cedar that fought against our forward movement like a battalion of soldiers. Even lunch was miserable. We ate sardines, rye crisp and cookies that were soggy and crumbled in our hands. We stood, because it was too wet and cold to sit down. We even managed to miss entirely the long hoped-for meadow that Mel had told us about which, from a distance, looked like a vertical bog.

Since there weren't any trails to follow, Paul led with his map, an altimeter and compass. The occasional trails we stumbled on were those of the many small deer who randomly traversed the peninsula. We actually saw a few of these deer, which were barely chest high and apparently ducked with ease under branches that had us stooping and squirming. It was late afternoon when we finally reached the actual crest of the mountain—some 2500 feet above the ocean. All vegetation of any height disappeared, and we walked quickly across the graveled, windswept terrain. At long last, we could see our destination below. This brought great cheer in the ranks but it looked terribly far to me, which indeed it proved to be. We started our descent and made rapid progress as we slid down the muddy slope, pausing only to drink from the streams and taste a few wild huckleberries or savor a handful of gorp. I kept thinking that it couldn't be much farther. By now it getting dark and we were all wet and chilled.

I was beyond fatigue. I might have been willing to stop and rest if only I could have convinced the others. But they knew better than I how utterly disastrous it would have been to be caught in the pitch black of night and have to make a fireless camp in this dank forest. Finally Paul Williams, who had us following barely discernable deer trails, brashly began walking in the middle of a stream, reminding us, *"Every lonely river must go down to the sea."* The rest of the group followed suit. About an hour later, and perhaps a mile and a half down this twisting, turning and endless stream, the group began to emerge onto the beach like refugees from a biblical flood. Although I was the last to arrive, I was thrilled to see my fellow hikers beginning to shed their wet clothes. Perhaps we were actually going to rest! They turned to welcome me.

"You call this a beach hike?" I groused. And then, because the worst was over, I couldn't help but laugh. Bill snapped a picture of me, completely drenched and bedraggled and happy to be alive. Everyone was smiling. We dubbed the beach, "Happy Five." A few of us gathered sticks and logs and made a giant fire. The heavy rain clouds began to break up and the faint light of the setting sun glowed in the west. We spent the rest of the evening hanging up our clothes to dry. I managed to char a pair of socks and a t-shirt and melt a good part of my foam mattress in the process. But life seemed awfully good, in spite of it all.

The next two days were sunny and lovely. It felt as though we might have been in Mexico or the Mediterranean or anywhere with sunshine, warmth, sandy beaches and spectacular views. The difference here was that we were alone in paradise. It felt like it was all ours, and we had a sense of infinite good fortune. We found the hippie cabins that Mel had told us about. There was a moment of disbelief, thinking about these young people who had been so adventurous as to try surviving in such a remote place, and so near a treacherous winter sea. We saw the work they had put into building their shelters and sensed what they might have felt on sunlit days and evenings full of stars. But we were terribly sad, knowing how it had ended for them.

On the fifth day, we reached Peddler's Cove. Mel deftly landed his seaplane near the beach and we climbed in and were whisked away. "How did you like the meadow?" Mel asked.

Bill, who was sitting next to him, replied, "Oh, we bypassed it."

"Really?" Mel sounded disappointed.

Bill turned around and gave us a mischievous grin. "Yes," he said, "we decided to climb a mountain instead." As Mel banked the plane and turned toward Tahsis, I looked out the window at the spectacular view. I had survived another Dougall hike, and the familiar glow of amnesia was already settling in. As the plane headed east, I watched the Brooks Peninsula slowly fade from view. It was the first step in our long journey home.

The Celebrated Macjack Trip
by Bill

The successful completion of the Death March led to a series of increasingly difficult beach-hikes over the years. One of these hikes, about ten or fifteen years later, was on a stretch of beaches in Canada on the west side of Vancouver Island. We had already hiked several beaches on this island, but this particular stretch had been left undone because, having flown over it, we felt it was full of unmanageable sea cliff difficulties. I personally felt for that very reason that we should therefore try it. Were we not real beach-hiking hotshots by now? I waited until those interested had a three-day weekend from their respective jobs, and then said, "How about trying that stretch now?" One volunteer, Paul Williams, was dubious about having only three days. He said things like, "Look at the map, there are more headlands than beaches along that stretch." But I said not to worry, we're all so experienced we can handle anything. We were young and feckless, and loaded with confidence.

By starting early and driving long hours, we made it up to a small village near the south end of our starting point by that Friday night, a village named Winter Harbor. There were seven of us, all experienced in Vancouver Island beach hiking. There was me, Bill Dougall that is, and Paul Williams of course, and then experienced beach-hikers Lucy Dougall, Bill Hanson, Pete Berliner, Barbara Yarnall and Ken Van Dyke. On the maps, this stretch looked like it could be easily covered (barring impediments like sea cliff headlands) in a couple of days. We planned to reach our destination by Sunday afternoon so we could be home for the workweek. We didn't know it then, but the experienced background of these seven hikers was going to turn out to be necessary, and the hike itself was going to add to our already lengthy experience.

A photo exists of this happy group, striding energetically out over a footbridge from that small coastal village near the north end of Vancouver Island. We reached our starting point and headed north on a long, friendly sand beach. It went for quite a ways north, but then ended up at a headland with a vertical ocean side. Not to worry! Weren't we experienced in navigating sea cliffs? So we scouted around on the land side, looking for bypass routes. It turned out there was a rising gulley behind the headland, which we went up until it ended close to a final, vertical cliff about 30 feet high. Paul Williams swung into action as the able mountaineer, and worked out a route. It did require a little scrambling and a little exposure, but was doable for reasonably agile hikers, and was not quite vertical. Paul went first and I went last, with me pushing occasionally on behinds. Once on top, the hiking was manageable and we made it past the barrier sea cliffs, but the terrain led to forest bushwhacking for most of the whole day. Toward late afternoon, an easy route down from these highlands led to a wonderfully sandy coast, with hard sand beaches and a grassy flatland about five feet above the beaches with occasional trees and bushes. The day ended with a great sunset and a cloudless sky. Spirits rose.

The next day went enthusiastically and enjoyably, and we covered ground rapidly. Wow, I thought, this is great! Everything is going so well, we'll easily make it out by the end of the day. All of our worries about impassable sea cliffs seemed to have faded. But even though we were on hard sand beaches with an occasional short low headland to scramble over, by the end of the day we still hadn't gotten to the place we would be able to connect with a logging road and hopefully get a ride back to our cars. Now we were facing being overdue by a day, which meant missing work and families wondering where we were. But everyone took it in stride. The weather had held, and we figured if we got up very early the next day we would make back to Seattle by early afternoon. But we had somehow not accounted for how little ground we'd covered on that first day. So even though we set out early, after miles of steady hiking (now well into the afternoon) we came to an anticipated river crossing that we had seen on the maps. However, this was a really deep, substantial river. It looked to be over our heads. It was also fairly wide and not something to try carrying a pack. We hiked on up the river to where it disappeared into the forest, hoping it would become shallower or more manageable.

We used most what was left of the day scouting up the river, hoping that some crossing would appear. No one was talking about the fact that we were now already a day overdue. The underbrush was so thick that we gave up trying to crash through it and simply walked in the river itself along the bank, trying to avoid projecting sweepers and brush. There is a photo of Barbara, up to her neck in the water, smiling! She was always cheerful, even in a dicey situation like this. We finally had a conference and decided that the widest part of the river was probably where it was also shallowest. We hoped it could be waded without the water going over our heads, and we also assumed that the current would be least there. It was now late in the day. We went back to the widest part and drew straws to determine who would try the wading. The wader would be tied to a rope that would do two things; one, give us a way to pull the wader back out if he or she went over their head or got swept away. Two, if the wading produced a crossing route, the rope could be tied or held at both ends, so that others could use the rope to cross with a pack on their back.

Ken Van Dyke and Paul Williams then volunteered to be the waders. Ken was the tallest so he tied on the rope and headed out into the river, with Paul Williams wading behind him and paying out rope, and me paying out a rope to Paul. Ken got to where it was really deep, even for him. So he and Paul came back to the south shore to consider their options. It was now close to sunset, and a crossing was starting to become a real necessity. We all had jobs and families to get back to, and were already overdue. It was beginning to seem as if there was no way across the river, and that we might be actually marooned, with no alternative but to retrace our route all the way back. That was a sobering thought. Ken went out again and the water rose on him. It got up to about his armpits and finally even deeper than that but he pushed on. He was about two thirds of the way across by then. He was the ideal one of us to be taking on this river crossing, strong and determined, and our tallest. Paul was out there deep in the water passing the rope on to him but it just got deeper and deeper, so Ken came back.

Then Paul, always the man of action, tied the rope around his waist, strode out into the river and when it got too deep, simply dove in and swam to the other side. He then tied the rope to a tree, looked around and found an old hatch cover that he attached and sent back over. From then on, we formed a ferry system, each person kneeling on the hatch cover with their pack, half submerged with the weight, while Paul pulled from the other side. We must have had a rope on either side of the hatch cover because I stayed on the near side, partly out in the water, paying out the rope while Paul pulled.

We finally all made it across, completely soaked, and the day was almost over. We scouted around for the trail and went up it a ways but it was now too dark to go on. We changed into clothes that, if not exactly dry, were not soaked, and then built a small fire. We were very hungry but short of food, so each took out what they had left and we lined it up and divided it among the group. Ken, who had the smallest most efficient pack, surprisingly had the most food. This was a happy revelation. After eating, we then put the tents up and got into our sleeping bags, which incredibly were still dry. Paul, in his sleeping bag, started chuckling. "What's so funny?" a wet and tired me asked. He responded that early tomorrow morning, about a half dozen of his clients would be meeting in his office to work out some financial problems. That humor escaped me. Especially when I realized that my students and fellow teachers were already wondering what happened to Bill Dougall?

The next morning, we ate the last little bit of food between us and hiked up the trail. We were, by this point, a little subdued. Everyone was tired and hungry and a few of us might have been worried about the consequences of not showing up for our jobs. We were now two days behind schedule. We finally made it out to the logging road and started plugging along, heading inland towards the nearest town. Shortly it seemed, a logging camp pickup truck rolled by. He stopped. I went up to ask him how far out we were, and also might he consider giving us a lift. He chuckled and said, "You people are the missing hikers! The Royal Canadian Mounties are about to start a big search for you. I'll call and tell them you're out and safe." That was a sobering moment, thinking about the cost of a search on our behalf. The truck driver added that that we looked tired and wet, but definitely alive. Then he took us all the way back to our original starting point where we had left our cars.

Our spirits rose steadily from the time we actually reached the road and met the logger. The idea of retracing our route had seemed really depressing, even ignoble, to me. So the fact that we had made it down this last stretch of unexplored (by us) beaches on Vancouver Island, plus made it across the seemingly unfordable river, buoyed our spirits. It's always true that when you're faced with a problem, you just deal with it and focus on the present moment. But once a problem (like fording the river) has been surmounted, in retrospect it turns into a great adventure—one you wouldn't have missed for the world. And so our drive home was full of enthusiasm and the wonderful feeling one has when something unexpected and exciting happens. That is how we came to call this hike the Celebrated Macjack trip.

As we round the headland, we find another shipwreck,
more recent—the bow of a large freighter.
We discover later that while its captain played cards
below decks, the ship struck a reef
and split asunder. When we saw it,
only its bow remained, bent and buckled
and that too would soon be gone.

from Between Storms on Hecate Strait, **The Simple Life**

Cape Scott
by Peter Berliner & Lucy Dougall

From the book, Cape Scott Story: *In March of 1897, an expedition of Danish pioneers led by Rasmus Hansen set out on the ship Floyborg settle the area, improve the land, and obtain leases from the Crown. Rounding Cape Cook, along what has been described as one of the most godforsaken stretches of coastline on the continent, the ship sailed into a storm and its main boom broke. In spite of this setback, the Floyberg was navigated north around Cape Scott to Fisherman's Bay. It later broke adrift and was irreparably damaged. It was the first of an unbelievable number of obstacles to the settlement of that promising land.*

Pete: We set out from Woodinville for Cape Scott on an early Thursday morning in March, 1976. Cape Scott is on the northernmost end of Vancouver Island in Canada, and was the site of a failed wilderness settlement that dates back to the 1890s. Bill Dougall had mapped an interesting route that involved a long drive, a plane ride, and miles of beach hiking. He persuaded the gullible that this would be an ideal late-winter excursion. There were nine of us in two vehicles, with supplies and equipment for a four-day camping trip. We had the advantage of seventy-five years of technology over those early settlers. But we were barely twenty miles from town when the shattering sound of the blown engine of my Chevy Carryall interrupted our journey.

Lucy: We left in the pouring rain. Shortly after Everett, about half an hour from home, we lost Pete's car, or rather, Bill went much faster and we soon noticed they weren't behind us. First we slowed down for several miles. Then we stopped, and when no one appeared, went on to the border and waited. We told our story to the border patrol and decided to continue on to the Vancouver airport to wait there, on the off chance that they had taken the other border crossing.

Pete: The Dougall's truck was hopelessly ahead. No help from them. I jumped out and started kicking tires and cursing. Steve and Ted, taking a more constructive route, stuck out their thumbs and hitched a ride toward the nearest service station. That left four of us to contemplate whether we would make the 8:45 a.m. plane out of Vancouver and what would happen if (or more likely, when) we missed it. Miraculously, twenty minutes later a car pulled up behind us carrying Steve and Ted. Apparently, they had found a welder on his way to work and persuaded him (by offering a hefty cash bribe) to drive us to the airport. They also arranged for the Carryall to be towed to a service station to await our return. Hearing that, we bounded out of the truck, crammed ourselves into the car and lit out for the airport. It was 6:40 by now and the airport was two hours away. We were all very tense. In the back seat were Fred and Tory Campbell, along with Karen and Steve Trafton. My friend Ted Steege, with whom I had done a lot of hiking in the Cascades, was in the front seat with me and Rolli, our heroic driver. We raced north and, with a slight delay at customs, at last reached the airport entrance.

Lucy: Bill was thinking out all the alternative plans and the loss of one day, when at exactly three and a half minutes before departure a car came screeching up, our six comrades poured out, and all of a sudden there was frantic running and throwing of packs and boots and cries of "hold the plane!" It was a rather hectic start. Strangely, the exact same thing happened on a similar trip about five years ago. That time we *did* miss the plane and had to stay overnight in a dreadful airport motel.

Pete: We could see Bill and Lucy and Paul Williams waiting for us as we pulled up. When we got to the gate we were greeted by the pilot who said, "Yes, we are *all* waiting for you." In a minute or two we were high over Vancouver Island. Upon landing in Port Hardy, we were met by a twelve-passenger van that would take us through Holberg, a logging town, and on another twelve miles to the trailhead to San Josef Bay. Being early in March, the road was covered by snow. The day was sunny but the temperature was below freezing. It was about 12:30 when we emerged from the van, slung on our packs and tightened the tops of our rubber boots in preparation for the snowy trail ahead of us.

The first hour or so of hiking is always a shock to the system. *What am I doing here?* the body seems to ask, as you hoist a 40-pound pack on your shoulders and start slogging through the mud. *This must be a terrible mistake!* On my previous hikes with the Dougalls, I've found this is a time for relaxing and accommodating yourself to the task ahead. Fortunately, the three-mile trail to San Josef Bay was well travelled. The skies were clear, but as we went deeper into the woods it was damp and cold, and the path was submerged in snow and mud. All around us were moss-covered trees and giant ferns. We slowed only to cross a stream on two logs that were slick with ice and to climb over fallen cedar logs.

Soon we were on the fine sandy beach at San Josef Bay, and at last it was time for lunch. We hadn't eaten anything since early that morning. Everyone started foraging in their packs. Bags within bags came out—cheese, sausage, peanut butter, crackers, rolls, bagels and nuts. Tory offered up home-dried pineapple; a delicacy. Just as we were beginning to feel satiated, a terrible thing happened. Instead of leaning back against the driftwood logs to rest, everyone started putting food away, rearranging layers of clothes, zipping zippers and tightening straps. Had I not looked up in time, I would have been abandoned. We were on our way again.

Lucy: The first obstacle we encountered was what appeared to be a large mountain that the trail climbed up and over, literally to the very top. The going up was arduous, carrying fully loaded packs through increasingly deep snow. We were following fresh cougar tracks and I couldn't help but wonder if Bill and Steve, who had surged ahead, might run into the owner of those tracks and what they might do in the case of a cougar attack. Pete, after commenting on the tracks, stopped to adjust his boot-laces (he later confessed he had decided to let Paul take the lead, in the off-chance of a cougar encounter) and I stopped as well—for the same reason.

Pete: We slowed a bit more as the trail took us to the top of St. Patrick's mountain—1,400 feet above the sea. In some places, the snow was a foot deep. Near the top, we walked out of the trees and onto a windy summit scattered with scrub pine trees, branches twisted and stunted, with greenery brilliant in the sun. It was a long way down to the beach. We could see coastal peaks of the Vancouver Island mountain range behind us. The rest of the group soon arrived, took off their packs, and we all struck heroic poses for pictures. With the wind blowing, it was very cold. We were soon hurtling down through the trees, sliding some of the way. At the foot of the trail was Sea Otter Cove. We decided to camp there—even though it was still light. It had been a long day.

Lucy: Spending the night at Sea Otter Cove reminded me of another trip that Bill, Debbie and I had taken there with eight Lakeside students. It had seemed like a very protected small cove, sheltered from the wind, and the students confidently put up their tents a little way inland from the beach. Bill and I decided to put up the red tent fly on the bench of ground just at the edge of the beach, sharing it with Debby and a girl student. An ominous portent of the violent windstorm to come started right after we'd cooked supper on our camp stoves. Rain began pelting down. Wind whipped and rattled the tent, tugging on the lines we had tied to a nearby tree. We got into our sleeping bags and hoped for the best.

I was not asleep for very long before I heard the sound of water lapping the foot of my sleeping bag. I grabbed the flashlight and saw a wave inching its way into the tent. I roused the other three and we all sprang into action, throwing sleeping bags and all loose articles into our packs. Bill dispatched Debby to run to where the other students were camped to see that they were okay while he was evacuating our tent. I climbed out on the tree to untie the knots in the guy ropes, my hands like ice and the surf surging beneath me. Hurricane force winds blew as we all gathered in the woods. Most of the student's tents had ripped or blown down so we just sat up for the rest of the night.

Pete: The next day was dry and cold, though a bit more overcast than the first. We planned to work our way along the beach to Goose Bay, which opens onto Hansen's Lagoon. We packed up early after a breakfast of hot chocolate and granola. A short inland trail behind a headland took us Lowrie Bay. From there we could see our destination—Cape Scott! The walk to Goose Bay lay before us. Amazingly, it looked to be only a few hours away. This observation produced some joy among the ranks but set Bill to muttering, "It won't be that close." He was right. It turned out to be seven hours of climbing in rubber boots over sharp rocks exposed by a retreating tide, desperately trying to avoid slipping on algae and ice. The gravel beaches offered some relief from the tension of tight roping over rocks and driftwood logs, but sinking into the stones with every step made our loads seem even heavier.

The nine of us were strung along the coast, going at our own pace. We occasionally collected at places where we had to edge around a precipice while trying not to look at icy water below, or contemplate what a misstep might bring. All things considered, we made good progress. Unlike some other stretches we have hiked, this one forced us up the banks and into the salal only two or three times. After the last of these forays, we dropped down to the beach by a stream for lunch, and lingered long enough to heat up some soup and coffee. A few miles later we began looking for a suitable camp near fresh water, managing to use up most of the daylight. We set up our tents on the beach and, after a long effort, got a good fire going. Then we donned more layers of wool and down and began to relax. That night we were treated to a crescent moon and lots of stars. We ate polish sausage and Chinese noodles and drank margaritas. We even managed to have a heated argument over the future of the country before finding our way to the frosty tents for the night. "I wonder what the poor people are doing," Bill said, meaning everyone but us. Who else had a private beach—even an entire ocean—at the foot of their beds?

Lucy: We began the hike the next morning wearing just our rain pants. The evening before, we had encountered what appeared to be the only real obstacle left; a large river, swollen by the high tides. Much to our relief, in the morning light it turned out to be two branches of a swift, but fairly shallow stream. We rolled our rain pants up to our knees and waded in the icy water, carrying our boots. It was thigh deep on me, but pleasantly short, sandy, and shallow, compared to other treacherous crossings we had done before. Nothing like the time I tried crossing the San Josef River, which was so deep and swift that my pack started floating and began to carry me downstream. I was rescued by a quick moving Pete on that trip, but once back on shore, Bill Hanson inexplicably handed me the 5 pounds of marinated steak he had been carrying, turned around and went home. Somehow, the sight of me floating downstream had soured him on the whole hike.

Pete: It took about an hour to walk to the remnants of the old settlement, which began with a crumbling dike. It wasn't much to see; a stretch of rocks three feet high at most. But the sheer effort it took to build it was apparent. A little beyond the dike, we walked into the marshy fields that had once been carefully segmented into plots by rough cut fence posts, still standing in straight lines along the settlement road. On the side of the road, now overgrown, was an ancient buckboard wagon. Up ahead was a metal tractor seat lying amid the weeds. Some of the first settlers had built their houses near the lagoon. There was nothing left of these. A quarter mile up the road, on higher ground, we found partially collapsed buildings; a barn, a house, a shed. It was snowy and quiet where these buildings had once been. We searched around and found a tractor, parts of stoves and the decorative cast iron hardware from an old-fashioned school desk.

From the book, Cape Scott Story: *By 1899, 90 colonists lived in the Cape Scott settlement in houses built with unpainted split cedar boards. There was also a parsonage, a church, a meeting room and a school. Children left home often before daylight to hike several miles to school, returning home after dark in northwest downpours. The adults were engaged in the incessant chores of survival—hunting, fishing, tending garden and livestock, building and chopping firewood. The arrival of the steamer meant unloading with no docking facilities. The livestock were lowered into the water in slings and forced to swim ashore. The storms at sea took their toll of boats and lives and made halibut fishing on any scale impossible. The lack of a road meant tedious time-consuming hikes to carry in supplies from cast-iron stoves to tools and dry goods.*

Pete: We emptied most of our packs at the settlement, hanging the food up in plastic bags out of reach of the bears. Tents and extra clothes were bagged and placed in an empty oil drum. With lightened loads, we sped down the trail back to head of the lagoon. Tonight we would be guests of the lighthouse keepers at Cape Scott, friends of Lucy and Bill's. The trail took us through the woods to a beach called Nell's Bight where we found a lone camper who had been there for five nights. From there, a trail took us through the salal and over the mud to Experiment Bight—another short beach—and then to Goose Bay where the wind, coming from the south, was blowing 30 to 40 mph.

It was raining and cold. We arrived at the lighthouse at about 3:30 p.m. There is no traditional lighthouse at Cape Scott. There is a huge light beacon, three well-kept white clapboard houses, a helicopter pad and a foghorn. There were two families living there—Don and Linda Weeden, veteran light housekeepers, and Gary and his wife and four year old daughter. We straggled into the extra house one by one. We took off our boots and wet clothes in the basement and found our way upstairs to a nicely heated home with nine mattresses, a bathroom, running water, and a pile of magazines. Utter luxury!

Lucy: Bill and I met Don and Linda Weeden through a very embarrassing mishap that occurred on our first expedition to Cape Scott, a few years earlier. Our group then consisted of Bill and me, Tory and Fred, Barbara and Steve Yarnall and Bill Hanson. We had chartered a floatplane and told the pilot to land us at the north end of Hansen Lagoon near the old Cape Scott settlement. When we arrived we found an old wagon, a boathouse, various antique implements and glass fragments from a church. The boathouse seemed like a perfect shelter for the night, saving us the trouble of putting up our tent. Half of the floor was missing so we put our sleeping bags and mats on the good side. The next morning it was raining so Paul set up our camp stove on the dirt side of the cabin floor. We had a good breakfast since we planned to walk to the lighthouse, several miles to the west.

Don and Linda Weeden welcomed us warmly and offered us delicious homemade cinnamon buns and coffee. We lingered, having a great informative chat with them and then started walking back. It had been a lovely walk because we had left our packs in the boathouse and were carrying nothing. On the last lap of the walk, we saw a little wisp of smoke coming from the beach ahead and wondered for a while what it could possibly be. As we approached, it dawned on us it was coming from the direction of the boathouse, at which point we all broke out in a frenzied run, arriving horrified to see flames consuming the structure.

Bill Hanson immediately picked up an old tin can from the beach, filled it with water and kept running back and forth trying to extinguish the fire. The rest of us realized at once it was utterly futile and just stood and watched the large structure burn up like a matchbox in what seemed like only minutes. We found out later that the supposed dirt floor was actually duff—decaying leaves and branches from the forest floor—an ideal fire starter. It seems that Paul's camp stove served as the igniting spark, and while we were away it spread through the entire structure. When the fire had cooled down, we surveyed the ashes; all that remained of our tent, sleeping bags, mats, packs, food and clothes. Bill Hanson found only one thing that survived, a blade from his Swiss Army knife, which he kept as a souvenir. Since we had no food, we returned shame-facedly to the lighthouse, where the Weedens again welcomed the seven of us, without a word of reproof, and treated us to dinner. We had kept in touch with them since then, and today they were as gracious and welcoming as ever.

Pete: No sooner had I sunk into an overstuffed chair than we were called over to the Weedens for coffee. It was like walking into heaven. Before us on the coffee table were hot, fresh baked cinnamon rolls, cookies and chocolate cake. The coffee was served in porcelain cups. We spent the next hour drinking hot coffee and plowing through the snacks while having a lengthy and informative local history lesson with the Weedens. The conversation finally got around to dinner. It was Bill's turn to cook and he had mentioned something earlier about freeze-dried macaroni and cheese (which is something like eating newsprint left in the rain). It was then that the Weedens insisted we stay. We happily accepted.

Before dinner, we hiked over the wooden walkway to the foghorn station. It was precisely five hundred and seventy six stair steps and a short walk on a suspension bridge that hung over a deep gorge. We finally were on the westernmost point of the island. On top was a huge foghorn comprised of twenty separate horns. The sound was jarring. Far below us in the surging sea was a herd of sea lion feeding on carp, diving, nuzzling and playing. We climbed down to the low rocks that were just beginning to be washed by the waves as the tide came in. The sea lions were only about twenty yards from us. In spite of the rain and the darkening skies, we stood there for a long time. I was impressed by how powerful sea lions must be to have such control in the rough waters. A boat would have been splintered on the rocks. To the sea lions, it was a playground.

Dinner was magnificent: hot chili and beer, homemade rolls and cornbread, cold roast beef, sausage, cheese, and apple pie for dessert. Afterwards, we had coffee and liqueur. The conversation was lively. We learned more about the area, with its population of bear and deer, cougars, wolves and other wildlife. We had asked Don to wake us up at 5 a.m. and it was still dark when we arose. On our way to coffee and rolls, Steve spotted Comet West, just over the horizon in very clear view. It was brilliant, like a large star with a distinct tail, stationary just over the trees. We took turns looking at it through Ted's binoculars.

After breakfast, Ted and I took off first, tramping through the mud by flashlight. An hour later, the sky was yellow and pink with the rising sun. At Nell's Bight we picked up the camper who wanted to hike out with us. After our good night's sleep, we were moving quickly. We had to cover nearly 20 miles to meet our driver who was to be on the logging road at 2:30. Within two hours we were back at the settlement loading our packs and eating a snack. We had passed two or three old buildings on the way including a church, completely caved in and quietly being reclaimed by the earth. A half-hour beyond the main settlement we saw the last of the houses. It too had collapsed.

From the book, Cape Scott Story: *It was not so much the natural obstacles that extinguished the colony as much as it was politics. The lack of a good harbor made it extremely difficult. But that deficiency might have been overcome with the building of the road the government had promised. The road was never built. In the settlement's third year, B.C. government stopped issuing leases to new settlers. By 1907, steamer service to Fisherman's Bay was suspended. Most of the settlers moved to more favored population centers, if they stayed on the Island at all.*

Pete: We left the last of the settlement behind us and marched in a line on the trail leading out. It was not raining, but we were sinking to our knees in mud in places. We avoided the deep holes by trying to walk around them or balancing on fallen branches. After a while we just splashed through the puddles and hoped for the best. In the woods, it was cold and damp. Slowed by windfalls, we scrambled over snowy branches. We kept moving because we were too cold to stop for long. As we neared our destination, we came to where the logging operations had moved to within a few feet of the trail. Every tree was down and gone. The ground was packed and rutted where big machinery had pushed the logs out. Here, we cut back into the woods on the old trail. We stopped short of the logging road to wash off our boots in the San Josef River. Finally we arrived, with time to spare.

"It would be terribly ironic," Fred observed, "if they were to build a road now, so that people could see the ruins of a settlement that failed for lack of a road."

On our way to Holberg in the van, we spotted an old man walking toward town.

"He lives out here," Bill said. "He was one of the settlers."

"Let's give him a ride, he'd be great to talk to."

"He doesn't want a ride. Just wave."

So we waved. The old man looked to be in his eighties, perhaps more, but seemed very strong and hardy. As we passed, he turned toward us; city folk, out for a weekend adventure that had ended in the ruins of the village he had grown up in. He didn't smile. He just watched as we drove by.

In the rain forest of Graham Island,
three hundred year old cedars co-exist
with butterflies that live for just one day;
water is everywhere, dripping onto carpets
of green moss, plunging down falls
or simply seeping through the spongy ground.

from The City and the Wild, **Home and Away**

Two hikes in the Queen Charlotte Islands
by Lucy

Since we had not been there before, Bill and I decided to go further north beyond the Olympic Peninsula and Vancouver Island to the Queen Charlottes (now known as Haida Gwaii). Access to those wild and rugged western shores was extremely limited and we looked forward to empty beaches to explore, and uncharted territory. Our group consisted of myself, the two Bills (Dougall and Hanson) and the two Pauls (Stocklin and Williams). Getting up there involved driving to Vancouver B.C., flying to Sandspit and then chartering a floatplane. It would be an hour-long flight to a spot Bill had picked out on the northern tip of Graham Island. As usual, we had no idea what we might encounter along the coastline but hoped we'd make it down to our pick-up spot five days later, a narrow indentation on the map further south. Floatplane pilots are always game for anything and this one readily agreed.

We boarded the plane with all our gear, eager for an adventure. The water was too rough to land us on the exposed ocean beach, so the pilot picked a small bay just inland of our starting point. He cheerfully dropped us there in the middle of nowhere and we were very happy. There were no cell phones and no GPS in those days, and we didn't miss them. It was fair weather and all was clear and beautiful and empty when we started walking south. The first beach was long and sandy. I spotted the remains of a huge Haida Indian longhouse, just inland from the shore, and was amazed at its size. In the old days there used to be large villages made up of rows of longhouses, all made of cedar logs and planking, facing the shore with the owner's carved totem pole attached to the front.

It was one of those rare beach hikes where everything just seemed to go right. The weather remained fine and the camping was superb. Unlike the dense salal and brush next to the Washington beaches, we found places just inland from the beach with a mossy, springy forest floor quite empty of underbrush and very comfortable for sleeping. Every day we walked along beaches that ranged from small rocky coves to wide sandy stretches, littered with shells. It felt to us as though we were the first explorers to have set foot on these rugged shores. The tides were in our favor and the headlands were easy to navigate. The weather held, and every night we camped on another beautiful beach and watched the sun slowly set into the western sea. At one point, Bill remarked that the trip was rather "non-descript," but the rest of us shot him down for being a killjoy and he replied with his usual cheerful question, "I wonder what the poor people are doing?"

The day before we were to rendezvous with our floatplane, we came upon the most remarkable beach I've ever encountered. When we were rounding a headland on some large rocks, we noticed that they were imbedded with smoky-clear pockets of what looked like golden glass. The bright sun shone and glinted through the veins and they looked just like precious jewels. After exclaiming over and examining them for a few minutes, I jumped off of the rocks onto a small beach of light colored sand. Immediately, I noticed several agates. And then several more. It quickly became apparent that the entire beach was literally covered with hundreds, perhaps thousands of agates, all glistening on the sandy shore. I realized at once that they were the polished remains of the veins of golden chalcedony we'd encountered in the headland rocks.

The agates were every size and shape imaginable, from pale gold to deep carnelian red. Some had swirls of white or banded multi-colored layers, and some were clear and totally translucent.

Bill Hanson and I became very excited. We got down on our hands and knees and started collecting them on a piece of driftwood. The others sat on a log and watched us, slightly bemused. Bill H. and I were astounded at the treasure trove and kept exclaiming over one or another stone, holding it up to the light and turning it in our hands. After about 15 minutes, we counted the ones we'd collected. There were more than 300 of them, some enormous in size and all extremely beautiful. We stacked them into a cairn and Bill took a photo. By now, the others had already set off around the next headland. Reluctantly, Bill and I decided to only take a handful each, both because the agates were heavy and also because we wanted to leave the little cove just as we'd found it. I scattered the cairn of agates and said a reluctant farewell to a beach I knew I would likely never see again. Years later, I told the story to a few friends, including one who sailed up and down that northern coast looking intently for the agate beach. Thankfully, they never found it. It was a magical place and I hope it always remains hidden.

The following day we arrived at the small inlet where we expected the plane to land. After four clear days, this last one was foggy and rainy, very difficult for a plane to spot anything. We spread out on the rocks everything colorful that we had including the red tent fly and prayed for an opening in the clouds. We finally heard the sound of a motor but could see nothing at all and were feeling a bit discouraged when suddenly the plane zoomed down through a brief opening. It landed dangerously close to the rocks and tossed alarmingly in the rough surf. The pilot shouted at us to throw the packs to him as fast as possible so we could take off. Paul, complying with the order, flung Bill's a little too far and it landed in the water. With great effort and a lot of cursing from Bill, he managed to yank it out then we all threw ourselves into the plane and the pilot took off like a shot. We all laughed in relief. The entire hike had gone so well, capped off by the marvelous discovery of the little agate cove, and we realized we might have been stranded for days in the notably uncertain weather of the Queen Charlotte Islands. The pilot agreed, and informed us that it was the last time he was ever going try another landing on the open shore.

~ ~ ~

Our second hike, many years later, involved renting a car in Sandspit in order to drive to the north end of Graham Island. Accompanied by our dear friends Tory and Fred, we decided to stop on the way and take a short hike out to Hecate Strait on the inland side of the island and camp for one night. Unlike our first hike, which had been in early fall, this one took place in the middle of winter. Not surprisingly, a major storm was brewing but we had the old red tent fly so I thought, why worry? However, the rain started coming down in torrents and even in the shelter of quite dense woods the wind was blowing at near-hurricane force. Bill and Fred struggled manfully to raise the tent fly, which kept tearing out of their hands and flapping noisily in sharp snaps. It was soon dark. Tory and I, both drenched, looked at the glistening red tent fly dubiously. We did not see how, even if they could secure and peg it down, it would be remotely possible for us to keep dry or to start a camp stove, much less a fire.

Tory and I left the men still struggling and set off walking, with the faint hope that we might come across some kind of a shelter. We had not walked far when, amazingly enough, we actually stumbled on a crude cabin and found the door open. We entered, with silent thanks to the owners, and found it neat and clean and then raced back to tell Bill and Fred. The four of us were soaked to the skin, but ecstatic to be able to get warm and dry so we broke out the over proof rum and lots of dark chocolate and proceeded to get hilariously drunk. I don't remember us eating any supper, but we did a lot of hysterical laughing and discussed important things (so we thought) and Tory and I recited poetry. That went on for much of the night, and in the morning we found the storm had passed over and the sun was out. Miraculously, none of us were even hung over. We walked back to our rental car and drove up north and then began our actual beach hike. It was just as glorious as the one Bill and I had taken years before (though we didn't go as far as the agate beach) and confirmed our sense of being the luckiest people on earth. On our last day, we came upon a small cove where the clouds and mist descended and the sea foam came up to our thighs and wobbled in the wind. Fred took a photo of the two of us, which he called Bill and Lucy in Heaven. I couldn't agree more.

Midwinter storms had raged
for days as we walked south in
drenching rain, leaning against
the relentless pummeling winds
while the seething ocean lashed the sand—

but suddenly there came a pause.
The wind stopped altogether,
sun came out and waves
lapped gently as lake water
on the shore.

from Halcyon Days, **Home and Away**

Cougar Annie

by Peter Berliner

The hardest part of any hike is the first 20 steps to your car. It takes a compelling reason or driving force to pry you from the comforts of home to venture into the unknown. Bill and Lucy Dougall provided both. After any adventure with the two of them, and whomever else they could cajole in joining, I always looked forward to the next—no matter how outlandish it might seem. One of the trips I remember best was in the fall of 1977. I was 30, feeling fit and strong, and under the irresistible sway of the Dougalls, who would entice you to attempt things you never imagined you could with the promise of experiences you would never forget. One thing you could be sure of was that at some point in the journey, perhaps while standing on a frightening precipice, in a driving rain, or underneath a cold and starry sky, Bill would turn and say "I wonder what the poor people are doing?" He meant by that phrase, anyone who wasn't with us right here, right now, experiencing the kind of thrill that lasts a lifetime.

This particular trip took us to a place called Boat Basin, on the rugged outer coast of Vancouver Island. It was accessible only by air or water. We left Seattle after work one Friday in October and drove all night to Tofino. From there we planned to take a floatplane across the Steward's Inlet, to a long beach from which we would surely hike through roaring streams and over impassable headlands. You know—something to make it interesting. It was pouring down rain when we arrived and to our dismay, the storm

85

was too treacherous for a plane to land. Improvising, Bill somehow arranged for the five of us (Lucy, Bill, Ken, Paul Stocklin and me) to hitch a ride on the lumber mill's crew boat to take us to the start of our hike.

We spent the next two and half days hiking up the beach in heavy rain, with winds gusting 40 to 50 mph. We experienced the unavoidable sensations of being wet and cold, enduring the aches and pains that come from hiking for hours over sand and rocks, leaning against the wind, and sleeping in damp bags on thin foam pads on a rocky beach. On the final day of the hike, it rained so hard that we had breakfast inside our tents. But at least we had the wind at our backs so the walking wasn't as difficult. Unlike other trips where we were stranded on one side of a raging river, we actually got to the rendezvous site with the plane earlier than we thought, with time to spare.

So it was that we found ourselves in Boat Basin—five bedraggled hikers walking up a long pathway made of rough-cut cedar planks, past a large woodshed, an even larger chicken shack, and an expansive garden still bearing green beans, beets and carrots, to the cabin where Cougar Annie lived with her grown son Tommy. They were, in fact, the town's only permanent residents. Nearly 90, her hair white, body bent, practically blind, Cougar Annie stepped out to greet us. We made our introductions and then, in a sure and steady tone, her soft eyes not seeing us as much more than shades of light and dark, she told us her story.

When I was ten years old, my father brought my mother and me from Sacramento, California to Johannesburg in South Africa. He was a surgeon and had been invited to come there. My mother was sick and had been for a while. My father thought the change would do her good. I worked very hard in the school there and passed three grades in one year. I even won the spelling competition. All the boys and girls entered. We had to learn the meaning of all the words in Webster's Dictionary. They gave me six gold farthings for winning. But I don't have them. We lost them in the Saskatoon River along with lots of papers and other things, so I can't show them to you.

When I was 13, the instructor told my father he hadn't anything more to teach me. This was during the Boer War that you might have read about in your history books. I was young then. I could hear the sound of guns, but I didn't know much about what was going on. Later, we came to live in Canada and I taught business classes in Edmonton. That is where I met my husband. He was Scottish. His father was the first Lord Mayor of the City of Glasgow. He was knighted by the Queen. I have the paper here saying so. It is signed by Queen Victoria herself. My husband would have been Lord Mayor as well, but being Lord Mayor doesn't pay the rent. I found that out. The man never worked a day in his life until he was 36.

Later, we lived in Vancouver. I had my own business and made eleven dollars a day. I hired two women, one to clean and one to take care of the children. They said I was the best mistress they had ever worked for. I used to buy and sell pedigree dogs. I found you could buy them quite reasonably because people would have these pups that were messy, and they were glad to sell them. My husband used to say that I could buy them at the back door for $10 and sell them at the front door for $25. My husband was working with the telegraph company then, but he spent more than he made and he spent what I made too. He had a problem with drinking, same as he'd had back in Glasgow, but I hadn't known about that. He would drink. Then he would take my money down to Chinatown to a place off of Patton Street, and gave it to a Chinaman. There was opium there, you see. The man would take fifty dollars and give him ten cents in return. That is why we had to come here.

Annie paused for a moment to pull back the hood of her yellow rain parka from her brow. Under the parka, she wore an ageless dress. She wasn't a big woman, probably about 5'4", but even then, seemed strong. Her hands shook slightly. She told us that after finding out about their brother's state of dissolution, his sisters arranged for the family to move to Boat Basin and Anton's Landing—property that had been preempted from a Russian family. They allowed him 10 crowns a month to live on. But her husband died soon after they arrived, and Annie had to live off the land. By then she was raising eight children.

I loved to garden since I was very young. My father brought me flowers from the bush in South Africa. He said that whatever I touched would grow. So I cleared enough land for a big garden. I trapped quite a bit; minks and martens and cougars. I shot ten cougars one season and sold them for forty dollars each. That's how I got the name Cougar Annie. I guess I could still trap a cougar or shoot him if I had to. I'd have to get up pretty close to see it though. I shot two martens in one day and sold them for $35. But I earned the most money raising flowers. I could pack and send a parcel of dahlia bulbs the same as a sack of potatoes. I sent them all over the country. After a while, I was doing so much business at the postal station that they made me its head post-mistress! I raised hens and sold the eggs. I still collect the eggs and check them for size and for cracks. I can't clean them though. I don't know which ones are dirty. The hens seem to know I'm blind. They used to peck me. Now they push out the chicks so I can give them their feed, and they show me where their eggs are. We've almost always been here by ourselves. There was another family for a while—a couple named the Wheelers. Mrs. Wheeler was just a girl really. One night she came over asked me if Margaret, my four year old, could stay overnight for company. I said, "Yes, if you make a fire and keep her warm and give her some breakfast in the morning."

"I'll have to chop some wood then," she said to me.

Now this was a little girl, frail. She wore a size two and a half shoe. I knew she couldn't chop that wood. I told her, "Why don't I come over and chop you some wood while you cook us something to eat?"

"I haven't got anything to bake with," she said.

Well. I got some flour and things and took it over. She didn't have anything in that cabin to speak of. She must have been near starved. I chopped some wood, and she made baking powder biscuits. Then I left Margaret there for her company. The next morning I looked out over there and didn't see any fire burning. I waited a bit, then decided to go have a look to see where they were. When I got there, Margaret was on the bed. One sock was on. One sleeve of her dress was on. There was no fire.

"Mommy," she said. "I can't get Mrs. Wheeler up. She won't wake up."

I did about everything I could think of. I got the place warm and got one of the boys to take Margaret home. I called the company where her husband was. Pretty soon, he came with another man in a boat. They jumped off and hurried to the cabin. But the anchor of the boat wasn't set. The boat washed away and later we found it broken up on the shore. Her husband tried what he could, but still she didn't wake up. He called the doctor, Dr. Bridges, in Tofino, but he said he had no way to get there. The doctor wouldn't come, you see. So there was nothing to be done. The men. Well, they did what they felt they had to do, and they buried her right under where those fruit trees are. She still had some color, and she didn't stiffen up the way you'd expect. I don't know. I did everything I could. But I just don't feel that she was dead. He was her husband and had to decide. He never came back after that.

We had been on the porch for some time now. She had been standing the entire time. Finally, Bill said, "I think we've interrupted your lunch. We should let you go."

"Oh yes," she said, "I've got to get Tom his lunch and feed the chickens after that. But you should come back sometime when I'm not so busy. You won't tell anyone about what I said about my husband will you?"

We assured her we wouldn't, shook her hand and said our goodbyes.

"Well, come back when you can," she said in parting.

Soon after, we climbed into the plane that would take us back to our car in Tofino. Civilization came on fast. We drove to Nanaimo, caught the last ferry and drove home. I didn't get home until four in the morning. I felt dog tired from the trip, and it felt good to be in my bed. I woke up late the next morning, drank hot coffee and devoured three days of newspapers. As I watched the rain outside my window, I thought about Cougar Annie, in her cabin amidst the cedars and the firs, warmed by the fire she built from the wood that she chopped herself. I would have never have known about her—or for that matter ever attempted the kind of trip we undertook were it not for Bill and Lucy. I guess some people are just born with intrepid spirits that makes them want to squeeze every bit of life they can from every experience. People like the Dougalls—or Cougar Annie.

A child can make an ocean from a puddle,
a mountain from a pile of stones. And so it was
for me when I grew up in the city.
Now, gray pavements and mind-formed lines
seem harsh to eyes and unforgiving to the body

while rock on a mountain is primordial,
part of earth and permanent. Knees,
thighs and ankles bend and give,
adapt to follow contours of the land;
shoulders and wrists twist to navigate
through brush and branches, thread
through vines and over fallen trees.

from The City and the Wild, **Home and Away**

High up on that mountain leave your sorrows down below...

Mountain Climbs

The Return

Waiting, pacing, ricocheting back
and forth; jumping at the phone's shrill ring,
watching hard for headlights through the black,
I conjure up disasters in a string
and calculate, as nervous stomach churns,
how long it takes to get you down the mountain /
down the river / from the sky / to then return
over the long miles home to where I wait.
Lights finally flare from darkness, brakes glissade,
the car door slams and you at last appear
smiling, unshaven, tired but flushed and glad,
laden down with pack and sopping gear.
The weight lifts from my heart, all knots untwine;
You leave your virile world and reenter mine.

from **Migrations**

Aconcagua, 1964
by Bill

Sitting here in the relative lap of luxury in the hotel at Puente del Inca, I feel the urge to fill you in on the events of the last few days. All this past week I have been up on the side of Aconcagua at a flat spot at 14,400' called Plaza de Mulas. Actually, I should say I have been climbing from there, because we spent several days acclimatizing at the basecamp of Plaza de Mulas. There had been a long period of good weather for Aconcagua, weeks in fact, which is very unusual. The summit of Aconcagua is nearly 23,000' and it is the highest mountain in the world outside of Asia. Monday, we decided to start up via a new, direct route that I had proposed.

There were six of us; Professor Vicente Chiccitti from Mendoza, and from the Seattle/Everett area, Paul Williams, Gene Mason, Ralph Mackey, and Dick Hill. We were carrying two mountain tents, climbing equipment and six days' worth of food, which made our packs weigh about 35 pounds. I had been against bringing the tents because of their weight. Because of various ailments, no one was in especially strong condition. Paul Williams was worst off. He had suffered from dysentery ever since arriving from the U.S. ten days before. Everyone was poorly acclimatized and had headaches all night. But we had to go because of the weather. It broke the day we left when a storm blew in.

We ground our way slowly through gullies and up cliffs. Around sunset, we reached a place under some massive cliffs at about 17,500'. This was an open spot on a frozen talus slope of about 450'. It was hard to stand on, much less traverse. Dick Hill scouted around and found a remarkably flat spot some distance away. We were even able to set the tents up end to end. It was cold. The wind was blowing, and it was snowing. Gene Mason and I cooked dinner between the tents, on Primus stoves. They kept plugging up because the white gas is so poor down here. It took forever to melt snow for soup. Paul got sick when he tried to eat. He was really low. It was hard to sleep. It was also hard to get up. Still snowing and blowing. The thermometer read 12°. Gene, Ralph and Dick (the Everett three) went to scout a route. Paul and Vicente were feeling low. The scouts returned and said they had found a gulley that would go through. We spent the rest of the day fixing a rope on a steep ice slope. Cooking dinner was hard again.

We were up relatively late again on Wednesday. No one had any great urge to take off. The Everett three packed up at about noon, put on crampons, and started hiking toward the gulley. I stayed back to watch Paul and Vicente. Paul wasn't going to make it, so I talked him into going down. He really was in bad shape, but he was reluctant to give it up. I sold him by saying it wasn't conducive to safety in the mountains. I was going to take him back down but Vicente, who was moving poorly, insisted over my mild protests that he would accompany him. I moved fast, and caught up to the Everett three where the gulley necked down to an hourglass part where they had fixed the rope and cut some steps. Above that, the gulley opened into a wide snowfield, and looked easy. It was snowing, but not blowing, and was foggy. Then Vicente appeared at the bottom of the gulley, climbing and shouting. Paul was down and in distress.

Gene and I debated. I decided I had to go back, and told the others to go on. We hesitated because Gene is a doctor, a pretty good one. I took everyone's picture, described the route to them above the gulley, and went back down. The reason I describe all this in such detail is that this is Monday, and that was last Wednesday, and I haven't seen them since. They had about four or five days food, a tent, and are fairly strong and mountain wise. But they should have reached the summit in two or three days, then descended by the standard route.

When I left the Everett three, I told them I would come back up the route to meet them. Then I went down to help with Paul.

By coaxing, Vicente and I got him back down to where we'd camped the night before and put the tent back up. We all got inside the tent and waited out the day and following night. The next morning we got up early, abandoned the food, and set off down the slope. It was slow and difficult to keep Paul interested and going, but we finally got back to Plaza de Mulas, and put the tent up again. It was windy through the night, but the next morning it cleared up, although still gusty. I decided to go for the summit using the refuges on the standard route. I told Paul I was going. Then I packed up my blue parka and wind pants, my sleeping bag and some food. I was looking at an over 8,000' gain in elevation from our base camp to the summit.

I started grinding my way up switchbacks with the wind blowing. I had that stupid wind meter, but as usual didn't dare use it because of the danger of exposing my hands. I should have been suspicious when I saw lenticular clouds forming over the smaller peaks (15,000 to 18,000') even though none were forming over Aconcagua. It started to snow and whiteout at times, but I plodded on. There was a long traverse at about 18,000' but the trail was obliterated by snow. I had only an aerial photo, which I studied from time to time, as a guide. Finally, in the late afternoon, I started up the final ridge. I was in a real storm and was looking for the refuge. One gust caught me taking a step with my foot in the air. It spun me around and I fell down on my knees. At about 19,000 feet I was really laboring. It felt like I was like lifting lead weights. At about 5 p.m., I got to approximately where the refuge should be, but couldn't find it.

For the first time, I had reached the end of my resources. I felt like a dumb pack animal and couldn't go on. So I gave up, and I knew I was giving up. Again, I'm going into great lengths because of the novel situation. Interestingly enough, I was never worried. Somewhere, struggling above me were three climbers, two of whom are now apparently dead. Not the Everett three, but the climbers I'll describe later. Anyway, I had my sleeping bag, and one of the plastic tarps I always carried. I knew I could dig in under a rock for the night. But even though I had come up 6,000' in eight hours instead of the usual twelve, I was quitting on a route that everyone but old ladies had done. Maybe my lack of energy had to do with the fact that I'd taken Paul down the mountain before coming back up, but at any rate, I was beat.

So down I stumbled. Because I couldn't see any distance, I couldn't get a bearing, and the wind had swept my tracks completely clean. I recognized some markers on the way but then hit a flat spot that felt unfamiliar. I continued to angle down but I felt uneasy. It occurred to me that to drop down on the wrong side of a ridge could put me in another valley, and perhaps in trouble. I waited for a clearing, but the wind got worse. I got out the compass, and checked to see that I was moving southwest. I moved tentatively, and then stopped, over and over. Darkness was approaching so I tried to hurry. Finally, I found some snowed-in switchbacks and bounded on down. The switchbacks gradually became clearer, so I raced and slid down, even though they still did not seem completely familiar,

Suddenly, the switchbacks ended in a good trail off to the left around a ridge of unfamiliar rock. I knew the trail I had come up did not do this. I was immensely depressed. I couldn't understand why there would be good switchbacks in another valley. I was too tired to climb back up, and I was going to have to spend the night out. The storm was getting worse. The wind blew down the mountain in great torrential gusts. Twice I had been knocked over. It cleared between great gusts so I could see down into the valley, which looked strange. The compass showed it running parallel to my valley. It made no sense. I assumed the switchbacks went up to a mine, so I labored back up towards the rocks hoping to find a sheltered place below them to sleep.

I waited with my back to the wind for each gust to end, and studied the valley as best I could. It pieced together much like my valley, but just looked different. Finally, to my happy surprise, I recognized definite markers. You don't think as clearly and logically in high elevations, but eventually I realized that two valleys could not be so much alike, and what was making it seem foreign is that I was seeing it through driving snow. There had been no snow on the valley floor when I left, only glaciers. But even the glaciers took on a different appearance. So I started down again, and on around the trail. It turned out that the great open slope on the northwest side was divided by a huge rock mass called the Condor's Nest, and switchbacks went up each side of it. So I smashed and slid down the rest of the endless switchbacks and plodded into Plaza de Mulas. To my pleasant surprise, everyone in the refuge had been worried about me and made me good things to eat.

It was cold in the tent that night. The next day I sat around and talked to Paul. My face was badly wind-burned from goggle-level down. I didn't dare blow my nose, or open my mouth too wide. It was bitter cold again the following night. On Saturday, I watched, squinting into the sun, for the Everett trio to appear. I had great confidence in Gene, Ralph and Dick, but the storm on Friday had defeated me, and it is a big mountain. They did not appear. On Sunday I sat against the refuge, still exhausted. Maybe it was the altitude, but I had a hard time accounting for my sheer lack of energy. The time was getting long. Out of nowhere, I heard a voice in English coming from the cliffs. I couldn't believe it. The cliffs above camp, cut by steep gullies, are over 500 feet high. I heard the voice again, but knew it wasn't one of my friends, and no one else around spoke English. Finally, the voice said, "Help me."

I answered, and heard rocks coming down an extremely steep gulley. I couldn't imagine how, but some stranger was up there so I ran to the refuge and got a rope. I then saw a figure half way up a precipitous gulley filled with loose rock and snow. I started up as fast as the altitude and my limited resources would allow. I had to stay to the side of the gulley because of rocks that were being knocked down. I passed a Mexican climber, also heading up the gulley. I shouted up meaningless, comforting phrases to the stricken figure like, *You're all right now.* Finally, I got close enough for us to talk. I asked his name, which was Rudy, and said, *How are your feet?* He answered, *Look at them.* I did, and couldn't believe my eyes. This young man, really a boy, didn't have any shoes on and his feet were torn to pieces. He said, *I won't be doing any more climbing.* I didn't know what to say. The Mexican climber reached Rudy and threw his arms around him like a mother to a child. I had this great lump in my throat and actual tears in my eyes, and felt a great longing to be like this Mexican in such a situation.

The boy's feet were awful. Not only cut and gouged, but green and white. They looked like they were frozen solid. His hands were also cut up, but I hardly noticed them. Rudy was German but spoke English, so I started talking to reassure him, meanwhile digging in my heels and holding him around the shoulders. He told me how, on the day of the storm, he and another young German friend and the Mexican priest—whom I had met at basecamp— had found the upper refuge full of snow, and spent the night out at 22,000'. The next day they hadn't made it down to the next refuge because the Padre had gone snow blind and couldn't walk, so they slept another night out. In the morning, Rudy's shoes wouldn't fit and his friend was gone, somehow having wandered off during the night. The Padre didn't answer when Rudy tried to wake him, so he walked barefoot in rocks and snow, from 21,000' to 14,000' where I found him in the gulley. Unbelievable!

I took off my shoes one by one, and held the German boy while the Mexican climber brushed gravel and skin from his feet, and put my boots on him. Paul had heard the commotion and had now arrived. With rope, and one of us on each side, we gradually walked and slid Rudy down the rest of the gulley, me in my stocking feet. The Mexican didn't understand English, so I translated about the snow-blind Padre as best I could, and sent him up to find him. Rudy, who was about 25, was superb. It took almost an hour to get him down. We tried to carry him across the flat area before the refuge, but he pushed us back and walked the rest of the way, supported on either side. The insides of my boots he was wearing were wet with blood.

At least two others, Rudy's German friend and the snow blind Padre, were in real trouble on the mountain at this point. But it was 3 pm., and there wasn't enough time to reach the lowest of the refuges before dark. Besides, we couldn't carry bodies, living or dead. I decided to walk out to Puente del Inca to get help from the army and high altitude mules. The Mexican climber had reappeared, and he decided to hike the 42 kilometers down with me. I was pretty beat by now, but running on adrenaline. Several kilometers down the trail we met cargo horses coming in to take people out, so we commandeered a couple, and rode what seemed an endless seven hours. Walking would have been faster. When you are saddled with a feeling of urgency, as I was thinking about the stranded climbers and that poor German boy and his feet, being only able to walk horses is oppressive. But the mule track down, with skeletons of mules at the bottom of ravines and so forth, is something you have to see to understand why walking them is the only alternative. The last part was in pitch darkness.

At the army post, I labored to report the actual situation in my poor Spanish. The Mexican climber kept toning it down because he couldn't accept the possible death of the Padre, whom he'd been unable to locate. I knew I had to rouse these army people out in earnest. From Rudy's description, I was sure that the Padre was dead, and probably the other German boy, but I couldn't say so, especially in front of the Mexican. Besides, Gene, Ralph, and Dick were up there somewhere too, and they were overdue. Somehow, I got across the urgency of the situation and the army swung into action. They sent me off to get dinner at 11 p.m., and gave me a room at the hotel. I had planned on riding back in to help, but I fell asleep about midnight after finishing dinner. The rescue party started on the trail at about 2 a.m. At 5 a.m. they sent in radios, and posted guards at the valley mouth to prevent any other climbers from heading up the mountain, so as not to confuse the picture. I got up at daybreak, found all this out, and went back to bed.

That day, today, once I woke up I spent hours telling my story in broken Spanish to various people. They called to Mendoza for a helicopter, which can't come until the day after tomorrow because of winds. At about 3 p.m., the radios made contact. Paul had sent the German boy, Rudy, out on a horse, so I went up to the mouth of the valley to greet and pay tribute to this foolish yet invincible kid. About 5 p.m. a car drove up to where I was sitting, and out jumped a couple of Argentines who came over and congratulated me. It seems the news had just came over the radio that Gene, Ralph and Dick had struggled to the summit today, and were safely on their way back to the basecamp, Plaza de Mulas. It was a big deal, these Americans making it to the summit on a new route. I was sorry I hadn't been a part of it, but I'd been busy going up and down the mountain to help people in distress, and that was a pretty fair trade-off.

The German boy arrived about 9 p.m. and an ambulance was waiting with me to rush him to Mendoza. His toes were already black. But his feet had been bleeding, so there had been circulation. As I was riding out on the horse the day before, I remembered that I hadn't asked if they warmed up his feet in warm water. There did not seem to be any signs of infection or gangrene, but his feet were in such terrible condition I couldn't be sure. I don't even know about his hands. After dinner, which was at about 10:30 p.m., I went over to the radio shack to listen in on the scheduled transmission. It came. The patrol on mules had found the Padre and the second German boy, sleeping the sleep of forgetting and forever in the snow where Rudy had told me he had left them, and where had he left his shoes. He had been especially concerned about his shoes, because his passport was carefully stowed in one of them.

The Padre will become something of a legend around here. Everyone has a story about him. This would have been his fourth time up the mountain. He was the type of person you couldn't ignore, good or bad, which you've met many times. A container of energy, pushing around to use itself up. Maybe like me, if the similarity occurs to you. I like to think I have high-minded goals, in addition to all my peripheral smashing, but then, the Padre had committed himself to the church in the main. Suddenly, as is usual with an unexpected death, I began remembering various things from our few days together at the Plaza de Mulas. How the Padre had fixed my head when I had knocked myself down on the low doorway of the refuge and was bleeding. How we had sung *Because* together, and he had drowned me out. How on the last morning before he went up the mountain, he had commented on how my leading the singing of *Alouette* had pleased him, and how I had taken pictures of him saying Mass last Sunday, with Paul as altar boy.

100

Well, this makes for a lot of reading. I feel better getting it off my chest. Writing it down this way makes a kind of record. In a year, when I'm back, I will be able to remember it more as it actually happened rather than in the generalized, intellectual way that time will push me into. There are of course many peripheral details of things and people that I have left out. Sitting here, cooling off in the Puente del Inca Hotel, makes me realize how I can only make moderate excursions away from city-type life before my body starts to show real wear and tear. The weather, especially the storm on Friday has made a mess of my face. I look like a leper, except for the fact that the hotel tourists look at me with a little awe instead of disgust. My nose is still swollen from breathing cold air, my fingernails are cracked and bleeding from cold and dryness. At least I've stopped smelling. I didn't realize how bad it was until I got into the hotel dining room Sunday night and started looking under the table to see what dead animal had been left there. I didn't like the smell, even if it was my own. So I took a shower, and joined the modern world.

Lucy's Postscript: About two weeks after Bill came back from Aconcagua, a taxi came screeching up to our house in Santiago. A man leaped out and ran up the driveway frantically with a telegram addressed to me. It was the telegram Bill sent when he got down off the mountain. The German boy, Rudy, was taken to a hospital in Argentina where he spent two full years recovering from his ordeal. He had multiple surgeries and lost over half of his hands and feet. Bill and I visited him in the hospital and took a picture of him surrounded by a group of very pretty nurses. His spirits were high and he radiated a joy of life, in spite of his physical loss. Some years later, we visited him in Munich. At this point, he had created some sort of device for his hands that actually allowed him to play guitar. He also invented skis for his crippled feet. He never felt sorry for himself. Years later, he wrote a book (in German) about his ordeal. Neither Bill nor I could read German, but we did find Bill's name and picture in the book. We kept in touch for years, and Rudy never failed to thank Bill profusely for giving up his boots and helping save Rudy's life.

The rope pinches taut around my waist,
caught by an ice-axe anchor in the snow above.
I hang suspended, dangling between sheer walls
of ancient ice, cold storage vault of winter,
ominous blue loveliness. Above, a narrow
slit of sky, below, a boundless darkness.
This rope can be my lifeline or my noose.

from Lure of the Glacier, **The Simple Life**

Noah's Ark
by Bill

Prologue, 1962: It all started one Sunday afternoon at the Moorings, our beach house in Mantoloking, New Jersey. My good friend Dick Barkle was preparing to face rush-hour traffic back to New York, wallowing in self-pity with a gin and tonic and a remark about his boss who was off having a good time on his sailboat. "And I'm left with this Noah's Ark thing," Dick said. I asked him to elaborate, not being especially surprised by the idea of Noah's Ark. After all, this was Dick Barkle—the public relations man extraordinaire for Pan American Airlines—who had done such things as take a monkey dressed in a tuxedo (named J. Fred Muggs) to some of the best restaurants in Europe. "Some man sold my boss on the idea of contributing to an expedition to climb Mount Ararat to confirm evidence of a find some Frenchman made there," he said.

Now this was something I knew about. A Frenchman, Fernand Navarra, had climbed this 17,000' glacier clad mountain in eastern Turkey in the 1950s and come whooping and hollering down off the mountain claiming he had seen the Ark buried in the glaciers. He even said he had been able to chop through the ice and extract a piece of wood and bring it home. Mountaineering is my avocation, and I read everything about climbs—this was simply one of the many articles and news stories that I had filed away in my memory. The Frenchman had written an account of it, and now some people in England—more interested in mountain climbing than biblical history—had decided to organize an expedition to look into his claims. At about the same time, a group of Seventh Day Adventist church members led by George Vandeman became the driving force behind the actual expedition. For them, it was important to find any corroborating evidence for biblical stories.

These men contacted the Frenchman and, in addition to discussing the story with him, they obtained a piece of the wood that he found in 1955 and claimed was from the Ark. It was about five feet long and seven or eight inches square. The Frenchman claimed to have climbed down into a crevasse in the glaciers, some 40 feet, and to have chopped it from a large structure exposed in the ice. He even got excited enough to decide that it was one of the ship's ribs. These Adventists decided to get the wood carbon-dated and a piece of it was sent to one of the two universities that can conduct such a process. In addition to the carbon dating, which involves actual destruction of the wood, they asked what type of wood it was, and any other details that could be determined. The report that came back got them quite excited, since it bore out the bible story in practically all respects. The age of the wood was put at about 4,500 years plus or minus 250 years. A detailed inspection of the wood indicated that it was hand tooled by a tool similar to an adze, that it was white oak of a type that doesn't exist any longer and that it had been immersed in water or ice for an extended period of time. This university had no previous knowledge of the source of the wood, and in fact asked what the source of the wood was after they compiled the report.

Based on this news, the group decided to organize their own expedition, which required both meeting with the Frenchman and raising a large sum of money for expenses. They set up a nonprofit, calling it the Archeological Research Foundation, and went about getting sponsors and donations. Meanwhile, the English expedition was having organizational difficulties, so the two groups ending up merging and sharing efforts. Dick Barkle came into the picture because Dick was doing work for Pan American Airways, which was a possible source of money or transportation or both. When Barkle's boss was shown a piece of this mysterious wood and the results of the carbon dating project, he became very interested and decided to give the project some support.

Now, jumping back to Dick and me on that Sunday afternoon. When I learned that Pan Am was going to support this expedition to a remote mountain I had always wanted to climb, I half-jokingly suggested that I be sent along as Pan American's representative. Dick, with great composure, replied, "Okay, you're in."

"Have another drink Dick," I said.

The next morning, I was just barely up and reading the New York Times when Dick called from New York and said he had been on the phone to San Francisco. The expedition needed another expert mountaineer and they would like to have me go.

"Well Dick, when would I leave?"

"Next week," he said.

This left me with something of a dilemma. Did I really take this seriously and make plans to go off to Eastern Turkey on the say so of one of my best friends—a friend who had once come to a costume party as the New Jersey Turnpike, and charged people 10 cents apiece to walk across him? I decided, with my engineer's training and experience, to do neither and both. I would make some motions in the direction of going, but not really assume I *was* actually going. The former led to telephoning Seattle to ask my good friends to pack and send my climbing equipment via airmail ($32 in postage). Secondly, I went to the American Alpine Club in New York City to read about Mount Ararat. I found several books and articles that were quite interesting. Most usefully, Lucy's mother—by some great coincidence—actually had one of the Frenchman's books, written in French. This was an account of his first trip and was a sort of old-fashioned, segmented paperback. I read it carefully, particularly where he wrote that he had traced out a dark shape buried in the ice, and that he found the shape to resemble that of a large ship. It turned out that I was the only one on the expedition who had actually read his book.

I kept in contact with Barkle, pressing him for details. He confessed that he didn't actually know the names of the people going on the expedition. Even so, I continued to assume I was (or wasn't) going and took care of details. I got a new passport, extra pictures and shots. My climbing gear arrived, papered with postage stamps. Dick told me the name of someone in Ankara to whom I was to send three photographs, my passport number, and my father and mother's names. This was for a clearance to the fortified military zone, where Russia borders Turkey. Foreigners were not particularly welcome in Turkey, and getting clearance to climb Mount Ararat was very unusual.

I still drove down to Washington D.C. with Lucy and the children as I had promised, so they could see the sights. We stayed with an old friend, a lawyer, to whom I mentioned the trip to Turkey and the goal of the expedition. He paused and said in a semi-concerned (but trying not to embarrass me) tone, "Bill, you don't really think there's an Ark do you?"

The following hot and humid day in D.C. I got a call from Barkle telling me to call a number in San Francisco. The man on the other end of the line said the expedition was happy to have me along, especially since I spoke French and could communicate with Navarra, the Frenchman. I had told Dick Barkle to inform the Research Foundation that in addition to being a climber, I read and spoke French. I meant the word spoke (in the past tense) literally because I hadn't spoken French in 15 years—not since my year of studying at the Sorbonne where I'd actually been noted for being very poor at speaking the French language. The man on the phone didn't know this. He said they were glad I had this skill and called me their official interpreter. I deprecated my abilities modestly, but still tried to make myself sound like a desirable asset to the expedition. Finally, this man on the phone asked, "Could you leave tomorrow?"

"Yes, I could. But where am I supposed to go?" I asked.

He told me to go to the Grand Hotel in Paris and meet a man named Bill Loveless. So the next morning I shoveled all the kids into the car, dropped them at Lucy's parents' house in New Jersey, and continued on to New York. Lucy and her brother Dick had

106

decided to come see me off. As we passed the last drug store before getting on the Turnpike, I stopped to get some film. As an afterthought, I got a roll of adhesive tape and a small bottle of aspirin. Later, when we were finally on the mountain and opened up a ton and a half of equipment and supplies, I realized that I had the only adhesive tape and aspirin on Mount Ararat.

Dick Barkle was to meet me in the Pan Am terminal in New York, but I still felt a little odd walking in with my ice axe under my arm and no ticket. Fortunately, he appeared and then took Lucy and her brother out to the plane where we were photographed in a way that the *Pan American Clipper* was in the background. As I got on the plane, Dick introduced me to Dave Baxley. Dave was also in Public Relations and was being sent along because things sounded too vague to Pan Am, which was funding a portion of the expedition. Dave had come in for an ordinary day of work without any idea that he was going to take the night flight to Paris and wouldn't return for another five days. Pan Am had decided to send Dave because of an enormous coincidence. During his military service he had been stationed in Bordeaux, and had lived at a rooming house that was run by one of the Frenchman who had gone on the first Mount Ararat trip. This became important because our Frenchman (Navarra) who had found the wood had suddenly grown very cool about going on the new expedition. But since this other Frenchman, Raymond Zerbini, had gone with him, it seemed that either one of them would do.

Dave Baxley and I sat up all night on the plane talking about the trip. We decided that Baxley would go directly to Bordeaux while I went to the Grand Hotel to meet with Bill Loveless. A Pan Am interpreter met us, expedited us through customs, and then I took a bus into Paris. By the time I arrived at the Grand Hotel I'd been up for a day and a half and was feeling pretty heavy-eyed. I inquired at the desk for Loveless. He wasn't registered, so I checked in and went up to my room. I still wasn't sure that all of this wasn't an enormous joke crafted by Dick Barkle. It was just the sort of thing he would cook up. Here I was in Paris complete with my ice axe, and so far I hadn't met anyone connected with the expedition. I took off my shoes, lay down on the bed and went to sleep. Almost immediately, the phone rang. A voice said, "Hello, is this Dougall? Come down to my room." No introduction, just that.

Being confused and tired I said, "I haven't got my shoes on."

"I'll come up," said the voice, and the phone was hung up.

I'd had just a half hour of sleep and was having trouble tying my shoelaces. The door burst open and in rushed a man who, without any introduction, pulled up a chair facing me, sat down and took out of his pocket a huge wad of American money. He counted off a large number of $100 bills, shook them at me and said, "Offer him $2,000." Then he put the other pile of bills into his own pocket and said, "If he won't do it for that, you can offer him the rest of the $10,000." All this time I was still bent over, trying to get my shoelaces tied.

For want of anything else to say I asked, "Who?"

"The Frenchman," he said in a semi-irritated voice. "He drove up from Bordeaux with his son, and he's waiting downstairs to talk to us."

"But why do you want me to offer him the money," I asked innocently.

"Because you're the interpreter for the expedition!"

This was almost too much to handle, but I was too sleepy to think of any face-saving device to extricate myself, or even delay the trip downstairs. Loveless went rushing out of the room with me several steps behind, one shoelace still untied. Under my breath I was trying out some French phrases such as, "*Bonjour*," and" *Je m'appelle Beel Doogaal.*"

On the elevator, which was dropping like a stone, Loveless said, "We think he's stalling, holding out for more money, or (and this was said with a dark look) someone's got to him."

We got to the ground floor and walked toward the lounge. There was the Frenchman and his 20-year-old son, Raphael, sitting in a couple of armchairs. Navarra was sound asleep. With a weak smile I went in, knowing that my French wasn't too hot but that I was going to try to talk them into going on the expedition. We pretty quickly got around to Navarra saying he couldn't go, because the business he had so laboriously built up after various trips to Turkey would suffer enormously. Having the preconception that Frenchmen didn't make large amounts of money, and thinking of that $2,000 backed up by $8,000 more, I felt pretty much in control of things.

"Well," I said, "and how much would you lose if you were to come with us?"

"One million francs a day," he replied, adding "that's $2,000 a day."

Staggered, but not defeated, I figured that we would just need five days of his time. I suggested that maybe we could fly him to the mountain, rush him up long enough for him to point where to dig, and then rush him back. "No," Navarra said grandly, "three weeks would be the minimum time possible for such a trip." That would make $42,000, a lot more than what we had.

"Well, how about your son?" I inquired, since I had heard that he had been with him when this piece of wood was found. No, it turned out that the son had slipped a disc in a skin-diving accident. By this time we had moved to Loveless' room and had been joined by Bill Dopp, a member of our expedition. He looked very unhappy over all this dickering. The conversation had taken up a great deal of time since I had to transmit to Loveless what was being said. I was a pretty poor interpreter considering I could barely speak French myself, and I couldn't insert my own opinion because right at the start the Frenchman had let me know that his son understood some English. My instinct was to like Navarra and to trust him, but there were some things about his story that were pretty hard to accept. Namely, finding Noah's Ark.

Finally, I off-handedly suggested the name of the other Frenchman, Zerbini, the one who owned the rooming house in Bordeaux. I was a bit concerned because I had heard that the two were close friends and if it was money Navarra was after, he might think that we were trying to get his friend to undercut him. Also, I knew I couldn't bring up Dave Baxley, who was already down in Bordeaux, because if Pan Am was mentioned that might smell like more money. Navarra dismissed the second Frenchman as being a good fellow, but apparently, although he'd been on a couple of earlier expeditions he had never been up by the Ark. This took me aback because we had sort of counted on the second Frenchman as an ace in the hole, and Baxley was down there already priming the pump. Navarra started to get restive, and allowed as how he ought to be getting back to Bordeaux. I suggested that he drop back by the hotel at about 6:30 when some maps and photographs were due to arrive with another contingent of our group from London. Surprisingly, he said he was willing to locate his find on charts. We bundled the Frenchman and his son out the door and then tried to decide where to go from this mess.

About this time the phone rang for me. It was Baxley in Bordeaux, calling to say he had spent the afternoon with Zerbini in a bar, where he was now, and that they were about to leave to come meet us. He insisted that I keep my Frenchman in Paris, because his Frenchman wouldn't do anything without talking to Navarra. Just as I was trying to cut in to say that was utterly impossible, he hung up. All I really wanted to do now was go to bed and make up for some of that lost sleep. The idea of more translating seemed onerous and I wasn't even sure I was communicating at a very intelligent level. I suddenly had the bright idea of calling the Pan Am interpreter who had hustled us through customs, and he agreed to appear when the Frenchman returned. Feeling that things were ready for the meeting at 6:30, I went up to my room, took off my shoes, and went to sleep. It seemed that the phone rang almost immediately. It was Loveless.

"Has anything happened?"

"How should I know, I've been asleep," I mumbled, and hung up. The phone rang again at 6:30 p.m.

"The Frenchman is arriving," Loveless shouted, "you'd better get downstairs."

Loveless and Dopp were waiting for me with one eye on the elevator and the other, nervously, on the front door. We went into the lounge and there was the Pan Am interpreter—the first good news of the day. I explained the payment situation (at which he snorted) and cautioned him that he couldn't be identified as being associated with Pan Am. Dopp guarded the lounge door, looking worried. Finally, looking like Genghis Khan had just arrived, Dopp rushed out into the lobby. Sure enough the Frenchman had returned. We all trouped up to Loveless' room and spread out the maps and aerial photographs. I told Navarra to show me where he'd found the Ark. He asked for a grease pencil and with a sure hand drew a circle on the aerial photograph. "It's inside that circle, or near it," he announced with great assurance. He drew a second circle on the map, which matched the aerial photograph pretty well. I was so relieved by this, I didn't look too carefully at the size of the circle. I discovered later it turned out to be about 2 miles in diameter.

Feeling elated, I let Navarra know that the second Frenchman was on his way on the train. To my relief, he accepted this very expansively and said he would give his personal okay to Zerbini joining the expedition. He even said he would drive us all over to the station at midnight to meet the train. I asked a few more fairly unperceptive questions like, "Was it a big crevasse?" and "Was the crevasse across the glacier or parallel to it?" The Frenchman happily answered my questions. He even had a few photos of him and his young son hauling the wood beam out of the glacier. I was impressed by the pictures. By the time he insisted on taking us to dinner, we were all sort of caught under his spell and feeling pretty enthusiastic.

The Frenchman had actually brought a couple of pieces of the supposed Ark with him. They were small—maybe 5 inches long and several inches wide—and dark, almost black. The wood looked petrified and very old. Navarra handed me one of the pieces and said he wanted me to have it. I was pleased to have an actual artifact to bring home and show my family. It was about 9 p.m. by now and I guess my brief nap had perked me up because I was pretty hungry. We wandered around in back of the Opera where we found lots of closed restaurants. The Frenchman and his son and I were in front, and the others walking behind us kept shouting at Navarra to find a place where they could get a real American hamburger. Some of them had been out of the United States for as much as two days, and the strain was starting to show.

We finished eating and then the Frenchman drove us high speed to *Le Gare du Nord*. In Paris, lights are only turned on at intersections. In the long stretch of the Champs-Elysee by the Louvre we got up to 60 miles per hour with the lights out, which was a pretty unnerving experience. We managed to find the second Frenchman, Zerbini, and Dave Baxley at the station and then took them back to the hotel and got them rooms for the night. Then Baxley and I went out and spent a couple hours at a sidewalk cafe feeling very expansive about the great coup we had just pulled off.

1962 Expedition: On Saturday, we boarded the plane for Ankara, the capital of Turkey. For the first time I met the other climber, an Englishman named Gordon Mansell. Apparently, a startled Pan Am public relations man in London had telephoned Dick Barkle in New York to say that a guy with a long, flowing red beard, a banjo and an umbrella, had just appeared in his office demanding to have a ton and a half of equipment flown to Turkey to look for Noah's Ark. I admit that the first sight of this man made me wonder what eccentric technique he would use to try and save me if I were at the other end of a rope dangling over an ice precipice on Mount Ararat. On the flight, Gordon mentioned another element that was to become a burden in Ankara. It seemed that there were some vague commitments from *LOOK* magazine and the CBS television network of money for the first options on any story of a find. The Archeological Research Foundation directors interpreted this as a requirement that the aim of the expedition should be shrouded in secrecy. It meant that I was supposed to say I was merely a casual tourist in Turkey—ignoring the ice axe and climbing rope that were strapped to my bags.

During the stopover in Istanbul, a small-time news reporter accosted us from Ankara. Since his English was poor, we convinced him that we were only tourists, but that if we did anything unusual we would certainly notify his paper. In Ankara, we were helped through customs by Pan Am and some contacts from the McWilliams Oil Company, which was to lend us a truck. While riding from the airport to Ankara, we got the usual inside dope from people working in a foreign country, notably that our chances of getting permission to climb Ararat were nil and we shouldn't ever look cross-ways at a Turkish official. We languished at a hotel in Ankara for almost a week. It was true that they normally gave no permits to visit Mount Ararat. Turkey had been invaded via the mountain about 12 times by Russia in the last 250 years and just this past spring, the US had installed Jupiter missiles on the southeast side of the mountain. So tensions were pretty high. Turkey was really not keen on civilian groups, particularly Americans, poking around in this area.

Our hope for the permits was through a Turkish lawyer who was a friend of a member of the Archeological Research Foundation. He had been head of the law School of the University, and apparently the heads of government departments were friends or ex-students. Without him, we would have had no chance at all. We diddled around day after day, hoping that mysterious forces were at work processing our requests. The temperature was over 100 F. and the humidity was about 30%. I got to know Mansell, the English climber, and began to appreciate how lucky I was to have him along and how he was going to make the whole trip a good one for me. We also met our last member—an electronics expert named McReynolds—who brought a piece of equipment that would detect buried articles. Since wood assumes small magnetic properties, McReynolds could use it to lay out the shape before we started digging—assuming we located the Frenchman's find.

The Ark, according to the Bible, was 300 cubits long. A cubit is the distance from the elbow to one of the finger joints—about 18 inches—making it some 450 feet long, or about as big as a ten thousand ton freighter. If, as described in the Frenchman's report, it were still intact, the glaciers on the mountain would have to be pretty enormous indeed. McReynolds, the electronics expert, steadily became stranger as time went on. He had already distinguished himself by trying to change money with black marketers in Paris where he was taken for $50. I was beginning to think that our second Frenchman was going to be a problem, since he and McReynolds became inseparable. I found them out in the hotel hallway, playing handball in their underwear. They said they were getting in condition. They both had extremely short attention spans and when you wanted to get them to do something the instructions had to be short, simple, and appeal to emotions rather than logic. I could see that this might be a problem on the climb.

Our expedition members included myself and Mansell, one of Vandeman's sons, a Seventh day Adventist named Bud Crawford, Sahap Atalay, McReynolds and Zerbini. After several days, permission came through for four expedition members (not including me), this being based on the number who had been signed up to make the trip last spring. These four started out in the truck with the supplies while the rest of us would fly to a little town called Agri, about 100 miles from the mountain. Mount Ararat was 800 miles east of Ankara over fair, but unpaved roads. After the four climbers got to Erzurum, they hunted down the military commander to get the additional permits. He said to have us come without them, so we did. That evening, we arrived at Agri, which looked like something out of National Geographic. There was a civilian governor over the military people who had to be bribed before we could go on. We stayed the night in the "traveler's hotel," which at 15 cents was overpriced. The only water was from a 50-gallon barrel with a spigot at the bottom, and the toilet was a hole in the earth some distance away. But our real concern was fleas and lice. Mansell found some DDT and we powdered our beds with it.

The next day I was thrown into the fray again when it turned out that the governor spoke only Turkish and French. His French was certainly better than mine and I commended him on his fine accent. Our expedition plans seemed okay to him, but he wanted us to take along a local guide. We agreed, but the guide managed to get us lost, as well as getting our truck stuck in a swamp. Rather than stay at the traveler's hotel another night, we started out for the mountain. We had arranged for burros to cart our stuff after we got to the end of the drivable land. They were to meet us early the next morning at a spot explained to our guide. On the way to the mountain, the drive shaft fell out of the truck and was cheerfully reinstalled by our driver/guide. He then led us over a long, devious route through little mud-hut villages, fields, a stream with volcanic boulders which had to be cleared by hand, along goat paths, into sand pits, and finally to the approximate rendezvous spot.

Mount Ararat is an inactive volcano that looms over the countryside. There are no other high elevations near it, and the mountain rises to 17,000' from its base at about 2,500'. The temperature at the base in the middle of summer can reach 120 degrees. On the glaciers at the summit it can be below zero at the same time, so on the slopes you can find almost any climate. In the morning, at sunup, the 23 burros and four drivers appeared. With loading and packing, it was 9 a.m. before they started off. This was the part I had been looking forward to—climbing a new mountain—and it was great to be walking and not even have to carry a pack.

In this temperate region there were various encampments of Kurds—nomadic shepherds that we were to run into several times. Besides being picturesque, the Kurd encampments presented the practical problem of having the meanest, surliest, most vicious dogs I've ever seen. Fortunately, I saw right away how the villagers dealt with them. They didn't say, "No! No, Fido!" Instead, they picked up a stone and hit the dog with it as hard as they could. These dogs were so mean, it was a pleasure to bounce a rock off them, and it was a relief to see that it wasn't going to offend the owners. These Kurds were a something of an unknown quantity. They rebelled from time to time, did not pay taxes and went back and forth across various borders. Not long ago, they preyed on travelers. We wished we could be sure that they had given up that kind of nonsense for good. But in fact, our contacts with them were extremely hospitable. One large camp got out their best rug and insisted we all have tea. We sat on this long rug with the villagers all facing us. No one said a word. At one point, when the silence got a little too lengthy, I got out my harmonica and played, *On Top of Old Smokey.*

By noon, some of the expedition members were beginning to show real wear and tear. They couldn't understand why it was so much more tiring than hiking back in good old Slippery Rock state park. McReynolds in particular looked close to tears. I finally got him a burro to ride. These were the dwarf variety that stood about waist high, so the sight of this 250 lb. guy on that small animal, with his feet almost touching the ground, seemed inappropriate. It did keep us moving though. Later, when the burro stopped and refused to go farther, I devised the technique of McReynolds hanging onto the burro's tail and being pulled uphill. He joked that when he tired of this, he would go around and pull on the burro for a while.

All this time we were heading for Lake Kop, which would be our base camp. The Frenchman Navarra had started from there, and we could orient ourselves on the maps from there. This was going to turn out to be some 15 to 20 miles of uphill walking, going from 2,500' to about 11,000' in altitude. Finally, at about 6 p.m. we seemed to be getting close. When we were almost to the base of the old moraines and ridges that wind down from the final pyramid of the summit, Zerbini went bounding ahead like a bird dog. As I looked down from the top of a hill, I saw McReynolds grasping the burro's tail and making his way up the slope. Meanwhile, Zerbini had disappeared over another hill with various people strung out behind him, so I set out to slow him down. I finally caught up to him at the end of a small valley. He was acting very strangely, looking around with suspicion. The sun was going down by now and the temperature was falling towards freezing. My shorts were starting to feel like a bad choice.

I waited for an hour while various members of the expedition (but no burros) showed up. Zerbini had wandered off and now reappeared, looking very disturbed. He was sure that we were being led into a trap by the Kurds. He said it had all been planned. I set off to find the burros, hoping to cross the track they would have left. In a short while I spotted McReynolds on top of a hill, waving a shirt. He came bounding across the rocks and acted as though he was going to kiss me. The drivers had taken his burro away and he had fallen so far behind he'd gotten lost. He figured it was all a big murder plot. He was convinced that the piles of rocks outlined in the fading light were lookouts for Kurdish scouts who were waiting for darkness to fall so they could attack and kill us for our clothing.

Zerbini and McReynolds were of no help in keeping the group calm. We were lost and separated from our equipment, but at least we were together. Earlier, when it had looked like the expedition had become detached, Mansell went off to try to find the lost burros or Lake Kop. All the others were with me now. We walked until it was quite dark, not seeing any sign of a trail, burro tracks or droppings. I decided that the only thing to do was to return to the last rest stop and wait until morning if necessary. The murder plot sub-committee had grown in size and didn't want to do anything. They huddled together, whispering and casting furtive glances over their shoulders. I told them I would just leave them there instead of putting up with this nonsense and headed back, walking as fast as I could to keep warm. My legs were like blocks of ice by now and to keep people busy, I told some jokes. I noticed that no matter how fast I walked, no one got very far behind. Finally I saw a faint light, and there in the darkness were all the burros. Mansell had not only found them, he had brought them back to the same place I was heading. I was happy to see him.

The next day we decided to set up our basecamp there, since we could see that this was within the circle the Frenchman had outlined. We were at about 11,000 feet, on the northwest side, where there is a fairly extensive, almost flat area, with a small lake in it, Lake Kop. There were some modest low ridges running away from the mountain, and the massive summit pyramid rose almost abruptly at the south end of this flat area. Some of the glaciers came almost down to this flat, meadow-like area. We made our camp right at the base of this summit pyramid, not only because it was flat, but also because it was located where a stream running from the snow and ice at higher levels was a source of water for cooking and drinking. In general these streams only ran during the day when the sun shone on the snow and ice and melted it and it became runoff water.

Mansell and I planned to set up a higher camp in the middle of the area circled on the map, and search for the Ark from there. This would mean hauling a lot of stuff up. We didn't feel it was good idea to have any of the others on the glaciers, but thought they could carry the gear up to the edge of them and then search the moraines for evidence that might have been washed out. After we left Lake Kop and started up the mountain, I could pick out the general area where the Frenchman said he went, on the western slope of the mountain. We studied the maps and aerial photographs as carefully as we could. The next morning we loaded up, ready to mount the final search.

Something mystical seems to settle over people when they are on Mount Ararat and sure enough someone got out a Bible, opened to Genesis, and read the account of the flood. He concluded with, "And on the seventh month, on the seventeenth day of the month, the Ark came to rest on the mountains of Ararat. . ." And with that, we set out. What with all the time spent encouraging our bearers, and making rest stops, it was late in the afternoon when we finally reached the high ridge alongside the glacier. Here we had them dump their loads. Zerbini, with his usual lack of insight, commented that this would be a fine place for a campsite. The area was strewn with boulders of all sizes from a cliff that towered overhead. We might have lasted all of one night without being crushed if we had camped there.

Mansell and I now had to cross the glacier. It was about a quarter to half mile wide and angled sharply up to a ridge on the other side. We planned to aim for the crest of the ridge and look for a point that would put us in the middle of the area circled by the Frenchman. We were at about 14,140' and on the northwest face. The glacier flowed down like a tongue onto the north, barren side of the mountain. While it wasn't a dead glacier, it was old, and showed little signs of any movement. Above us, toward the summit, towered an almost vertical ice cliff that was maybe a thousand feet high. Apparently the ice was moving over the cliff and the glaciers were fed by it. A great deal of snow probably fell here. Even now, in the middle of August, it snowed or hailed every night. But August was also when the melting was at a maximum and the new snow a minimum, so that any conceivable exposure of the Ark would be taking place now.

We pondered how to get all this equipment to where we planned our high camp across the glacier. Daylight was fading and it would take at least two or three trips to get our equipment

118

across. We told the others to head on back to the base camp, and decided to pack in just the essentials. Even with crampons on our boots, we were going to have to be careful since walking on steep, inclined ice is always a danger. There was also the problem of carrying a heavy load at this attitude while picking a path through the crevasses—the huge cracks in the ice. When we finally got our equipment loaded, Mansell and I had to help each other on with the packs. My load was so heavy I was somewhat concerned that the straps would break. We labored across the glacier with slow ponderous steps. After a while we saw what looked like a couple of a dark sheep cross our projected path. We mused at what they might be doing on ice at this attitude. If we had not been so burdened when we crossed their tracks we probably would have been more concerned. It turned out these were not sheep, but bear tracks. I had heard that there were bears on Ararat, and during the nights in our high camp, when the wind was whipping at the tent, there were times when visions of hungry bears crossed my mind.

By the time we crossed the glacier we were dripping sweat—in spite of the freezing temperature—and drained of energy. We were on a very steep incline at this point, using our ice axes to maintain balance. Mansell, in trying to step from the hard blue ice to the moraine, slipped, and started sliding. The moraine on Ararat was a treacherous combination of crushed lava, volcanic dust and rocks of various sizes. He smashed into a giant boulder after 10 or 15 feet. Fortunately, it stopped him. My pack prevented me from moving quickly enough to help him, and after that rock there was a long steep slope that would have meant real trouble. As it was, he had to carry on with a bruised thigh. I was much more careful as a result.

Mansell decided to carry his load up the side of the ridge in stages. I was determined to get mine all the way in one trip. I proceeded to painfully inch my way up the rocks. The high altitude was really taking its toll and I was gasping for breath. At the top, I lay on my face in the pumice and didn't get enough strength back to stand up for several minutes. It was now dark, but with the help of moonlight reflected by snow, I was able to find a level place and set up the tent while Mansell went back for the other half of his load. His idea had been the better one. I had the worst case of altitude sickness I'd ever had, from overexertion. All I wanted to do was to curl up and die. I crawled in the sleeping bag and tried to sleep, while Mansell hummed away and made tea and food.

The next morning we got our climbing equipment ready and surveyed the search area. There were only three short glaciers involved—none very wide or long. Because of the state of the glaciers we could immediately see that it was very unlikely that we would find any that were 40 feet deep, as the Frenchman claimed the one he had descended into was. The glaciers here were in an advanced state of recession, just as I had seen them all over the world—except in New Zealand. Nowadays you could stand on ridges that used to mark the top of the glaciers, and look hundreds of feet down to where the glacier started. Because the Frenchman's discovery had taken place nearly ten years ago, I quickly realized that what things looked like back then would be of no help. In fact, it was beginning to dawn on me that the actual glacier he described might have disappeared altogether, or the crevasse might have closed up.

We spent several days plodding around, peering down into crevasses, looking into dark areas in the ice and working our way down into the great hollow caves at the sides where the ice melts away from the rock. One moderately likely hole was near a rock wall, and subject to regular bombardment with rocks as the sun melted them loose. We went there early one morning and fixed a rope into the cave. I rappelled down into it and searched around among the great icicles without any success. Suddenly, rocks and pieces of ice came ricocheting down. I huffed and puffed my way back up the rope out of harm's way. One of the glaciers was below a rock wall, and during the middle of the day, rocks bounded down it constantly. These are what mountain climbers call widow-makers. Even one as small as six inches in diameter can take your head off if it hits you directly after accelerating down the ice.

The only thing I found of interest during our whole exploration was a length of steel pipe embedded in the ice. It was unclear what its purpose was or how it had gotten there. At any rate, it certainly wasn't a part of the Ark, unless they had been manufacturing steel pipes back in Noah's day. After we had explored the glaciers, we went back down to the base camp to see if they had turned up anything in the outwash of the glaciers. The hot rumor going around was that a Kurdish shepherd knew what we were looking for. He claimed to have found some pieces of wood, but was mysterious and reticent about showing us where he had found them. After we sent the interpreter down to stay at his camp, he communicated that if we were to give him money first, he might recover his memory. When we refused, it became clear from his defeated smile that there wasn't really any wood.

The other men in our expedition hadn't found anything while searching the moraine below the glaciers. Mansell and I spent a day walking around the area, seeing Lake Kop in daylight and getting the lay of the land. The following day we went back up to the high camp. This time it took only three hours instead of all day. The next morning we got up early, and made an ascent to the summit. This meant making a long traverse under the ice cliff to a ridge that led around the cliff, and then following it to the gneiss. Early in the morning the ice was hard. It meant we had to cut steps and do some careful climbing since we couldn't afford to lose our footing and start sliding. The only problem was picking our way around crevasses on the big plateau, which was the source of the ice that gradually flowed over the ice cliff. This was a tremendous vantage point from which we could see all the way to the Caucasus Mountains, the Black Sea, into Russia and Iran, and back into Turkey. We could faintly make out the Russian town of Erevan, where the missile base was supposedly located. But we didn't see any signs of Noah's Ark.

The plateau with the twin snow domes seemed like a possible hiding place, but it was definitely out of the area indicated by the Frenchman and higher than he had said. We sat there for a while and took some pictures, including one of me as possibly the first American to climb Mount Ararat. I didn't know it then, and never claimed recognition, but it turns out I actually *was* the first American to summit the mountain. It had not been a remarkably complicated climb, but then neither was Mount Blanc the first time De Saussure climbed it back in the 18th century. At 17,000', Ararat is in the category of being a modestly high mountain but certainly not one of the highest peaks in the world. Even so, the altitude presented a problem and after a while, Mansell and I returned to our high camp, picked up our equipment, and retired back down to the base camp. I could see there was nothing to do now but leave the mountain, and for me to go back home or go to Bordeaux to talk to the Frenchman. Having been on the mountain, I would be able to ask some probing questions. However, time was a considerable element. Summer was ending and soon snow would extend all the way down to where we had been dropped by the truck.

Zerbini and McReynolds had apparently been stewing about the Kurds the whole time Mansell and I were up on the glacier and summit. They had been talking to the others about being attacked or taken hostage. So it was no surprise that they were greatly relieved when we all agreed it was time to go, and sent for the burros. The next day we hiked out to where the truck was going to meet us. This meant going back through the Kurdish villages, stoning dogs and suffering under the intense sun and heat. My shoes didn't fit as well going downhill, and I could feel blisters developing on my toes after many miles of going downhill. Finally, we arrived at the little village but there was no truck to meet us. I reconnoitered a couple of miles in one direction with no luck. Back at the village we found our famous guide, the one who had gotten us lost, at the little army outpost. I was pretty sure he had been hired to guide the truck back to pick us up, but he seemed clueless.

Our Pan Am interpreter, who was supposedly with the truck (wherever it was) had never memorized any Turkish other than counting, and a few phrases like, "Where is the bathroom?" while we were in Ankara. I knew something was amiss, but didn't know exactly what. The guide telephoned on the army telephone line— the only one in this whole area—back to Dogubayazit. I assumed he was looking for the truck, but I was still suspicious. I walked up the road a ways, but finally the heat drove me back to the army post. I was tired and irritated by now. I wanted to know why the guide shrugged his shoulders when I kept using one of the few Turkish words I knew, "Truck? Truck?"

122

Finally, I was mad enough and firm enough to get the guide to point. It turned out he had led the truck driver on a shortcut through a swamp, and the truck was now bogged down in the tall rushes—out where there were rumored to be poisonous snakes. I looked him right in the eye and in good English said, "You stupid son of a gun!" This seemed to break through the language barrier. We followed him out, and sure enough, there was the truck sitting on its bottom in soft mud. We spent the afternoon jacking up the wheels and putting rocks and boards under them, all to no avail. I even got the local peasants—about 30 or 40 in all—to help push. Interestingly enough, some of the peasants didn't want to help us when they found out we were mostly Americans. They were so much in the backwash of things, they thought it was still World War I when it was best to be German, and then possibly English. The only other option was to be towed out, which meant getting the army to help. Now it was revealed that this was who our guide had been telephoning. He had been trying to borrow a tank.

Our Pan Am interpreter, who had been waiting with the truck, went off on the back of one of the midget burros to find a tow, looking like Hopalong Cassidy. I climbed onto the truck to get away from all the snakes, and tried to go to sleep. I finally took my boots off to look at my feet, and found it was going to be difficult to get them back on. One foot in particular looked pretty bad. The skin was completely gone, top, bottom and sides. Toward midnight, a Jeep and a large truck came down the road. In the Jeep was a Turkish army major in charge of things. While the truck was smashing into the swamp, I talked to the major through the interpreter. He was interested to hear that I had climbed the mountain. It turned out that he had been the one that had imbedded the length of pipe I had found up on the glacier. We got to be great buddies, and while they were dragging out the truck, I hobbled back to the army post and got out a stove to make some tea. In Turkey, you thank someone by offering them tea. I figured that even at one a.m. I could be the perfect host.

Our journey home was uneventful, at least compared to the rest of the expedition. I felt pretty good about having climbed a new mountain and been to a country that was usually off-limits to foreigners. We hadn't found Noah's Ark, but I had found a life-long friend in Gordon Mansell. Dick Barkle was happy I'd made it to the summit of Ararat and returned to tell the tale. I tried to explain to him the mystique of the mountain. When I was there, poking around in the glaciers, I'd really been hoping we'd find some corroboration of the Frenchman's find, whatever it actually was. Dick agreed—after all, he was the Director of Public Relations at Pan American Airlines, and this would have been the story of the century. He said, "Bill, you might see Noah's Ark sooner than you think." It took me a minute to realize he was talking about what he planned to dress up as for our next Barkle-Schneider party.

1964 Expedition: After the end of the 1962 expedition, I didn't hear anything for almost a year. Then, towards the end of 1963, I got a message asking me to come to New York for the annual meeting of the Archeological Research Foundation, of which George Vandeman was the chairman. Mansell was flown in for the meeting and he and I shared a room in the hotel. It was wonderful to see him again. The business of the meeting was to review the 1962 expedition and to make a decision on whether to fund another expedition to Mount Ararat. There was great enthusiasm for continuing the search, and the decision was made to begin planning for a second expedition, to occur in the summer of 1964. My plans for the coming summer were complicated by a Fulbright grant I had been given to teach in South America for a year. At this particular time in my life, I was very involved in climbing, and part of the idea of going to South America was to make it possible to do climbs in the Andes Mountains, the highest mountains outside of the Himalayas. I stayed in contact with Gordon, and with the Pan Am friends, and let them know that I was interested if it could be arranged.

The plan was, as soon as the Lakeside school year ended, to take Lucy and the five children—mostly grown adolescents—in our Carryall and drive to South America. This was complicated by an unexpected event just at the end of the school year. A small group of us planned to climb Mount Rainier on a route which had never been done and which was very difficult, involving glaciers, aid rock climbing and steep ice fields. We reached the summit successfully, but on the descent a big snowstorm struck the mountain. For several days we were trapped, sheltering in snow caves we had dug. Because we hadn't planned on being out that long we quickly ran out of food, but it was the bitter cold that became a real hardship. In fact, a rescue team was finally sent out and we ended up in the newspapers. But before the team could get to us, the storm finally ended and we actually met them on the way down. When I got home and took my climbing boots off, I found that my toes were frostbitten from the time spent in the snow caves and I was unable to wear any shoes. I lost all the skin off the toes and some toenails too. This added an awkward complication to the plans for the drive to South America, but too much was involved to not find some way to go ahead.

It took about three weeks to reach the Panama Canal, and by that time I was able to wear oversize shoes and function. I got a telegram from Dick Barkle saying that Pan Am was going to contribute to the 1964 expedition and they wanted me to go, if it all possible. I consulted with Lucy, and she agreed that we should sell the Carryall and she would go on ahead on a ship heading for Chile. I then got on a Pan American plane heading for New York, and continued on to England. I met up with Gordon Mansell and we got some climbing equipment together. We purchased some double thick boots to protect my feet, which were now extremely sensitive to cold (and always would be) because of the frostbite.

This expedition was full of good intentions and enthusiasm, and was designed to avoid all the mistakes and shortcomings of the 1962 expedition. There were more experienced climbers, including one from Denver who had the previous year been a member of the first American ascent of Everest. The expedition also had a doctor along, also from Denver, who knew something about climbing. The 1964 Ararat climb would be bigger and much more complicated, but unfortunately, clumsier as well. The planning seemed somewhat haphazard to me in that people were arriving at different times in Ankara, some as much as weeks apart. The Archeological Research Foundation had the best of intentions to create an expedition that could accomplish the search more effectively. But a group of men sitting in a room planning something this complicated had its shortcomings. This year, for instance, an airplane was included which the organization hoped could land at the Kip Gol (alternately called Kopgel, meaning Lake Kop) base camp and scout the glaciers. On paper it was an imaginative idea, but the altitude and reality served to make it more of a burden than help.

I felt a sense of urgency, not just because of my obligation in Chile, but also because of the weather on the mountain. I pressed for getting going with whatever climbers had already arrived in Ankara since we were coming up into August already. At this point, some of the climbers were drifting off to Istanbul to be tourists while the rest of us marked time in Ankara. George Vandeman had been the drive behind this expedition, hoping to make it bigger and better and more successful. He had found the doctor, for instance, and organized the airplane in the project. It was big thinking, but the idea of landing a plane at 11,000 feet was complicated. As a pilot, I knew the problem. At that altitude an airplane would have to land substantially faster, and would take almost twice as much distance to land or take off. I found out years later that the airplane idea was actually a ruse by the CIA, who wanted to take pictures of Russia. They had offered the plane to Vandeman to search for the Ark, but in fact had sent along a CIA photographer with another mission entirely.

Gordon and I were familiar with the country and its customs from the 1962 expedition, so we started out ahead to set up a base camp. The atmosphere in Turkey had changed radically, politically speaking, since 1962. For instance, driving out with the supplies, we were stopped in Erzurum and told that there was an American military post where we were welcome to stay. This would not have happened, even remotely, in 1962. We continued on to the mountain and instead of staying in hotels or in the town, set up a camp in a farm field on the west side of the mountain. Enough climbers gradually arrived so that we could move up the mountain to the base camp we had used in 62'. We used horses and mules procured at a local village to transport our supplies. Then it was a process of waiting for people to arrive, of more supplies being carried up to the base camp, and waiting for the plane to arrive. The plane was kind of a grandiose idea, and if it had been able to operate out of the base camp, it would've been a marvelous tool to have for the search. But it was simply impractical for it to land and takeoff at that altitude.

A new problem arose from the first day we were up on the mountain. As soon as word got around that we had a doctor with us, every morning outside of the doctor's tent there would be as many as perhaps 200 locals waiting hopefully and patiently for the doctor to look at their problems. Some had walked for days to get there. In that remote area of Turkey, doctors were simply unheard of. And like people everywhere, these locals had all had kinds of major and minor health problems—diseases and injuries that were straightforward enough to take care of, but required substantial amounts of medical supplies, and more importantly, the doctor's time. The first thing the he did was to go through the trunk of medical supplies from 1962 and throw most of it away, most being outdated or unlabeled. That left him with only a very modest amount of supplies. The complication of these local people needing medical attention was very difficult for him as a doctor being that his role was to be available and useful to keep the searchers functional.

Some new people had arrived, and one of them had a project I was assigned to deal with, a photographer who wanted to take some pictures as high on the mountain as I could get him. He seemed like a reasonably fit, friendly, pleasant man between 30 and 40 years of age. Wherever we could climb to and then return to camp in a single day was his goal in this project. He wanted to take pictures from the north side of the mountain. I had a reasonable, general sense of the structure of the mountain on the north side from my previous trip, and since this was to be a one-day project, neither of us was carrying much weight. We were able to move fairly steadily, and soon reached a large, relatively flat rocky area beneath the glaciers. We talked some along the way, but he offered me no information about who he was or what he was doing, or what these pictures were to be for. He was a cheerful, friendly, ordinary kind of person but did not seem to be someone who would have a hobby of climbing mountains to take pictures. I simply assumed that he had something to do with the Noah's Ark search, and was happy to get him safely wherever he wanted to go. That was, after all, supposed to be my way of contributing to these expeditions.

The photographer didn't want of go up onto the ice and glaciers above this higher rocky area, and I worked him around to the northeast side where he indicated he wanted to go. At this point, he simply took some pictures looking over towards Russia and that's all he wanted to do. I offered to take his picture, or pose for him to take my picture, which is what anyone in the tourist mode of living would do, but he comfortably refused these suggestions. Then we basically retraced our steps and went back to camp, and the next day he left. It had been a long, friendly day of small talk with an amiable person. Later, after leaving the mountain and getting back to Ankara, someone explained the photographer to me. He was working for the CIA, gathering information on the production of missile fuel in Russia. The photographs he took were on infrared film, which would, by the brightness of the picture, be a measure of the level of energy in the factories in the city he took pictures of. The goal of the project was to return to that same place a year or two later and take a second set of infrared pictures. By comparing the two pictures, the increase in infrared radiation energy could be used to see how much more missile fuel the Russians were manufacturing. This would give our government an idea of how many new missiles were being made.

While I was with the CIA photographer, a critical event happened. Gordon, who had also been up on the mountain in another area and been careless about wearing sunglasses, got his eyes sunburned and went temporarily blind. When the whites of the eyes get sunburned, your eyes sting so much you can't keep them open. So he had to get down to the bottom of the mountain, away from the high altitude sun, riding a small horse. On his way down he passed by one of the Kurd villages. The Kurds have incredibly vicious dogs that wear sharp, metal pointed studded collars to protect them from bears and other dogs. As Gordon rode by the village, stone blind, these vicious dogs erupted from all sides making the horse bolt. Gordon fell off but one foot caught in the stirrup, and he was dragged for quite a while before the horse stopped. The doctor came to help, and his comment when he saw Gordon lying on the ground, blind, with one foot still caught in the stirrup and weeds and grass caught all over his clothing was, "You poor bugger."

At this point, the expedition—with its drive and experience and direction gone— simply faded away. The airplane, for instance, had been an idealistic notion but it was simply unable to perform at that high altitude. After a couple of sweeps around the mountain the plane made two landings at Kopgel and then left. Then, when Gordon went out of action and I had to leave and head back for South America, the expedition simply died. We could have been effective and used if the expedition had all come together and been ready to go when I first arrived, but it was simply too complicated and theoretical for all these things to hold together. By this time I had spent almost as much time in Turkey as I had in 1962, and had essentially done nothing new on the mountain. When Gordon and I left, all the experience and background went with us. No one else was prepared to step decisively into a leadership position. In retrospect, it was clear that part of the problem in those days was the complication of mounting an expedition in such an incredibly remote and difficult area. Today, tour groups commonly go there, and ascents of the Mount Ararat are made by inexperienced and not especially vigorous people, not unlike the commonplace ascents of Mount Everest.

The 1962 and 1964 Noah's Ark expeditions happened because of the energy and the drive of George Vandeman, the televangelist for the Seventh Day Adventist church. He thought in big terms and was able to talk to big-time people in their world. His enthusiasm was of course predicated on the biblical story of Noah's Ark. To have a mountain named Ararat where the Ark supposedly landed really fired up his imagination. Also, there had been a few discoveries over the years that fueled the hunt. One was of course the Frenchman's find in 1955, the five-foot wooden beam hauled up from under the Parrot Glacier on the northwest slope. In 1959, a Turkish army captain flew over Ararat and took an aerial photograph that showed what appeared to be a huge, boat like structure. But for me, these trips were just a very exotic and interesting experience, and I always felt fortunate to be included in them. I wouldn't have minded finding Noah's Ark, but it was the adventure that drew me in. And when the opportunity came up to go on another expedition in 1966, I jumped at it.

1966 Expedition: The 1966 expedition was made significantly different from the two previous ones by the presence of Alva Appel, who was a Seventh Day chaplain for the U.S. air force. Alva and I met on the 1966 expedition, and we have been friends ever since. He was a very effective and forceful personality, and both of the other two expeditions would have been significantly more productive had he been a member of them. He had exactly the right personality to energize and move the expedition to an operational phase in Turkey. His presence added a quality of effectiveness that had been missing on the two previous expeditions. George Vandeman remained an enigmatic figure in the background. He was a nationally known figure, with a very successful television program directed towards a national audience of people who believed in the literal writings of the bible. He was the founder of the Archeological Research Foundation, and his name was always associated with any expeditions to Mount Ararat. The only time I ever was in contact with him was after the 1962 expedition. He was wearing a very formal three-piece suit when I saw him in Ankara where he made me an official member of the ARF.

Going from a Pan American round the world flight to traveling across Turkey was always an abrupt event. Pan American in those days had a level of sophistication that doesn't exist today, not even in First Class. The planes themselves were less fancy, but the size and quality of seats, the food and the attention from stewardesses seemed like the realm of show business people and the wealthy. On the other hand, as the 1960's went forward, travel across Turkey also steadily improved. The 1966 expedition was quite different from the previous ones in that not only was the traveling easier, but the military situation was markedly different. In 62' and 64' I had a clear feeling that the military did not want us out there. In 1966 we almost seemed to be encouraged and supported by both the American and Turkish military. For example, upon arrival in Ankara, instead of resistance in getting our equipment through customs we were actually helped with it. In Ankara, both the Turkish authorities and American military personnel contacted us and offered to help in various ways. I first met Alva Appel in Ankara, and he was a wonderfully forceful personality in arranging getting the transportation for our equipment out to Mount Ararat. Needless to say, after the last, over-planned yet haphazard expedition, this was a welcome change.

Alva headed east in a truck with the supplies in early July this year rather than into August in past years, and I was able to have the luxury of flying to Erzurum to meet him. The plane was a DC-3, and the in-flight meal was a glass of lemonade, but this was traveling in luxury compared to previous trips to Erzurum! The early start to the expedition was another real luxury. It meant more time on the mountain, when the last snows were melting and the climbing season had just begun. Our previous expeditions had taken place in August, where we were working under the gun of winter storms beginning and getting in the way of our search. Once in Erzurum, I joined up with the overland party in the truck and we drove on to Dogubayazit, and then on to the small village at the base of the mountain where previous expeditions had also hired the horses or burros to transport supplies. The outfit also provided mounts for some members of the party who were happier riding than walking. I couldn't help but remember the ignoble image of McReynolds riding the midget burro, his feet dragging on the ground, or worse, being pulled up the mountain by the burro's tail. We were heading to the same base camp we'd used at Lake Kop in order to be as close to where The Frenchman said he had found his wood. In reality, it was as good a lower base camp for exploring on the northwest side of the mountain as could be found.

From almost any other side of Mount Ararat, the slope rises relatively gently and in essentially the same angle all the way to the actual summit. All of the commercial tours of recent years take hikers to the summit on these simpler sides of the mountain. On the southeast side, there is a lower summit called little Ararat, a cinder cone summit, where apparently the Jupiter missiles were installed and which had created the complications that we'd encountered in 1962. On the northwest side where we were camped, there is a large flat shoulder at about 11,000 feet. The mountain rises abruptly from the shoulder and there are small, old glaciers located in this steep area. It's what you would expect on the north side of a mountain, simply because of less exposure to sunlight. In the northern hemisphere, the south side of a mountain generally has a more comfortable angle and the north side is usually steep with rock cliffs because of the weathering effects of snow and ice.

Water in any form in eastern Turkey, is a real gift. The area is very brown, and very little vegetation is present. The rocks and stones themselves are basically the result of frost action during the winter, which shatters the bedrock. The boulders and rocks created from this are generally sharp edged because there is very little running water during the summer months. I was surprised to see that the area we had created as our base camp on the previous expeditions was now filled with wild flowers and the stream was running. There were Kurdish shepherds in the area because this was apparently good grazing ground, and one of them even had a bagpipe, which he played periodically. He was quite a friendly fellow, and hung around our camp wanting to have his picture taken.

The base camp was set up very quickly compared to the last expedition. Having all the members present made a huge difference, and people scurried around busily, taking care of tasks. One guy had the idea of using the lumber from our crates to build an actual outhouse. This was immediately deemed a waste and then dismantled to build an outdoor kitchen. I was restless and eager to get climbing, so Alva Appel and I went off to explore. We climbed up to the Abich glaciers area, which, along with the Parrot glacier, was considered a place of interest in the Noah's Ark search. The glaciers were steep, so Alva and I roped up as we crossed them. We wanted to get a look over the edge where the mountain fell away, so we took turns anchoring each other. I was impressed by the vertical drop, and happy to retreat a ways up the glacier so Appel could take a look. I thrust my ice axe handle into the glacier to anchor myself and could tell immediately something was wrong. The handle just slipped down into the ice like butter, a sure sign of an impending avalanche. I shouted at Alva that the glacier was ready to go and we'd better get the heck out of there. I was proven right a couple of nights later.

Alva and I decided to go on an extensive overnight exploring expedition along the base of the summit pyramid to get a sense of the geography along the north side of the mountain. The Navarra story was always in the background of everything we did, as it was literally the motivating force behind all of these expeditions in the 1960s. Along the north side were various small valleys scraped out by glaciers, some of which had snow and ice in them. We did a very rough check into each of these areas, partially to develop a sense of the geography, and also to look for anything that even approximately resembled what the Frenchman described in his book. We continued along the whole of the north side, finally coming to a great gorge, which was called the Ahora gorge. It had once had a major glacier in it, which would have filled the whole of the gorge with ice right up to the rim where we stood. Now, there was perhaps a several hundred-foot drop from the rim down to what remained of the glacier. At the high end, the headwall was solid bare rock, almost vertical, several hundred feet high. It was like a great semi-circular wall around the top end of the glacier in this gorge, being the cirque that still held the remnants of the beginning of the glacier. It was very imposing mountain scenery, a gorge dropping perhaps a thousand feet in vertical height along its length, with very steep sides.

My feeling was that we should drop down to the valley at the bottom and do a little exploring. It was going to be a lot of work going down, and even more work coming out but Alva, with his enthusiastic energy, agreed to this without any objection or hesitation. We descended hundreds of feet down a moderately steep slope of scree—loose, broken stones—and finally reached the valley at the bottom. We were a few hundred feet from the end of what's know as the Black Glacier, which rose immediately from this moderately level area. Much further down this valley was where the historical Saint James monastery and spring had been located. The great volcanic explosion in the 1840's that had enlarged the Ahora gorge had also destroyed the monastery. There are stories that the monks saw the same rocky promontory on the east side of the headwall of the gorge that produces a lot of present-day sightings of the Ark. They apparently so firmly believed it to actually be Noah's Ark, no monk ever went up to confirm its existence.

It was now close to dark, so we set up the tent, boiled some water and had a quick supper. I really admired Alva for holding up and keeping up, and never complaining during a very long day of demanding mountain hiking. He was a beginner in mountain travel, but was very fit, very willing, and never lost his enthusiasm. We crawled into our sleeping bags and fell asleep quickly, after all of that difficult walking and the long descent to the valley floor. When you are near the end of a glacier, always in the back of your mind is the possibility of avalanches. Since they typically happen in the late afternoon, I had turned this possibility off in my mind. I had also forgotten the incident a couple of days earlier, where I instinctively felt the glacier was about to go. Sometime after we both were asleep, I heard the characteristic rumbling of an avalanche, and in the dark, anything like that is far more ominous that it would be in the daytime. I was instantly awake and tried almost frantically to get out of the sleeping bag and unzip the end of the tent. And then the rumbling stopped. Alva had woken up, either because of the rumbling or my thrashing around, and he seemed to think I had going to the bathroom in mind. I told him I'd been trying to get us out of the tent before an avalanche struck us. It seemed futile at this point to move our campsite, so we just lay awake in the dark, not talking and hoping for the best.

When we got up the next morning and checked on the avalanche debris, I found it a little sobering that it had stopped less than 100 feet from our tent. The massive amount of rocks, snow and ice would have crushed us instantly and I felt responsible for putting us in the line of danger. I was supposed to be competent about these things. We explored the area a little around the Black Glacier and Alva found a small, handmade metal bowl poking out of the ice. He was quite pleased about this. Then we ate, packed, and laboriously plodded up and out of the valley. We worked our way along the base of the walls of the great summit pyramid until we were back to base camp. Again, I was impressed with the physical energy and enthusiasm of Alva. This kind of mountain travel tends to bring out the ability to complain and be clumsy in people, and I don't remember a single negative instance with him, or ever having to wait.

Alva and I spent a few more days searching the Parrot glacier, the area where the Frenchman had made his find. I had already searched the area extensively with Gordon Mansell, and Alva and I didn't turn up anything new. Meanwhile, back in camp, someone had apparently been ferreting away all our canned fruit and there was a big to-do when it was discovered hidden under his cot. I just shook my head when I heard. Somehow, the idea of a grown man on a paid expedition stealing food from his fellow climbers seemed sort of pathetic. After getting back from our exploratory expeditions, there was nothing specific for me to do so I usually retired to my tent to read. I read something like 11 pocketbooks on this trip. I am a teacher by trade, and you can never read enough to continue having background information for teaching.

After a couple of days, an intelligence officer from the Turkish army arrived, obviously a city person and well educated. He asked if he could share my tent, and I welcomed him and we became friends. He did not speak English, but like me he had studied in France, and we would lie there on cots in the tent happily speaking broken French to each other. He was from western Turkey, which from my experience is where the educated elite come from. They look like an entirely different race in physical appearance from the farmers and the Kurds, who inhabit the eastern part of Turkey. In the military for instance, the officers are generally from the west, and the soldiers are generally from the east. In addition to the uniforms, the physical appearance of officers and enlisted men was striking, almost as though they were from different races.

The Turkish army officer turned out to be helpful to us. The local Kurds resented our being on their mountain. I don't really blame them, but on the other hand, we were there legally and officially and not bothering them at all. One day, one of them came riding over on a big horse and was, for some unexplained reason, quite unfriendly. It finally came to a head when he rode his horse right into the stream where we got our drinking water and made a mess of our water source. I tried through sign language to get him out of the stream but he wouldn't budge. This led to a real confrontation involving a lot of shouting. The Turkish officer came out of the tent and managed to calm things down to where the Kurd ended up riding resentfully away. At this point the Turkish officer went back to the tent, buckled on his revolver, and walked off in the direction of the Kurdish camp. Whenever he said, the Kurds never came back. After a few days, the intelligence officer said he had to go back to his military post at Dogubayazit.

After he left, I decided to go up on my own to camp, and explore the area on the north side above the Ahora gorge on my own. This would be easier, in the sense that I didn't have to worry about inexperienced people being with me. I took a tent, some food and a sleeping bag, and set up camp in an area free of snow and glaciers, beneath the summit. After a few days, a cheerful Swiss climber appeared from the German area of Switzerland, meaning he spoke no English or French. By mostly sign language, we agreed that we would go up to the summit the next day. I sort of conveyed the idea that I could beat him up to the summit, both of us laughing in a friendly way about the idea of competing. The next morning we got up, and with no packs, walked over to where the glacier started, put on our crampons, and then raced up to the summit in something like an hour and a half or two hours. We shook hands on the summit, and then started running down, and ran all the way back to the tent, laughing happily all the way.

The Swiss man got up early the next morning, we shook hands, and he went on down the mountain. I was then left alone in the tent, content to read one of my paperbacks. The next day, a couple of Kurds appeared with old, primitive looking rifles. After the unpleasant confrontation about the drinking water, this made me uneasy to say the least. Even worse, we couldn't communicate about what they were doing up there and what I myself was doing. I knew just enough words in Kurdish however to say that my friends were coming up soon, something I made up right on the spot, and that they would bring the Turkish officer with them. At least I think that's what I was conveying. The Kurds talked to each other briefly, sort of seriously, and went off without even a nod. I assumed they were out hunting, probably bears, but happily now, not me. As soon as they were out of sight, I packed up and headed down to the main camp, pretty clear now about the drawbacks of being alone.

By this time, the goals for the camp high on the mountain had been accomplished, and my usefulness as a mountain guide had come to an end. Early one morning, I said goodbye and, carrying all of my personal possessions in a daypack, headed for Dogubayazit. I wanted to get there before dinnertime, because the Turkish intelligence officer had invited me to dinner in the officers club on my way back. It was a long walk, maybe 30 miles, but mostly downhill for the first half. Every time I passed a Kurdish camp, here came their hostile and ferocious dogs with the steel pointed spikes on their collars. The dog's role was to protect the goats from bears and people. They came charging out, truly looking as though they were going to eat me. I had already developed the technique on my previous expeditions of picking up sizable rocks as I neared the village, and hitting the first dog that came out with the largest rock I could find. I did it with vigor, as a message to the others. But I was pretty unnerved, being on my own, with these vicious dogs snapping and snarling, with foam dripping from their jaws. Once I passed the Kurdish camps, I felt energetic and happy about life, swinging along the trail, and I made it all the way to the military post without a single stop. Even picking up rocks and throwing them at dogs I did on the move. I found my intelligence officer friend and had a happy dinner in the officers club, a marvelous experience in itself. The next day I made it west to Erzurum, and then on to Ankara by DC-3 (with another glass of lemonade) and then by Pan American's jet set luxury back to New York.

For me, an ordinary person, this indeed represented a remarkable experience. I have climbed mountains all over the world, but this experience of having a purpose on a mountain, other than simply getting to the top of it, made it a different and a very satisfying journey. In addition, I felt I made a contribution to the goals of these expeditions to Mount Ararat with my outdoor skills and experience. I maintained a reasonably open minded feeling about the search for Noah's Ark, meaning having neither a for-nor-against attitude. I could not help but have some feelings of sympathy for those who either wanted the Ark to exist, or those who wanted to disprove any of the stories In each case, they only saw what they wanted to see. Of course, at the end of this 1966 expedition, I still had the frustration of where had Navarra found that wood? The wood, which had been carbon dated to a time that reasonably fit within the Ark story, had been used to energize all of these expeditions in the 1960s. So for me, it was still a story without an ending. But at least now I could read the Frenchman's book with a clear knowledge of the geography of the mountain, and try to fit it into the puzzle that was Navarra's awkward descriptions.

Several more expeditions were to occur before the Frenchman's information and stories were finally laid to rest. This alone is a remarkable commentary on the power of the idea of Noah's Ark. In 1968, The Archeological Research Foundation mounted another expedition and I was again asked to go along. I stopped in Paris along the way to visit my eldest daughter, Lucy Anne, who was in college. The latest idea on this new expedition was so far-fetched I had a hard time believing they were serious. Someone had gotten the not very bright notion of taking thousands of feet of black plastic to try and melt the glaciers. The idea was that the sun would warm up the plastic and then the ice underneath would melt, revealing the Ark. Simple science shows that ice exposed to air melts faster than ice wrapped in plastic, so I thought it was a pretty stupid idea, not to mention a huge waste of money and time. But as always, I was happy to go for an all expense paid expedition to climb Mount Ararat. The best thing about this climb was the fact that the Frenchman Navarra was actually going along. I was finally able to have him take me up to the glacier where he said he had found the wood. I had him show me exactly where on that glacier he had found it and was then able to satisfy myself that there was no more wood, and that there was no conceivable place where something the size of the biblical Ark could exist. However, the fact remains that Navarra brought back a hand-hewn beam of wood that dated back 4,500 years. I still consider that to be a real mystery, how a piece of wood that old ended up at an elevation of 14,000 feet on Mount Ararat.

Penelope

She wove the shroud by day
unraveling it by night
to make the time stand still
until he should return.

Women devise stratagems
when forced to wait and hope;
they turn to homely tasks,
they knit and bake and fold.

I had my time of waiting,
of being left behind,
but then adventure called
and I left my shroud undone.

from **Home and Away**

The Rescue
by Bill

I was a member of the Mountain Rescue organization for many years, and this particular rescue took place back in the late 1960's. Lucy and I were having one of our classic high-energy parties in the kitchen of our old farmhouse, the one I accidentally set fire to later. Our parties consisted of friends like the Stadlers, Hansons and various others, with modest drinking and a lot of activities, like singing and charades. Paul Williams, a climber friend, was there. He had joined our group of energetic friends after coming with us on our strange and unusual beach hikes and figured our parties might also be interesting.

About 11 or 12 o' clock in the evening Paul received a telephone call. Paul was a key member of the Mountain Rescue organization, so he always left the number of where he was. He told me that there had been an accident over by the Alpine Lakes area and asked if I would come along. I wondered aloud how I could leave a party at my own house, and he said, "They won't even know you're gone." Then he suggested bringing Lucy, startling me even more. Lucy was not a member of Mountain Rescue but Paul knew she was always game for an adventure, and sure enough, her face lit up and she said, "Let's do it!" She didn't seem to have a problem with leaving a houseful of guests at our own party, and just like Paul said, they didn't seem to mind or even notice that we were leaving.

We collected some simple outdoor stuff, got into Paul's car and hustled over to Leavenworth where we found a small group of rescuers who were waiting and set to go. It was about 1 a.m. when we set up the trail, heading into the Alpine Lakes wilderness area.

We plugged away all night, carrying minuscule flashlights. There was not a lot of talk. We reached the lake at the end of the valley just as it started to get light. Although we hadn't slept or eaten, adrenaline kept us going, and the thought that there were people who needed our help. We kept on walking right up to the col (the lowest point on a ridge between two peaks) where one way goes to the Alpine Lakes and the other up to Mount Temple. That was where this accident had happened. All we knew was that a woman had fallen onto a ledge and was pretty badly hurt.

We discovered later that this woman and a friend had been sitting on a cliff, waiting for their boyfriends to come back from climbing Mount Temple. She tried to grab for her hat when the wind blew it off and fell about 50 feet, hitting a sloping rocky ledge. That knocked her unconscious and broke several bones, at which point she rolled and bounced over the edge and fell another 50 feet, landing on a second ledge. Her face, arms and hips were all broken by this time. The friend shouted for help and the two returning men climbed down to where the unconscious woman was on the ledge. Not knowing how hurt and damaged she was, one man stayed with her while the other hiked out and called the sheriff, who then called Mountain Rescue.

But all we knew as we hiked up in the dark was that this was a life or death situation. I was very impressed with how Lucy kept up with Paul and me, since this was one of those rescues where you have to go at a good clip, trying to get there as soon as possible. The route now went quite a ways up along an easy rocky ridge, with an impressive drop down to the lakes on the right side. But the walking was easy and solid. After a while we reached the serious, solid mountain. The route was still rocky. It followed an obvious line into a steep looking gully, with a solid rock face on the left and the almost vertical wall of the summit pyramid on our right. At this point Paul told Lucy not go any further, but to wait for us there. It was difficult to actually see in the dark and our flashlights were of little help. Paul and I scrambled up this increasingly steep gully, where you had to use your hands to climb over large broken rocks. We came to where it opened on the left side into a flat, slightly sloping ledge, maybe 15 feet wide.

We found the woman's boyfriend and a doctor waiting for us on this ledge. They had strapped the young woman onto a wire mountain rescue type stretcher and wrapped her in blankets. Both the doctor and Paul had radiotelephones and they had both gotten in contact with a helicopter that was now on its way. The injured girl's face was swollen and cut and dark blue. She moaned and moved every now and then. We asked the doctor if the girl could be carried on the stretcher down the gully, since the steep rock face prevented the helicopter from hovering close enough to lift her out from there. The doctor said that he was afraid that if she were carried any distance, the jarring that the motion might kill her. He indicated that she was in very serious shape, perhaps on the verge of death. Any rough motion might push one of the broken ends of bone through something vital. She was bleeding internally and suffering from the shock of the fall, and her breathing and heart might just stop at any instant.

Paul swung into action. He only said a few words but it was clear he was in charge. He understood that we needed to find a way to get the stretcher down to where Lucy was waiting for us below the cliff. He took out a couple of pitons and hammered them into cracks in the vertical cliff at the back of the ledge. He looked so impressive, we all just stood there and watched, ready for instructions. Paul then had us move the stretcher over to the edge of the ledge where he brought out a climbing rope and some carabiners. He handed me the climbing rope, then threaded part of it through the carabiner in front of me in the cliff face, then back through a carabiner he had attached to the front of the stretcher. Then he led it back to the cliff wall and tied the rope to his other piton. He did this quickly and confidently, as we watched. The girl moaned occasionally, reminding us of how serious her condition was.

Paul then fastened himself to the back of the stretcher, picked it up and said, "Okay, lower me down now," and then backed off the cliff. In a moment, he disappeared down the rock face. I braced myself against the back of the ledge and started paying out rope that I had threaded around my back. It quickly became a substantial pull load on me, and with my feet braced I could just barely handle lowering Paul and the stretcher. The rope stretched and got thinner, which made it harder for me to keep hold of it. It started out being about the size of a man's thumb, and soon went down to the thickness of a clothesline. It scraped across my back and I started wondering if the rope was long enough to reach the gully. I worried about what would happen if the stretcher was not all the way down and the rope ran out. I saw the coils disappearing down by my foot to the last one. Suddenly, the pull went off the rope.

That could mean two things—either they were down or the carabiner had failed and they had fallen off the rope. Then Paul's confident voice came up, shouting to let go of the rope. He needed some slack to get the stretcher flat on the ground and away from the cliff. I scrambled down to the gully and there he was, with Lucy. The stretcher lay flat on the ground. Paul told me to grab an end while he picked up the other, and we carried it down and away from the cliff face. The helicopter was now hovering several hundred feet above us. We had to find some open spot where the cable that was hanging down from the helicopter could be attached to the stretcher. Paul hunted around and found a small rocky overhang projecting out from the cliff. The top of it was not much bigger than the stretcher, and it fell off vertically on both sides. We cleared off the rubble and then carried the stretcher out to the end of the overhang. The injured girl groaned and thrashed a little, making the stretcher tilt ominously. At this point we were in a pretty precarious position, what with there being almost no room for Paul and me to stand. The sheer drop off on either side was at least a couple of hundred feet and so even that small amount of motion was unsettling.

There was a cable swinging freely under the helicopter and just as I was reaching for it Paul said very sharply, "Don't touch the cable, you'll get shocked!" Finally, after some maneuvering from above, the cable touched down on a rock and grounded. A spark jumped. Then the helicopter pilot eased it gracefully toward us. Paul grabbed it. "Give me any webbing you have," he said. I dug my trusty, dirty white climbing webbing out of my pack. Paul quickly threaded it through the end of the helicopter cable and then attached to the four corners of the stretcher. He got on the radio and said, "Take it away," and immediately the cable went taut and lifted the stretcher up a few feet. Then it swung away from the cliff face. We stood and watched the helicopter race away down the valley toward a hospital with the girl on the stretcher dangling below. Paul and I were stunned by the sudden loss of the emergency atmosphere and didn't do anything for several moments. Then Paul said, "Let's get off of here," meaning our little rescue platform with its horrific drop-offs. We made our way over to where Lucy was standing and the three of us sat down for a while and didn't say anything. I lay back on the rough rocks, feeling upbeat but exhausted. Although I'd been on previous rescues, this was the first time I'd dealt with an actual life or death situation. The tension that went with it made me more tired than the all-night hike.

The story had a happy ending. Paul was at a party for Mountain Rescue people about six months later. He told me a really good-looking young woman came up to him at the party and said, "You don't remember me do you?" Paul was kind of embarrassed and replied, "I really don't. Where did we meet?" She said, "I was the young woman you rescued off Mount Temple." When Paul looked carefully at her face, he could see white lines on it from surgery. Somehow, in spite of all her terrible injuries, this woman had not only survived, but also seemed perfectly fine. That made Paul feel very gratified, and of course, Lucy and me as well when we heard the news. All of those hours driving, hiking in the dark, and the tension and danger of the rescue left us feeling grateful to be of service—especially knowing we had saved a life. When we got back to our home in Woodinville the next day, our house was littered with the aftermath of the party. We had almost forgotten about it. When we next saw our group of friends, most of them didn't even recall that we had left our own home quite suddenly, in the middle of the night. Some of them thought that when we disappeared, we had just gone to bed. They were very impressed to hear about the dramatic life-or-death mountain rescue. They also said we missed a really great party.

Our first hike in Kenya ends
like so many others before—
a hair's breadth from an untimely death.

from Nandi Rock, **The Simple Life**

Climbing Mount Kenya
by Lucy

Bill loved books on mountaineering. Back in 1954 we both read an intriguing account of a climb of Mt. Kenya by three Italian prisoners of war. They broke out of a nearby prison camp, improvised their own equipment, used a drawing from a tin of Oxo (a popular beef cube) as their only map, climbed the mountain and then broke back into the camp. This was our primary inspiration for deciding to climb Mount Kenya during our sabbatical year in Kenya, from 1972-3.

Our friend and teaching colleague at the Lirhanda Girl's School was a lively English woman named Margaret. Her mountaineering boyfriend, Eric, was keen to climb Mount Kenya, as was Charlie Sleicher, our Seattle friend then living in Nairobi. That meant that with Bill, they made a climbing rope of three. The two highest peaks, Nelian (17,057') and Batian (17,021') are rock towers for experienced rock climbers only. As a novice, I would aim for Point Lenana (16,355'), the third highest peak. The plan was for the four of us to hike up the mountain until we reached the starting point for the three summits, then split up.

Someone had suggested that it would be a more interesting approach from a farm on the north side that crossbred zebras and horses and arranged for trips up the mountain. For variety, we could then come down on the regular Naro Moro route on the west side. It was a long (nearly 300 km) drive in our land rover and we were delighted to finally locate the farm. We didn't give any advance notice, but when we arrived the trip proved easy to arrange. The unusual crossbreeds, zebroids (which looked like horses with stripes) were used for packing supplies. They looked sturdy and docile, and we admired them from behind the fence as our guide made arrangements to take us up the next morning.

The ascent we had chosen was more gradual and longer than the Naro Moru route and we hiked, accompanied by the zebroids carrying supplies, to a camping spot for the first night. The walk took us through bamboo forests, which gradually thinned into a rocky subalpine terrain with sparse vegetation. By the end of the day I felt exhausted by the altitude (around 11,000') and lay down in the tent to rest. The smell of meat cooking over the open fires permeated the air and added to my intense nausea. Although I knew I needed the calories, I just couldn't force myself to eat anything. I spent a restless and uncomfortable night, tossing and turning with a bad headache. Bill, on the other hand, ate a hearty meal, slept well and was ready to go the next morning.

Shortly after dawn, we set off for the base camp, a hut located at around 15,000'. I felt pretty terrible by this time, too sick to eat or drink, and gradually began to lag behind. Bill and the guide leading the zebroids persuaded me to ride instead of walking and I readily agreed. Somehow, through sheer force of will, I managed to sit upright and hang on for however many hours it took us to slowly make our way up the mountain. When we finally reached the hut, the zebroids were unloaded and the guide departed, leaving the four of us on our own. By this time, the others felt the altitude as much as I did. We had a small camp stove and cooked something (which I didn't eat) and then tried to sleep. This second night was worse than the first, and all of us had headaches and were nauseous. At first light, we got up and attempted to eat something, and then Bill, Charlie and Eric roped up and set off to climb the two peaks, Nelion and Batian. I sat alone, torn between my desire to climb Point Lenana and hesitant to go by myself. After a while, a Frenchman and his son appeared who were headed that way. I asked if I might go with them and they politely agreed.

Point Lenana is the peak most people climb because it doesn't require technical skill. Nevertheless, it has steep parts and scree, which acts rather like ball bearings under your boots. In my somewhat weakened condition, I felt very reassured to be with the two Frenchmen. We hiked and then scrambled up the scree and reached the peak in a little over two hours. When we arrived back down at the hut, the others had not returned so I picked up Bill's camera and looked through the close-up lens to see if I could spot them.

Both Nelian and Batian rock towers are dangerously steep. I began to worry, especially after I finally located Bill, Eric and Charlie part way up and could see that they were not moving. They stayed that way for the longest time before finally, to my great relief, started down. I walked out to meet them and to find out what the trouble had been. Apparently Eric had the only rope, which was not a regular climbing rope but a much shorter rope he had scrounged from somewhere. That had meant the men had to move closely together and at a faster rate than was wise because Eric, much younger than Bill and Charlie, was leading. It seems that Bill had had an attack of tachycardia (dangerously fast heartbeat) and they had stopped to wait while his heart rate went down and they could move again.

We spent another night at the hut, still suffering from altitude sickness, with the additional worry of Bill and his heart. The next morning we started down the Naro Moru route, very relieved to be going downhill and feeling immensely better as the altitude decreased. At one point we passed a man going up the trail on crutches because he had only one leg. This was a reminder of what is possible when you really want to do something. Although the Naro Moru route is the most popular, we didn't run into any other people on the way down. We did, however, run into a Cape buffalo, an incident which Bill recounted many times afterwards and with good reason.

Cape buffalo are considered to be the most dangerous animals in Africa, especially to humans. They are very aggressive and unpredictable. Bill and I were walking unconcernedly down the trail (the others had disappeared ahead) when all of a sudden the buffalo appeared, standing stock still right in the middle of the trail, glaring at us. I was stricken with fear and instantly scrambled up the steep hillside next to the trail in order to give him a very wide berth. Bill, on the other hand, got out his whistle and blew a loud blast. The buffalo jumped straight up in the air and charged over the steep lower edge, disappearing with thunderous crashing into the brush. Bill, triumphant, decided to give him another blast for good measure. But instead of scaring the buffalo further, it aroused all his aggressive instincts. He shot up out of the brush and landed, snorting in anger, back on the trail. Bill abandoned his whistle and clawed his way up the hillside, following my route, where we both hid behind a tree until the buffalo finally disappeared.

We resumed our hike down the trail with great trepidation, discussing whether Bill should blow his whistle again (I said no, of course not, Bill said he would only blow it once, not twice). But soon, the buffalo was forgotten as we reached yet another obstacle, the so-called "vertical bog". We had been forewarned by the guide about this steep quagmire of wet moorland into which our feet kept sinking. It went on and on and seemed to pull with deliberate malice at our boots, step after tiring step. We were more and more thankful that we had chosen this side the mountain to come down rather than go up. We were also even more impressed by the feat of those Italian prisoners who, besides breaking out of prison, had to face wild game and thick vegetation, all without trail or map, in order to climb Mount Kenya.

Bill and I often talked about the many reasons why people climb mountains—most of them fairly irrational. Mallory's comment, "Because it's there," has been called the most famous three words in mountaineering. To subject one's body to the punishing nature of high altitudes, just to reach a summit, must seem bizarre and foolhardy to those who haven't heard the call. In the case of Mount Kenya, we wanted to know what had driven those Italian prisoners to actually break out of prison camp and attempt such a feat. They must have been inspired by their daily view of the mountain and devised this ingenious scheme, a crazy and wonderful act of pure defiance. But as Bill and I stood at the base and looked up at the rocky peaks from which we had just descended, we were sure that it was simply their desire to feel like free men again, if only for that one moment of glory.

We reach the summit, cold and tired
but fueled by memories
of those rowdy banquets
high on an African mountain.

from Spaghetti at 12,000 feet, **The Simple Life**

Mount Kilimanjaro
by Lucy

We were coming up on the Christmas holiday in 1972, when Bill had the happy idea of inviting Jonathan to join us in Kenya for his vacation from Swarthmore. The idea was to spend a week exploring game parks and then to hike up Kilimanjaro, at 19,341', the highest mountain in Africa. Friends told us to write to the manager of the old hotel from which trips traditionally started and make a booking, which I did. We were going to be joined by a climber friend of Bill's, and his family, who would be coming from Dar Es Salaam.

Bill, Jonathan and I flew from Nairobi to Arusha in Tanzania, and arrived at the old hotel in the morning expecting to start right up to the first hut. But as usual, nothing went exactly as planned. There was a bedlam of noise and activity in the hotel lobby as other trekkers were matched up with guides and porters and assorted food items. I managed to squeeze through the crowd to a small German woman who seemed to be in charge and told her we were ready to go. She looked surprised and said she had never heard of us. She seemed unaware of our booking but told us not to worry; after everyone else had left she would organize something.

So there the three of us sat, impatiently waiting for all the others (including Bill's friend and family) to leave. The German manageress then informed us that all the porters were taken and were on their way up but she would try to get three boys from a nearby village. After a long delay the boys appeared, food was packed, and each of us was given a walking staff. With a sigh of relief, we finally set off. After hiking for about half an hour, the porters simply vanished into thin air. Since they were carrying our sleeping bags, extra clothes and food for the entire climb, we were rather nonplussed and sat down, wondering what to do next since we didn't even know where the real trail started.

Eventually the boys reappeared, indicating that they had gone to their homes to get their own food for the climb. By this time, it was so late that the afternoon rains began. As we happened to be hiking through a rain forest, this was a not an ordinary shower but monsoon rain coming down in buckets. The porters disappeared again, leaving us without anything, including our rain gear. We tried cowering under a tree but since that proved useless, we decided to push on and continue up an old rutted road that gradually narrowed into a trail. We found out later that the porters are supposed to go on ahead and put one's stuff on a bunk in the next hut to reserve a place. This piece of information would have been helpful to know, especially when we came to a branch in the trail.

Jonathan and I were certain that the right fork was the main trail but Bill, being contrary, insisted we take the left one, even though it was clearly "the road less traveled." There ensued a rather heated discussion, whereupon Jonathan announced he was going on the right fork and promptly took off. Even though I was absolutely certain, and became more sure as we went along, that Bill was wrong, I simply had to go with him because I knew I would do nothing but worry if he went on alone, especially since darkness was falling. I was worried enough as it was, fearing we might get completely lost if we kept on. I didn't dare say anything more though, knowing that Bill's stubbornness and increasing frustration might make him persist. The trail got fainter and more overgrown until finally, to my great relief, he reluctantly turned around.

By the time we rejoined the main trail, it was almost dark and this is where the staffs came in. We poked along like blind people, barely able to follow the trail and were overjoyed to finally make out a light in the distance. We had reached the Mandara Hut (9,000'). It was pitch dark when we finally arrived, and all the other hikers (including Jonathan and Bill's friends) had long since eaten and were in their bunks. Since we were the last to arrive there was only one bunk space left, which Bill gallantly let me have while he stretched out on the floor. The kindly cook dished us up some soup, and then we managed to get a little sleep.

The next day we started at a reasonable time and the going was easy, though slower since we were beginning to feel the altitude. This time, our porters reached the next hut (Horumbu at 12,000') in time to reserve us spaces, which happened to be on the top of one of the three-tiered bunks. There were two on each side of the hut with a narrow walkway in between. We settled into our sleeping bags and were just drifting off when the door burst open with the shouts and laughter and singing of a very cheerful bunch of Italians. Completely oblivious to the sleeping hikers, they rigged up some sort of a table in the space between the bunks, put a red checked table cloth over it and unloaded a large quantity of spaghetti and sauce, cheese and loaves of bread and, of course, wine. They started at once on the wine, which heightened the volume of singing and laughing, which went on until around 2 a.m. Bill sat up on his bunk and made not very subtle comments about people who were trying to sleep, which they completely ignored.

The third day we walked steadily upward until we reached a high plateau, dry as a desert, and could see the summit cabin off in one direction and Little Kilimanjaro in the other. By this time, Jonathan was strongly feeling the effects of altitude. Bill and I had been living in the highlands of Kenya for several months and so were somewhat more acclimatized. The porters kept saying, *pole, pole (slowly, slowly)*, an entirely unnecessary warning. Since it was still early, Bill suggested climbing Little Kilimanjaro as well, so as not to miss anything. I said, *no thanks,* and continued doggedly on the trail. Jonathan felt lousy but could not admit it to his father who was 30 year older, so reluctantly went with him. They spent several hours going up the smaller peak and then back to the main trail.

The walk up to the next hut seemed endless because the air was so clear that the final cabin (Kibo Hut, 15,500') appeared closer than it was. By this time we all had real altitude sickness and Jonathan and I had severe migraines as well. Jono felt so sick and so tired, in fact, that he hadn't had the energy to take off his boots or gloves when he went to bed. This was an advantage when the porters woke us up around 2 a.m. because all he had to do was hop down and start walking. It was very cold and we were bundled up because the final ascent was all in snow. It was also quite steep, with an endless series of switchbacks. We trudged along for hours, stopping periodically to rest but unable to do any idle talking. We passed a few of the Italians, actually crawling on their hands and knees up the trail. I didn't disdain them because I myself sat down at many of the final switchbacks. In fact, I thought they were pretty game to be continuing at all, after their carousing down in hut #2, but one by one they all dropped out. At one point, while resting in a cave, one of our group showed up in some sort of dire pain. It turns out he had dislocated his shoulder falling. We watched as someone else wrenched it back into place while the poor man screamed in agony. Somehow, he seemed to want to go on after that, which made my altitude sickness feel petty in comparison.

We finally reached the summit and had a spectacular view of the tropical savanna stretching out in all directions below us. A guide, who was with another group, announced that the real summit was on the other side of the crater and was 14 feet higher. He sprinted off in that direction and naturally, Bill felt honor bound to follow him. But Jonathan and I felt we were quite high enough to call it a day. After all, we were on top of the world.

The Highest Mountain in Norway
by Lucy

For some years, my cousins Warren and Aase had been inviting us to visit them in Norway and do some hut to hut hiking in their mountains. We flew to Oslo and were taken to their apartment in the city. They proposed driving north to their cabin, located near the two highest mountains in Norway. We stopped to get grocery supplies and then proceeded to their charming cabin, entering by the kitchen door. We were forewarned by Warren that houses this far north, rather than having refrigerators, customarily stored perishables in a small concrete room under the kitchen, accessed by a trapdoor.

Warren went in ahead of me and opened the trapdoor in readiness for our cold items. I followed with great enthusiasm, carrying a large carton of groceries that obscured my view, and stepped right through the trap door's open hole. I plummeted nine feet and hit the cement floor on my back with a thud, groceries flying everywhere. Although I miraculously escaped major injury, the accident resulted in rather severe pain, leaving me flat on my back the whole next day while Bill, Dick and Dixie paid a visit to the spectacular nearby fjords.

We were forced to revise our plans, as I could not carry a pack. As an alternative, Warren and Aase suggested that we make our headquarters in one of the larger nearby hostels and walk out from there for the first few days, and then go on the famous Bessegen hike in the same area, in Jotunheimen National Park. Aase, being Norwegian, and having been part of the resistance to the Nazi occupation during World War II, was an expert skier and knew the mountains well. Her role had been to escort fleeing refugees through the mountains and over the border into neutral Sweden, for which she was finally caught and put in prison in solitary confinement for over a year.

Warren and Aase drove us to the hostel and then returned to their cabin. On the first day, I attempted a trial hike over more or less flat terrain. I was still extremely sore and uncomfortable and couldn't imagine going up a mountain. So the next day, Bill and D & D left me to recuperate while they set off to climb Norway's second highest peak, Glittertinden. The hostel was large and comfortable, providing a huge Nordic breakfast, but I soon got bored and decided to go out and take a short hike on my own.

It so happened that by simply crossing the road, I could walk up a well-traveled trail. I could only carry a fanny pack containing a sandwich so the going was easy. I thought I'd just go up little way, and plugged on until reaching a convenient rock where I sat down to eat my sandwich. Food revived me and I decided to walk on a bit further. There was now snow, and quite suddenly a dense fog settled in. As I was deciding whether or not to turn back, a young French couple appeared on their way up so I asked if I could accompany them, to which they readily agreed. I figured it was much safer and more comforting to be with people than blundering down by myself in a fog.

Although my back was really aching at this point, I kept going, thinking as one always does that the slope just ahead must lead to the top. Eventually it did, and there was an actual hut where you could get hot cocoa (Norway being very civilized in that way). The French couple and I didn't linger but made our way down the mountain and back to the hostel. I retired to our room, happy to rest and have a cup of tea and await the return of my companions some hours later. Bill, Dick and Dixie finally arrived, exuberant after their invigorating climb up Glittertinden. They were very apologetic for having left me for so long until I told them how I had spent the day.

"You took the trail across the road and went all the way to the top?" Dick asked. I nodded, feeling a bit confused by his expression. "Well," he looked over at Bill and Dixie, "so much for feeling sorry for Lucy. She just hiked up Galdhopiggen, the highest mountain in Norway."

A journey can take weeks or months or even years,
transcending time,
and space is the sand beneath your feet
or the horizon of infinity.

from Caravansary, **Home and Away**

When the stars are fallin` and the thunder starts to roll...

Adventures
Around the World

Masai Mara

Over the wide plain of the Masai Mara
the sun burns like glass.
The golden land is steeped in midday silence
as we watch gazelles and elegant impala
blend like copper pennies
into the tall grass.

Nothing moves but their twitching tails,
heads on alert. A sudden shuddering rocks the ground,
noise like distant thunder rattles the sky.
The antelope wheel and scatter
while we stand frozen, listening

to the pounding hooves——a human island
surrounded by a stream of zebras howling, barking,
baying, streaking by on either side
in a black and white blur——
the great zebra migration from the Serengeti plain.

And then, they are gone. Gazelles
and impala return to grazing, silence flows back
and we, released from our trance,
turn to each other in wonder.

from **The Simple Life**

The Journey to Kenya
by Sorrel North

In the late spring of 1972 when I was 13, my parents—Bill and Lucy—announced they would be taking a sabbatical year to live in Kenya. Because my older siblings had all left (or were leaving) home, I would be the only child to accompany them. The thought of being parted from my friends and beloved horses to go and live in darkest Africa seemed like a fate worse than death. But in spite of several months of vehement protest, including running away twice (to a nearby friend's house), I found myself hustled onto an overnight flight across the pole to London.

The idea for going to Kenya had come about when Bill felt the call for another yearlong adventure, this time in Africa. Kenya seemed like the most stable country at that time and, by fortunate coincidence, Lucy's mother knew that Kenya had the largest Quaker Meeting in the world. She obtained the name and address of a man who was the head of the Meeting in Kenya's Western Province, near Lake Victoria. It seemed there was always a shortage of teachers in the mission schools, and despite the fact that this man never responded to Bill's letters, he decided to go anyway and trust in fate. Lucy was always game for another adventure, so away we went.

When we arrived in London, my parents decided that they might as well take a weeklong detour to visit my mother's ancient, argumentative cousin who lived in Ireland. By now I was extremely lethargic and could barely keep my eyes open, something my mother chalked up to jet lag until she felt the huge hard lumps in my neck. A trip to the doctor confirmed I had mononucleosis. I spent the entire week in Ireland, including my 14th birthday, so weak and tired I could barely participate in any activities. When we arrived back in London, Lucy went prowling around the city looking for a "bucket shop," a place that sold ultra-cheap plane tickets. She purchased three tickets on Egypt Air to Nairobi, by way of Cairo, Egypt.

When we boarded the Egypt Air plane, we all thought there had been some mistake. This was an old Soviet cargo plane, without any frills like padding on the metal walls or reclining seats, and the only door was at the front of the plane. There weren't even any emergency exits. I felt an instant sense of claustrophobia that lasted the entire loud, rattling, smelly five-hour flight until we touched down in Cairo. Bill uttered periodic platitudes about the safety of cargo planes while my mother kept trying to locate the stewardess to ask about food. There didn't seem to actually *be* a stewardess until just before we landed, at which point she suddenly appeared and directed us out the cargo door and down onto the stifling runway.

The Cairo Airport of 1972 consisted of a series of low, small buildings, none of which had any identifying signage. It was now the beginning of September, and the temperature outside registered 108 degrees. The 40 or so passengers were herded into a small room with no air conditioning where our passports were taken away, after which, all official personnel vanished into thin air. We were left in the airless room with the other equally irritated passengers, unable to vent our frustration on anyone. Two sweltering hours passed in what to me seemed like the inferno of hell until finally, an official appeared and announced that the plane was delayed until the following morning. The good news, he said, was that we'd be put up in an airport hotel. The bad news was, our bags were to remain on the plane. We were taken in a small bus to the hotel where we spent a broiling, sleepless night with the constant deafening roar of planes taking off or landing.

In the morning, the bus brought us back to the airport where we found ourselves once again abandoned in the oven-like room. There were only enough wooden benches for about half the passengers and no airport personnel to tell us when our flight would be boarding. At this point, Lucy took matters into her own hands and began rushing down the warren of passages that led throughout the primitive airport, searching in vain for someone to tell us what was going on. Meanwhile, a woman finally appeared and announced that our flight would be delayed until the following morning because the plane had a "slight mechanical problem."

This time, the bus took us all the way into downtown Cairo where we were unceremoniously deposited in front of a shabby, run-down hotel. We had no spare clothes, no toiletries, and hadn't eaten since the day before. I was too tired and miserable to notice anything except the searing heat and a constant, nagging thirst. The passengers trouped disconsolately up the steep narrow staircase to our assigned rooms. Ours had two single beds with no bedding except stained bottom sheets. The bathroom had a toilet that the manager told us in broken English not to flush as it leaked into the room downstairs. The sink faucet was broken, he added. When Bill asked how they would manage the toilet contents, the manager assured us it would be removed after we left according to "the highest standards."

I immediately collapsed onto one of the beds. It was so unbelievably hot and I was so sick from the mono, I literally wished I were dead. That is, until I was awoken at about 3 a.m. by the loud chanting in the streets below which alerted me to a strange shadow on the wall. When I discovered its source, I let out a blood-curdling scream, causing my mother to leap up in a panic and shout "Fire! Fire!" (her worst nightmare). But in fact, what I'd seen was the largest cockroach known to humankind. It was at least three inches long and made a sort of clicking noise as it traversed the floor. Lucy's and my screams had woken Bill, who grumbled irritably and then took his shoe and smashed the monster cockroach. By now, the religious chanting wafting through our windows (which had no glass) was so loud, we resigned ourselves to being awake. Bill brought out a deck of cards and we moved the beds together because I was afraid to touch the floor.

The little airport bus picked us up the next morning and once again the passengers, now looking haggard and slightly deranged by the heat, were deposited in the airless room. After an hour, when no one had appeared to tell us what was going on, a heavyset man began shouting and swearing and banging on the desk while his distraught wife tried to calm him. Eventually, a beaming official arrived to escort us across the hot tarmac and back onto the smelly cargo plane for our five-hour flight to Nairobi. By this time, even my normally cheerful mother seemed out of sorts when she discovered that the one bathroom on the plane was out of order. "Where are we supposed to go?" she asked the stewardess.

"Oh, you can still use the bathroom," the stewardess replied, "the toilet doesn't flush, but that's all right."

Finally we were on our way to Kenya, and even I began to feel better when Bill told me it was much cooler in Nairobi. An hour into the flight, when the plane banked sharply over the Aswan Dam, we all looked with interest at the huge structure in the desert below. And then the plane banked again, so sharply that we were thrown sideways, causing all the passengers to begin murmuring apprehensively. Bill, who had been peering out the window, shook his head and remarked, "That's odd. They just dumped a bunch of gas." The plane was now clearly headed back toward Cairo but there had been no announcement from the pilot, nor any sign of the stewardess. Bill added, "They can't land with a full tank, so that must be why they dumped the gas." He then went on to assure us that this particular make of cargo plane was one of the safest ever built, even in an emergency landing.

By now, I was pretty much terrified. I had never liked flying in the first place, and my worst nightmare—a crash landing—seemed to be coming true. Suddenly, the stewardess appeared, her face white as a sheet, arms full of pillows. "Fasten your seatbelts VERY TIGHT," she shouted. Then she sat down in a vacant seat and proceeded to pile the pillows all around herself. Bill asked what the problem was and she told us there was a leak in the hydraulic lines, meaning the brakes might not be operational. Even my dad seemed sobered by that piece of news.

164

For the next 30 minutes or so, all of the passengers sat in what I assume was mute terror, awaiting our impending doom. When we began our descent into the Cairo airport, I could see that the runway was literally covered with emergency vehicles; some sitting in one spot, others racing along with lights flashing. "That's not a good sign," Bill commented, but when I moaned aloud he added, "It's probably just a precaution." The plane descended more quickly than I'd ever experienced, and when the stewardess shouted, "Brace yourselves!" there was a collective gasp. Miraculously, the plane touched down, screeched to a halt, and the pilot flung open the cargo door and hustled us out onto the runway. We were pretty far from the terminal, but here was the little bus, waiting to take the shaken passengers back to the hellhole of the Cairo terminal.

This time, we were told the "slight mechanical problem" would delay us until the day after tomorrow. I really wanted to die when I heard the news, and even more so when we were dropped back off at the cockroach hotel in downtown Cairo. After another miserable, sleepless night, both parents disappeared. Lucy went to find something for breakfast, and Bill to find a way to get out to see the pyramids. He figured that if we were stuck in Egypt, we might as well do something interesting. Bill came back with what he called great news; he had found an outfit where you could rent a camel to ride the 10 miles out to the Giza plateau. Lucy thought that sounded like a terrific idea, even though the morning temperature was already over 100. Naturally, I elected to stay behind and spent the entire day in a comatose stupor. I couldn't even rouse myself for dinner when the folks appeared late that afternoon, exhausted, but elated by their camel ride. They were covered in red dust, and pretty much filthy, but so was I. We hadn't changed our clothing three days.

We finally arrived in the blessedly cool air of Nairobi the following night. The journey to Kenya had been one of the worst experiences of my life. But, as it turned out, the actual year in Africa was just the opposite. Bill managed to find a teaching job at a Quaker mission school, and (to her surprise) got my mom one as well. The landscape of our new lives was red earth, brilliant blue skies and riot of color and sound. Like the natives, we lived in the present, and moved in the rhythm of our ancestors. Our home was a mud hut with no electricity, where armies of ants crawled in the window holes, across the floor, and out the other side. We read by candlelight and fell asleep to the sound of chanting and drumming. Every night, my dad and I went out to look at a sky blazing with stars, and he taught me all the unfamiliar constellations. My mom threw parties for our Peace Corp friends and introduced them to her favorite games—like pushing an orange across the floor with your nose.

During our year in Africa, I got to know who my parents were when they weren't being parents. On school breaks, we went on safari for weeks at a time and camped amongst rhinos, cheetahs, wildebeest and hyenas. We watched lions mating in the moonlight and walked through the middle of a zebra migration. Bill chased a bull elephant with our landrover into a grove, and shot back out with the elephant in hot pursuit, narrowly escaping being gored to death. Lucy swam in a lake teeming with crocodiles and hiked through a sugar cane field in the pitch dark—where several less fortunate people had been killed by boa constrictors. Danger lurked everywhere in Kenya, but as my dad said (after one particularly harrowing encounter), "I'd rather wrestle a Cape Buffalo than be one of those people who drive around a Sears parking lot for an hour trying to find a parking place closer to the door."

Even after all these years, I can still remember a classic Bill Dougall moment where he decided to set up a shot for a home movie that involved Lucy chasing wild animals. "Faster!" he shouted, "Wave your arms!" When she glared at him, Dad said to me, "Your mother doesn't like to be told what to do." But there she is in our home movie, running across the African savanna behind a herd of wild giraffe. She turns to look at the camera—and smiles.

Magic!
by Lucy

During our year in Kenya, at every school break we would load up our land rover and go on safari. We usually crammed in as many friends as could fit to go explore the amazingly varied countryside; game parks, tropical coastline, the Great Rift Valley, lakes, deserts and anything else of interest along the way. The last school break before we departed to fly home came at the end of June, in 1973. By marvelous good luck, it happened to coincide with a total eclipse of the sun passing over Lake Turkana (formerly Lake Rudolph), in the far north of Kenya. Jill was with us, ready to take over my last quarter of teaching, and also several teachers from our school.

We organized two other land rovers to accompany us, one from our school Lihranda, and one driven by Ken Van Dyke, who had flown to Kenya with a bunch of Lakeside students for this very unusual occasion. In fact, hundreds of people came from all over the world to see it. Most went to Lodwar on the east side, which had a small airport, but we chose the primitive road going north through the desert. We had taken this route once before and barely made it through. The road crossed numerous dry river beds, requiring all hands to push our vehicles through sand and rocks. We saw wild camels and sweltered in the barren desert heat, pouring buckets of water over our heads to cool off. Finally, we arrived on the west side of the lake at a tiny local village where the chief of the Turkana tribe held sway.

After camping overnight in a small structure, we were awakened very early by a forest of hands coming through the shack's windows from the native people. They held small artifacts and trinkets they wanted to sell. There were scores of small children, shouting and crowding in, hanging on our arms and legs. The women wore the customary neck rings to elongate their necks as a sign of beauty. It looked extremely uncomfortable to us, but they stood tall and elegant. The Turkana were a beautiful tribe, led by a most formidable and impressive chief.

We walked out to the shores of Lake Turkana, the largest alkaline lake in the world. The lake was brown and had actual waves, like an ocean, rolling up on a sandy shore. I decided to go in for a dip to cool off. What a shock! It was like immersing myself in a large vat of warm soapsuds. I later found out the lake was infested with Nile crocodiles, the second largest reptiles in the world. Our group gathered on the beach, had a sort of picnic, and then got out our smoked glass-set-in-cardboard sunglasses for the big event. It was truly a unique, once in a lifetime experience, and we were all deeply moved and impressed.

After the eclipse was over, the Turkana chief, surrounded by members of his tribe, walked up to Bill. He had singled out Bill as our leader, in whatever mysterious ways chiefs have of identifying an equal. They shook hands cordially, and then the chief asked Bill to explain why the sky had gone dark in the middle of the day. Bill, being used to teaching American students, launched into a complicated scientific explanation about the moon's umbral shadow sweeping across the earth's surface and the Path of Totality. The chief waved his hands cheerfully but dismissively and said, "Simpler." Thereupon Bill shortened his explanation considerably. The chief shook his head again and said, "Simpler." So Bill decided to use stones, placing a large stone on the sand as the sun and a smaller stone as the moon, and moving "the moon" between "the sun" and the earth. Still cheerful, the chief said, "No, no, no. Simpler."

Bill, in desperation, finally shrugged his shoulders and said, "Magic!"

"Ahhh, of course!" The chief turned triumphantly to his people and pointed to the sky. "Magic!"

The elephant is tied up next to my bicycle
contentedly munching at a large stack of hay.
He appeared suddenly last week,
led or ridden by his small master
over all those mountains
from India, to the south.

The pilgrim did not act as though
this were anything special,
just a journey of several hundred miles
over mountains
on an elephant.
He was coming to the festival of Shiva Ratri
to pay his respects
to the god.

One day, I wake up and look out.
Maiti Devi seems strangely empty.
Where are the hay and the elephant?
People keep on walking, walking
slowly around the little temple.
And acrid smell of smoke wafts over
from the burning bodies on the Ghats.
The sun beats down relentlessly on the dusty city.

I would not mind having
the kind of faith it takes
to ride an elephant over the mountains
for days and days
and miles and miles.

From Maiti Devi, **Migrations**

Last Trek in Nepal
by Lucy

Toward the end of the most exotic year of our sabbaticals spent living abroad, a young student of Bill's turned up out of the blue at our little flat next to the temple of Maiti Devi in Kathmandu. *You must go to Gokyo*, he said. We were shortly due to return to the U.S. and had already walked around the Annapurnas, and over most of the trails in the Kathmandu Valley and the area north from Pokhara. *Why Gokyo?* we asked. We were also very busy getting ready to leave after a year away from home. Also, the monsoon season was due to start with its torrential rains at any moment. But the longer we tried to talk ourselves out of it, the more we knew we just had to go. Bill and I could never resist a challenge.

We departed on May 6th, 1981, and in order to make sure we had enough time for the trek, took a small plane from Kathmandu flying east to Lukla. At 9,383', Lukla is listed even now as the most dangerous airstrip in the world. It lies on an angle and was not paved until 1999. The setting, in the heart of the towering Himalayas, is extremely dramatic. Lukla is the starting place for the Everest Base Camp and other expeditions, but we most definitely did *not* want to go on that route of tourists and garbage. So we started walking north from Lukla to Namche Bazaar, where we stayed the night at a very primitive hostel.

Namche used to be a major trading center where grain from the south was exchanged for salt from Tibet. It was a very busy and interesting town but we had no time to linger. We quickly discovered the hotel "bathroom" (and indeed the only public convenience for the whole town) was several blocks down an unlighted street. It consisted of a wooden platform with a hole in it, built out from the hillside and supported unsteadily by stilts from the street below. There was a vague sort of shed for privacy but naturally, no door. The whole operation, including locating it, was a real challenge—especially in the dark.

The next day we took a side trip northeast to see Thyanboche, site of a beautiful Buddhist monastery built in 1916 by Lama Gulu. We had the good luck of seeing it before it burned down (it has since been rebuilt). The Everest route continues to the northeast, but we cut back west to Phortse and the route north to Gokyo. On the trail to the tiny village of Phortse (12,000'), we met a man herding goats who beckoned us insistently to come with him to his house, which we did. He introduced us to his new wife and baby son and led us into the house, which was small and made of rough stone with no windows. He then made us tea and potato pancakes cooked over an open fire. We were hungry and welcomed this unexpected hospitality, thrilled that he wanted to chat with us. He told us he was a Sherpa guide and I wondered if the three highly polished brass plates in their open cupboard had been given to him in thanks for his services. His name was Sonam Tenjing, and it turned out that he had been the guide on two Everest reconnaissance expeditions, in 1935-36, for the famous English explorer, Eric Shipton.

This fascinated us because Bill had always admired Eric Shipton. In fact, we had actually met him in Chile in 1965 when he was on his way to walk across the ice cap in Tierra del Fuego. He had been denied leadership in the successful Everest expedition of 1953, even though he knew the area better than anyone and was a tough and experienced climber, especially in high altitudes. The English Himalayan Committee was caught up in a competition for the prestige of being the first to climb the highest mountain in the world and they were planning a large, organized military style maneuver with armies of porters and sherpas. They appointed John Hunt, a senior army officer, as co-leader with Shipton, but as

Shipton abhorred large expeditions as well as any competitive element in mountaineering, he resigned.

This was an outlook completely shared by Bill, who disliked doing anything in a large organized group. The Noah's Ark expeditions had showed him the shortcomings of too much planning. He came from the old tradition of individual or small, informal expeditions like that of Mallory (who romantically disappeared in the mist, leaving us the mystery of whether or not he got to the top of Everest). Sonam Tenjing showed us his old Sherpa guide record book which I took pictures of. These little books serve as recommendations of character and experience for future expeditions, rather like a resume for a job nowadays. Shipton had this to say about Tenjing: *Most willing and good-tempered. Conduct exemplary. Recommended for any expedition.*

After this wonderful and unexpected episode, we went straight north toward Gokyo, reaching Dole (13,400') in the late afternoon. The trail was sometimes alarmingly close to the edge, with a vertical drop down to the Dudh Kosi River far below. At other times it was so steep that it became a rough stone stairway. Oddly enough, I never felt any fear because Bill took everything so confidently and casually. Somehow, it just seemed normal to be hiking along a crumbling mountain precipice where one slip of the foot could plunge us to certain death. The trail was like a small ribbon cut across the huge barren slopes that towered above us. When we arrived at Dole, spectacular snow capped peaks spread out ahead of us. We realized then we were almost as high as Mt. Rainier, and yet the peaks we were looking at were twice as high. It was an amazing sensation.

Dole consisted of a "tea house," a very small stone building, in the care of a woman whose husband was off as a Sherpa guide to a group of climbers. She ushered us into the room where we were to sleep on the bare floor, a little below the level of smoke from the cooking fire. As the Nepali always cook inside with no chimney, they are continually inhaling smoke (which led us to speculate on what must be a major lung problem in Nepal). Our hostess was very lively and efficient as Sherpa women usually are, since they have to do everything while their husbands are off on expeditions.

She had even led expeditions herself. In broken English, she told us that once she had seen a figure by the nearby mountain stream and upon going down to investigate later, had seen the footprints of a yeti; what we in the Northwest would call Big Foot. The Sherpa woman was deadly serious.

The next morning we started up the final stretch to Gokyo, over very bleak and rocky terrain—so rocky there was no clear trail. The large boulders dotting the slope to our left were remainders of landslides. The weather turned cold with sleet and snow, and Bill and I were still completely alone, having seen no other trekkers along the whole way from Phortse. It was a desolate scene and I began to feel rather nervous and apprehensive. We were in a hurry to get to shelter but when we started to get wet, I took the time to stop and put on rain gear. With difficulty, I persuaded Bill to do the same. We finally arrived at the hut, euphemistically called a "hotel," one of three small buildings in Gokyo (15,720').

In reality the place was just a summer pasture for yaks. The hut had two rooms, one for the yaks, which kept poking their heads in the door and windows until they were let in, their shaggy coats covered in fresh snow. We went into the other room, which was completely filled with smoke. A voice speaking English rose up from the dirt floor suggesting we join him down there, as lying down was the only way to actually breathe. Then a woman materialized and offered potatoes, which she was cooking in a small fire. That was the sum total of the meal, as it had been at Dole, and they tasted very good to us. It seems that only potatoes grow near that altitude. After a friendly chat with the young man on the floor, we spent a rather fitful night, coughing and choking intermittently from the smoke.

The next morning was glorious and clear. Our English companion suggested we climb a small peak, Gokyo Peak, next to what turned out to be a ravishingly colored turquoise moraine lake a little farther along, so as to get the sensational view. We were now close to the Tibetan border. The panoramic view, considered by some to be the finest in Nepal, encompasses six 24,000' peaks: Cho Oyu, Makalu, Lhotse, and the north, west and south ridges of

Everest. Bill experienced some altitude sickness so we did not linger, and started back down to Dole where we spent another night.

The next day, we stopped at Khumjung to visit Ang Lakpa, the sirdar (leader) of our previous 28-day trek around the Annapurnas. It was a happy reunion, especially for Bill and Ang Lakpa, who celebrated with a goodly number of rounds of the very potent local beer called chang. They were having a great time, but we realized we had to leave to get down to our next stop at Khunde. I walked behind Bill, who was weaving his way cheerfully down the trail to the little village where Edmund Hillary had sponsored and help build a hospital and school. Hillary has contributed much to this region, which we were happy to see because so many climbers come just for the mountains and do nothing for the people—the sherpas and porters and their families who make it all possible.

We spent the night at Namche Bazaar and then descended to Lukla to catch the plane back to Kathmandu. As it happened, the monsoon had begun and no plane could land because of clouds and rain and the state of the airstrip. The person at the little hotel near the landing strip said, *Just wait, maybe it will come later or tomorrow.* The problem was that the plane was small, the reservations were full, and waiting trekkers just kept piling up. The next day was just as bad, and the following one as well, so we decided that we simply had to walk out or we would miss the plane from Katmandu back to Delhi and all the connections leading back home, including Istanbul, Athens and Rome.

At this point we were rather tired. High altitudes take their toll, so the prospect of carrying our gear all the way back to Lamosangu, a trek that normally takes 12 days, suddenly seemed like a lot of work. However, the hotel lady said not to worry, she would hire a porter to carry our packs and to act as a guide. We thought that sounded great until it turned out that the young man only knew the way back to his own village, less than a day away. Walking out meant walking west, against the grain of the land, as the main rivers run north and south. This meant that we would be either going up or down the steep valleys, never on the level. It is

150 miles from Namche Bazaar to Lamosangu, the end of the road, and where we eventually could get a bus back to Kathmandu. The walk involved a series of descents that total 35,200' and a series of ascents that total 26,100'.

Our first night (May 16th), the porter found us a smoky shelter with barred doors. We got up at first light the next day and moved fast, trying to cover as much ground as possible. The next night we spent near a cheese factory on top of a mountain. As usual, we slept on the floor (this time listening to the owner, who coughed all night, and the scurrying mice). The third day we got lost. Our supposed guide/porter had never been along the route in his life and led us, by mistake, off the main trail and up a path that gradually dwindled into nothing. This is very easy to do in Nepal, as there are many side trails and no signs. I kept thinking I saw a structure in the heavy brush and trees but it always turned out to be just more trees. By this time it was approaching dark and I began to be seriously worried. There was no trail whatsoever and Bill took over the role of guide. We dropped down into the valley, crossed the river on stones, and then started up the other side. We kept climbing and finally, to our immense relief, spotted a single light in the now pitch darkness coming from a small building.

We walked eagerly towards it for what seemed like a long distance, knocked at the door and were invited into a room lighted by one candle. Amazingly, the owner turned out to be the teacher at the tiny local school. He had a bare thread of English and welcomed us, saying we could sleep on the floor. We were so happy to be under shelter and with a friendly Nepali that we didn't mind sleeping with no mats and going without dinner. We chatted for some time, Bill telling him that he was also a teacher and asking what it was it like at the local school. Bill also told him that we had to get to Jiri the following day because it was the only village with a bank, and we had no money with which to pay the porter.

In the morning, the Nepali schoolteacher told us how to get to Jiri, and this time we put on even more speed since we had no idea when the bank closed. The trail continued going steeply up or down, making for interesting but tiring walking. Along the way we met one, and then another, lone trekker who struck me as the old-fashioned type of very educated, 19th century young Englishmen, who traveled on their own seeking adventure. We made it to Jiri in time to get money to pay off our porter, who seemed glad to be rid of us. Since it was getting late, we stayed overnight in some sort of a guesthouse, and the last night we slept in Kirantichap. We left the next morning for the final hike out to Lamosangu. From there, we caught the bus back to Kathmandu, arriving home mid-afternoon on May 21st, less than a week before our scheduled departure back home. The rugged, 150-mile hike from Namche Bazaar to Lamosangu had taken us only six days, half the normal time. Missing the plane had, like so many of our unexpected adventures, allowed us to see even more of the spectacular mountainous landscape of Nepal and meet a number of interesting people.

During our last few days in Kathmandu, Bill and I climbed Shiva Puri (9,000') with our closest friends—Alton and Elizabeth, Stuart and Bina, Janet, and Stuart's Nepali lawyer friend, Ner Kamar. Shiva Puri is a sacred mountain, has its own sadhu (holy man) who lives near the top. We then had a final party at our little flat, cooking for our friends on tiny electric hot plates, while they sat on the floor (because we had no chairs or tables). The following day, our rented bikes were returned, bills were paid and bags packed for the afternoon Air India flight to Delhi. Suddenly, and very inconveniently, I was struck down by (what turned out to be) 2 types of amoebic dysentery and giardia. I went to the hospital and was dosed with flagyl, which allowed me to get on the plane. As I looked out the windows and watched Kathmandu recede into the mists, I felt an immense gratitude for this most amazing and exotic year. Our last trek in Nepal had involved danger and suspense, and taken an unexpected (150 mile) detour at the end. But somehow, everything had worked out—as it always seemed to do. Bill and I often thought of ourselves as the luckiest people in the world. And somehow, perhaps even because of that, our luck always held.

Why is it that the polar lands
draw searchers on their quests
like iron filings to a magnet?

Those 19th century men sailed and walked
to barren wastes of ice and snow,
the frozen solitudes of the poles, knowing
they might be locked in for years
through winter's blackness, knowing

their dreams could turn to whitened bones.
And we, too, felt the pull
and followed it, wanting to know

that sharp edge of danger
without a reckless giving up
of all we left behind.

from North and South, **Home and Away**

Searching for Franklin
by Lucy

People often remarked that Bill lived in the wrong century. He would have felt so much at home in the golden age of exploration when there were still great mysteries to be solved—like the route through the Northwest Passage, the fate of Mallory on Everest or standing on the North and South Poles. His library is filled with the classics of exploration; original journals and accounts of famous early expeditions. He always wanted to do something that hadn't been tried before. As Bill liked to say, *If you know the outcome it's not an adventure.*

And so it happened that two of our greatest adventures together were in search of the fate of Sir John Franklin, a great English explorer whose mission was to find a route through the Northwest Passage. For many years Bill was a member of Mountain Rescue in Seattle. Returning from a rescue one day, Bill entertained the young climber at his side, Steve Trafton, with the story of the mysterious disappearance of Franklin in the Arctic Circle. English traders and explorers had long dreamt of a shortcut to India and China to replace the long and dangerous sail around Cape Horn. In 1845, Franklin was commissioned by the English Government to search for the fabled Northwest Passage, a route through the forbidding Arctic seas in Northern Canada that linked the Atlantic and Pacific Oceans. After three years with no word, England sent out the first of many search parties.

Steve Trafton became so fascinated with Bill's account that he launched a number of expeditions over the years to the Arctic Circle; two that I went on, plus several others that Bill was a member of. Our first expedition in 1983 consisted of Steve, Al Errington, their wives, a friend of Steve's named Mark, and Bill and me. We flew from Vancouver, BC, via Edmonton and Yellowknife, to the Inuit hamlet of Resolute in the Canadian High Arctic. There, we chartered a small plane to take us north to King William Island, where Franklin's ships were beset in the pack ice in1845. Steve had bought two inflatable rafts in case we had to change plans for where we landed. Flying over the channel on the west side of the island we could see that it was blocked solidly by ice, just as it had been for Franklin. This caused us to alter our plans. We landed instead on Bylot Island in Lancaster Sound, much nearer the Atlantic Ocean and indeed the actual beginning of the Northwest Passage.

Once we unloaded our gear from the plane and it took off, we managed to find enough driftwood to make our first cup of tea. The weather was a snowy drizzle and the land a bleak desert of stones. It was truly *"wild and savage,"* as Stan Rogers' famous ballad, Northwest Passage, describes it. We pumped up the boats, named Erebus and Terror after Franklin's ships, and were relieved to find the engines started right away. Bill strutted around in his yellow survival suit like an overstuffed rooster, issuing commands as though he were Franklin himself. We obeyed, donning our own suits for our first perilous voyage on the Erebus and Terror.

We cruised through the open waters, circling one particularly beautiful iceberg—but not too closely as we knew that most of it lay underwater and might easily topple over and swamp us. We stopped at a couple of other islands to hike, and even stumbled upon an old, unmarked grave all by itself in the empty landscape. Then we decided to visit a weather station on the Borden Peninsula, perched high on a cliff and manned by a fellow called Steltner. His job was to track icebergs by radar. He invited the women in our group to spend the night with three charming Inuit women who were already staying there. The men camped on the beach, slightly disgruntled to have been shunted outside.

180

The next day we crossed Navy Board Inlet, which involved three perilous hours threading our way through ice floes. A sudden fog sprang up, turning the sky and sea into a wall of grey, obliterating all landmarks. The Terror became stuck in the ice. It was unnerving, being in a tiny inflatable raft in the Arctic sea. I felt swallowed up by the heavy skies, the inability to see more than a few feet in front of me. And though we finally managed to extricate our raft with long poles, it reminded me of Shackleton's expedition to the South Pole, one of the greatest survival stories of all time. His ship, the Endurance, was trapped in the pack ice and slowly crushed over the course of a year, leaving three lifeboats that the crew dragged and ultimately sailed to Elephant Island. From there, Shackleton made an astonishing 720 mile open boat journey to South Georgia Island where he was able to find help, ultimately rescuing his entire crew.

I was acutely aware of how small and insignificant we humans were in this vast, inhospitable landscape, and how swiftly an adventure could turn into a harrowing survival story. I remembered an experience Bill and I had canoeing with Duke Watson on the Stikine River, from Telegraph Creek in northern BC to Wrangell, Alaska. When we emerged from the river into La Conte Bay, one of the paddlers in Duke's large Northwest Company Voyageur canoe suggested we turn in toward La Conte Glacier to travel through the icebergs. At first we encountered only small ice cakes. Those gradually thickened into ice floes, which we fended off with paddles. Then, huge icebergs loomed out of the mist, calved from the glacier ahead of us. What we had not considered, but which the appalled officials in Wrangell told us later, was that if the wind had shifted, we would have become trapped in the ice and our canoes crushed. All of these memories and warnings ran through my mind as I stared blindly into the fog while Bill and Steve maneuvered our rafts through the ice floes.

Once back in camp, Bill announced a characteristically bold plan to go west and cross the wide Prince Regent inlet, and then north across 50-mile wide Lancaster Sound to be nearer our goal of Beechey Island. When we consulted Steltner, the Borden weather station manager, he was adamantly opposed to the idea.

He insisted it would be far too dangerous to make these crossings in our flimsy rubber rafts because of swells, icebergs, currents and bad weather. He advised us to get the Twin Otter plane to drop us on Beechey. That was a great relief to all, except of course Bill, who was greatly disappointed to miss out on following the route Franklin would have taken.

Pilot Paddy Doyle dropped us on Beechey Island, a bleak, barren and desolate place made up of sharp, flat rocks and fossils. More lines from Stan Rogers' haunting song ran through my mind; *"Leaving weathered broken bones, and a long forgotten lonely cairn of stones."* From Steve's research we knew that Franklin had camped on Beechey the first winter of his trip, 1845-1846, and that there were three graves belonging to the first three crewmen from his expedition who died and were buried there. The government of the Northwest Territories recently declared Beechey Island to be a National Historic Site of Canada. We camped quite near Franklin's site, where there was no protection whatsoever from the wind. Bill's and my tent survived the night but Trafton and Errington's ripped in two.

As I looked out across the barren landscape the next morning, I could imagine what Franklin's expedition members thought when they arrived at this desolate island as their first stop on the search to find the Northwest Passage. It was a lonely, depressing place. Approaching the graves, we saw a sign lying on the ground that stated:

The Sir John Franklin Encampment, 1845-1846. PLEASE DO NOT REMOVE ARTIFACTS. Each grave had a marker saying: *Sacred to the memory of: John Torrington, aged 20, John Hartnell and William Braine.*

In 1984, Canadian forensic anthropologist Owen Beattie and his team got permission to dig up the graves and exhume the bodies of the seamen for clues as to why they died when they had sailed with provisions for three years. Beattie melted the ice on the first coffin, opened it, and was dumbfounded to find the almost perfectly preserved body of John Torrington staring up at him with his eyes wide open. It must have been an eerie sight to see the actual body of a member of that doomed expedition. It was preserved by permafrost and through some initial tests, Beattie concluded that the men had probably died of lead poisoning from the newly discovered canned method of preserving food. They may have also had lung disease. As I looked at the graves, I felt pity for these young men who embarked on what they probably hoped would be the adventure of a lifetime.

The next day we explored the nearby remains of Northumberland House, erected in 1852 as a depot for further searches for Franklin. We saw the marble memorial tablet written by Lady Jane Franklin and carried there by American explorer Elisha Kent Kane. Lady Jane financed and sent out several of her own search parties. She was aided by the readings of two remarkably accurate psychics, which led to the discovery of Franklin's camps on King William Island. There, in 1858, the search party found bodies lying face down in the snow, decapitated skeletons inside a boat filled with weighty and useless items, and abandoned heaps of clothing. The many searches for Franklin's lost party resulted in the mapping of almost the whole northern coastline of Canada.

Later that day a storm blew in, so we overturned one boat for a windbreak and spent a cold and uncomfortable night huddled together for warmth. The next morning, despite high winds, we motored into Gascogne Bay. To our amazement we saw three houses, rubber boats and men in diving suits who were even more surprised to see us. The leader told us they were doing environmental research but we suspected they were a secret military operation, laying cables to detect submarines. He invited us into their shack for tea, and when we questioned him about the research he was evasive, confirming our suspicions.

We camped that night on Devon Island and another tent and poles were ripped to shreds. For three long days, the seven of us were trapped inside our one remaining tent through a series of storms consisting of wind, rain and snow. Time felt interminable, and once again I couldn't help but admire the fortitude of Franklin and his crew. After all, what was three days compared to three years in these inhospitable conditions?

Bill and Al rigged up poles for our radio in order to get reception, and had to manually hold them steady in the fierce wind as we checked in with our pilot Barry at Resolute every two hours. But the radio yielded a lot of static and shouting and finally, getting more and more impatient, we decided to try crossing Wellington Channel to get to Resolute by water. The storms had subsided by the third day but pack ice near the shore forced us ever farther out to find a clear channel. Compasses don't work this close to the magnetic pole, fog obscures the land and the continual dodging of ice floes further confuses the heading.

I was so absorbed in the immediacy of the experience that I didn't feel any fear—just a determination to get back to civilization. After an hour in the floes, we were very relieved to sight land. However, it turned out we had just made a complete circle and were back on Devon Island where we had started. There were a number of responses to this dismal discovery, ranging from a string of swear words, to Bill's scientific excuse of the Coriolus Force which veers an object to the right in the northern hemisphere. We radioed Barry, who warned us in no uncertain terms not to try the open crossing again. He would try to somehow get his plane in, in spite of the low visibility.

We dismantled the boats and sat on the shore under the completely overcast and leaden sky, hoping for the best. We weren't seriously worried, due mainly to Bill's relentless optimism and his infectious sense of humor. In all of our adventures, I always felt complete trust in Bill's leadership. He exuded confidence and showed time and again how we could extricate ourselves from whatever predicament presented itself—a swollen river, flooded tent, an impassable cliff, or even a drive up into the mountains by way of hairpin turns heading for Tubal Cain Mine. On that icy and perilously steep road, he rolled down his window, leaned out and shouted to the car behind us, *"Isn't this great!"*

After what seemed like ages, a plane suddenly appeared out of the north. Barry had found a hole to drop through and get under the fog layer. We loaded the boats and all of our gear into his plane at record speed and took off immediately for Resolute and home. Our first trip to the Arctic Circle in search of John Franklin ended on a dramatic note, but left us yearning to know more. And so, six years later, in 1989, we planned another expedition. This time we had a much more specific objective, one that would lead to the heart of one of the greatest maritime mysteries of the ages. Thus began our second search for Sir John Franklin; or more specifically, his grave.

All signs pointed to King William Island, the nearest land to where Franklin's ships were beset in the pack ice. According to reports from early search parties, Inuit tribal members had seen one ship sink off of King William Island (the Terror) with great loss of provisions and lives, causing the remaining crew to come ashore. Some time later, other tribe members came across another ship (the Erebus) that had been piloted to an island in Queen Maud gulf and recently abandoned. The Inuit found dead men in their bunks, which they left, and assorted useful tools such as knives, utensils and wood, which they took. They found the tracks of four large men and a dog in the snow. Other Inuit reports told of a white man who had been buried on land with great ceremony in a hole, afterward covered by what they called white stuff, which hardened. We decided we would base our search on this information.

Members of our current expedition consisted of Steve Trafton, Paul Williams, Jim Brathoude, my cousin Gard Holby, Dick and Dixie and Bill and me. We flew from Edmonton on June 30th to Yellowknife and on to Cambridge Bay, expecting to fly out immediately to King William Island. Unfortunately, our bags didn't arrive so we camped for two days in the airport, putting mats and sleeping bags on the floor and living off of airport snacks. For diversion, we hiked into the tiny town each day and bought mosquito lotion, stove fuel and Inuit art objects. Finally, the bags arrived and we loaded up the Twin Otter. Pilot Duncan flew us over Victoria Strait and McClintock Channel, both completely covered with beautiful lacy patterns of ice floes. We saw King William Island below us, a flat desert of stones interspersed with many lakes. We landed near the north end, about a mile inland.

The wind was blowing fiercely so we hastily unload all our gear. Our pilot jumped back into the Twin Otter, calling out,

"Have fun!" before slamming the plane door. Bill chuckled. Duncan had never asked why our little group wanted to be dropped on a desolate island in the Arctic Circle, being that a bush pilot's job is just to do what he is asked. I suspected he must have thought we were a rather bizarre group, setting off on a camping trip in that bleak and barren landscape. And as we walked vainly in all directions to try and find any shelter from the wind, I concluded he was probably right. We quickly got to work putting up the tents, tying the guy ropes to large rocks. Dick and Dixie, Gard, and Bill and I had brought the red tent fly for sleeping and the yellow tent fly for us all to eat under. It proved invaluable against the wind, and even quite homey with the plastic food containers for seats.

That first night on King William Island was a fitful one for sleeping. We could hear the tent lines being sawed away by razor-sharp rocks, and not surprisingly, it was Dick who dragged himself out of his sleeping bag to go out into the wind and rearrange the lines, tying bits of cloth around them for protection. Since the object of this trip was to find Franklin's grave, Steve had made a rough map of possible sites to explore around the island. Our first goal was an area he had named Franklin's "summer camp." It was unclear where Steve had gotten this notion until the next day when we walked to the site. There, by a lake, was a circle of large flat stones and a suspicious looking mound. Completely unfazed by the concept of respecting the dead, evoking a curse or perhaps just committing an actual crime, the men in our group start wielding picks and shovels to excavate the mound. When no sign of a dead body emerged, they continued digging a grave-shaped hole into which Trafton inserted himself, and then emerged part way for a photo. The women looked on with a mixture of amusement and disdain.

We knew from the only official written report from the actual crew—found in a cairn at Victory Point—that both of Franklin's ships had been beset off of Victory Point, King William Island, in May, 1847. A second message on this unique document, appended 19 months later, reported that in June 1847, Franklin had died and that the remaining crew and officers had left the ship and were heading south on foot to the Back River, their only hope for a white settlement. In recent years, both of Franklin's ships have finally been discovered. Divers found the HMS Erebus in 2014, under 11 meters of water on the sea floor near Queen Maud Gulf. The HMS Terror, Franklin's flagship, was found in 2016 in Terror Bay off the south end of King William Island. The ship was in pristine condition, her three masts broken but still standing, with all hatches closed and everything stowed. Researchers believe the remaining crew may have re-manned the vessel after she was originally abandoned in a desperate attempt to escape south.

After our men had their fill of digging graves, Jim brought out his metal detector and checked the whole "summer camp" area as well as other possible sites, but it yielded nothing. We decided, since all else had failed, to build a cairn. It was very satisfying and we wished we had thought to bring a bottle with a note in it. Then we walked north to check out Cape Felix, which also had a cairn and tent rings and so was another possible site to explore. Cape Felix had a dazzling view of the beautiful frozen polar sea, dotted with electric blue small lakes near the shore. From there, Dick, Dixie and Bill and I decided to head east across the island hoping to find the cairn marked on Steve's map as being of possible interest.

We finally saw a number of loose piles of stones, but nothing that looked high enough to be a significant cairn so we kept walking. And then Bill stopped us and said, *"We'd better check out that scattered bunch of stones we just passed while we're up here—it may have once been a cairn."* We turned around and went back. He started lifting up stones while the rest of us looked on with skepticism. It certainly didn't look like a gravesite and in any case, we hadn't brought the shovels. Just as I said, *"I suppose you think you'll find a bottle or something,"* Bill lifted up a stone, under which was a very old looking green glass bottle. We were stunned. I then joked, *"Now I suppose you think there's a message in it."* He examined the rusted top and the ancient cork stopper, at which point we could actually see the tip of a rolled up piece of paper.

We were thrilled and hooted with excitement. An actual discovery! Because we would have never found the cairn without Steve's map and diligent research, we replaced the bottle in the cairn and walked in high spirits all the way back to our camp. Bill could hardly contain himself, and fairly hustled Steve and the rest of us back up to the cairn where Steve had the honor of "rediscovering" the bottle. Steve began to pull out the curled, ancient parchment and it started to crumble immediately. Bill was adamantly against this, due to the obvious extreme antiquity of the note. He felt we should wait until we were back in civilization. But that night in his tent, Steve simply couldn't resist the temptation. He pulled out the tattered piece of paper and carefully unrolled it. The note was written in pencil and deposited on July 5, 1879. Amazingly enough, we had discovered the message in the bottle on July 5, 1989, exactly 110 years to the day!

The note read:

Cape Felix, King William Land, July 5, 1879
Franklin Search Party of 1878-79 reached the above point July 3rd. Found this cairn today in good order but containing nothing. Found Lieutenant Irving's remains in bay just north of Cape Jane Franklin June 27th, identified by medal awarded him at Royal Naval College. Found part of his skeleton between Franklin Point and mouth of Collinson Inlet. No other remains, graves or records have been found. Start southward on return trip July 7th. Party all well. Fredk. Schwatka, Lieut. U.S. Army Commdg.

I later found confirmation of the authenticity of this note in a book written by Schwatka himself called The Long Arctic Search, the Narrative of Lieutenant Frederick Schwatka, U.S.A. 1878-1880.

On July 5, 1879 I found a large cairn about three miles inland from our camp, standing upon a very prominent ridge. It was built upon a flat granite rock and was about seven feet high and three feet diameter at the base. There was no doubting the fact that it was the work of white men from its careful construction. As I recognized this fact at a great distance, I cannot easily describe my feelings of suspense as I approached it. But upon nearing it, the unmistakable signs of being despoiled prepared us for our finding nothing, As it must have been visible from the ships with the aid of the good marine glass, it was probably a monument erected to establish and measure the rate of drift.

Schwatka's search from Hudson Bay to the northern tip of King William Island was remarkable for being the longest sledge journey ever made (by a white man), both in time and distance, through the heart of an exceptionally severe arctic winter. The party consisted of four white men plus 14 Inuit, including five children, three large sledges and 44 dogs. The white men lived in igloos and subsisted entirely on the same diet as their Inuit friends. Theirs was the first to make an extensive summer exploration of the ground covered by Franklin's crew in their doomed attempt to find aid. Schwatka's party found numerous articles of all kinds and spoke to the locals who had actually seen the boat filled with skeletons near what Schwatka called Starvation Cove, plus bones clearly cut with a saw (evidence of cannibalism).

Although we didn't find Franklin's grave, finding the note in the bottle was the highlight of our trip and left us all in high spirits. It was July and the beginning of the short arctic summer. Ice near the shore had begun to melt and Dixie, feeling reckless and brave, decided to go in for a dip in her underwear. We decided to celebrate our last day with a rendition of explorer William Parry's play, first performed at Winter Harbor, Melville Island in 1819. Ours may have been its only other performance. Steve had found a copy of the play and the eight of us were both actors and audience. We played our parts with great gusto. I was the bear, Dixie the Inuit, and both of us the waiting wives of the sailors. The men played all the other roles. We then had more fun and games, including a "boot shoot." All of our boots were by now torn to shreds by the jagged stones, so they were tossed in the air while the men shot them. No one could remember why we brought the two guns along, but this turned out to be a splendid use for them.

The next day our plane arrived to return us to civilization. Pilot Duncan was his taciturn self, merely raising his eyebrows at our bullet ridden shoes. As we loaded our gear into the Twin Otter and got into our seats, he finally turned to me and said, "Looks like you had fun." And as we flew back and I looked down on the pure white ice floes floating in a sea of turquoise, I thought, *Yes, we certainly did have fun.* We had gone in search of Sir John Franklin's grave, and instead found an ancient message in a bottle from one of the original search parties. It was an outcome none of us could have imagined. In Bill's way of thinking, that made it a true adventure.

Lady Franklin wrote a haunting song, when it became clear her husband would never return from his search for the Northwest Passage. Her grief is the sorrow of all those who have been left behind by the great explorers. I have felt it myself, when Bill would set out on an expedition that involved danger and hardship, when I feared he might not return.

I was homeward bound one night on the deep
Swinging in my hammock I fell asleep
I dreamed a dream that I thought was true
Concerning Franklin and his gallant crew

With a hundred seamen he sailed away
To the frozen ocean in the month of May
To seek a passage around the pole
Where we poor sailors do sometimes go

Through cruel hardships they vainly strove
Their ships on mountains of ice were drove
Only the Eskimo with his skin canoe
Was the only one that ever came through

In Baffin Bay where the whale fish blow
The fate of Franklin no man may know
The fate of Franklin no tongue can tell
Lord Franklin with his sailors do dwell

And now my burden it gives me pain
For my long-lost Franklin I would cross the main
Ten thousand pounds I would freely give
To know on earth, that my Franklin do live

The Silk Road
(An Accidental Circumnavigation of the Earth)
by Bill & Lucy

Bill: The idea for the Silk Road adventure came about in July of
1988, during an evening at the home of Bill and Elen Hanson. I
had been carrying on about the mysterious part of western China
and northern Pakistan, a remote area known as the Silk Road. This
area was an isolated, nearly inaccessible mountainous region in
Asia, a sort of ancient network of trade routes connecting the East
and West that had existed for well over two thousand years. The
Silk Road had played a major part in the development of
civilization in China, along with India, Arabia and Persia. Explorers
coming from Europe in the primitive Dark Ages, into a world in
its prime—eastern China—had to either come by ship or on foot.
With no canal from the Mediterranean existing in those days, the
only sea route was to sail around the south end of Africa. The
other access route was to travel across Europe and western Asia
on foot; a long walk. We thought it sounded romantic and
worthwhile to try following this ancient trade route, and a several
of us said, "Hey, why don't we do that?"

    Lucy: Both the Bills began recalling the romantic tales of the
wild and mysterious area of western China and northern Pakistan,
the Hindu Kush, the Karakoram Range and the ancient caravan
routes collectively known as the Silk Road. This network of roads
got its name from the lucrative silk trade during the Han Dynasty,
but it had been in existence long before that. For Bill Dougall, it

was the lure of the early explorers and climbers in the Himalayas—Mallory and Conway—and stories of the years of British–Russian rivalry known as The Great Game. For Bill Hanson, it was *News from Tartary*, a book by Peter Fleming that he read at age 14 while living in China. The Bills converged on the idea of the four of us taking off as soon as possible for a new adventure, to retrace a part of that romantic route. We decided to invite Dick and Dixie along as well. I loved the idea of an adventure with good friends to a totally new place, and was drawn to it also because of the Kipling stories about India I had grown up with, especially Kim. Since childhood, I had heard the romantic names from the time of the Raj, like The Khyber Pass, which connected Afghanistan to Pakistan, and was the route of Alexander the Great and Genghis Khan. We learned later that that route was also an integral part of the ancient Silk Road.

Bill: Our modern world approach was to fly to far western China via Pakistan, and for all of us to meet there on an agreed date. From there, we would somehow figure out how to travel north across a very undeveloped and mountainous part of Pakistan and cross a 14,000 foot pass into western China. Once we got to far western China, the plan was to figure out how to travel east across the whole of China, a distance roughly the same as crossing the United States. The part of the ancient route from Eastern Europe to western China, we agreed was left to be done at another time. It all sounded very romantic and simple in Bill and Elen Hanson's comfortable living room, while drinking a glass of wine.

Lucy: On July 7th, Dick & Dixie and Bill and I boarded a Pan Am flight bound for Karachi, Pakistan via Paris, Rome and Riyadh in Saudi Arabia. All went as planned until Riyadh, where we spent an unexpected eight hours in the most beautiful airport I've ever seen. It was also the beginning of what Bill henceforward referred to as Bamboola, those screw-ups which often become the most interesting and memorable parts of the journey. From the air at night, the Riyadh Airport looked like a space station. Shafts of brilliant light streamed skyward in every direction from geometric apertures, the only light to be seen for miles in that vast desert. We entered a high ceilinged polyhedron of white stone, overwhelmed by a feeling of spaciousness. It could have been an Eastern image of the antechamber to Paradise. Floors were pure white marble. In one corner of the building, extending from the ground floor to the upper ceiling, were giant palm trees, splashing fountains and wide white marble steps with waterfalls cascading down to a clear green-tiled pool.

We spent hours in that airport. There were no signs of any sort, no airline office, no Information Booth, no flight attendants, no announcements on the intercom, no intercom, no officials to ask, no food. Just emptiness and beauty and silence. Suddenly, two airline officials materialized behind the desk. Chaos! Silence was shattered by dozens of voices as the frantic crowd descended like a swarm of locusts on its prey. I raced up to be among the first. We were told that a U.S. military plane inadvertently shot down an Iranian civilian plane over the Persian Gulf earlier that day. The U.S. had deemed it advisable to cancel all civilian U.S. flights over The Gulf and shift passengers to another airline. Caught in this unexpected crisis, the poor besieged officials were overwhelmed and finally handed out boarding passes completely randomly in two colors, red and blue. Bill and I get red, which turned out to be first class, while Dick and Dixie got blue, tourist class.

Bill and I were ushered up a winding staircase to the upper deck of the plane where we sank into reclining seats, down pillows, blankets and soft lights. Each passenger was given a tray covered with a glistening white tea cloth and dainty china cups and plates. Next, came a china teapot of aromatic tea, a bright brass coffeepot of sweet dark coffee, and little pots of sweet sticky fruit preserves planted with tiny spoons. We ate, drank, relaxed and dozed. Some time later, feeling guilty, I descended the staircase and offered to trade places for a while with D & D. Bill, not feeling in the least guilty, stayed where he was. Dick, gallant as always, said he was fine but Dixie enthusiastically traded places with me for the rest of the trip.

It turned out that the trade was worth it for the entertainment provided by the man sitting in the window seat next to Dick. He was a small, wild eyed Muslim dressed in dirty white pajamas who leaped to his feet suddenly at odd moments, stood on the seat and climbed across or into our laps in his bare feet, and then into the aisle, pursuing food trays pushed by a harassed attendant. He grabbed pastries, stuffing them joyfully into his shirt, gesticulated frantically to a compatriot a few seats ahead and then returned to his seat again, following his route over our laps. When he wasn't jumping in and out of his seat, he was either praying or reciting, bent over a small volume on his lowered tray table, or eating paper. When he ran out of his own supply, he reached over and helped himself to our newspaper, which he tore into strips before crumpling into balls and popping into his mouth.

After landing in Karachi, Pakistan, we expected to take a train or plane immediately to Rawalpindi but were foiled again and ended up in a modern looking hotel for two days. At first we were intrigued by the lavish spread of exotic looking dishes for the luncheon meal. At dinner, there was again an array of many different dishes of curries and spicy sauces. The following day we noticed that the very same dishes as the day before were on the table for both lunch and dinner. That night I became violently ill. I concluded that the hotel policy was to simply leave all food where it was on the serving table until eaten up, no matter how many days that took.

Bill: We finally arrived in Islamabad and headed for a hotel where we had agreed to meet with the Hansons. Bill Hanson had spent his early adolescence in China, so this was a sort of homecoming for him. As the expedition leader, I was really happy to have Bill along, since he could understand and actually speak the Chinese language. My plans had not included the complications of temperatures well over a hundred degrees, and what that did to a normal person's drive and enthusiasm. I had assumed Bill, in arriving before us, would have some kind of transportation arranged. But the heat and time change had apparently beaten him down, and nothing was set up. We were all pretty affected by the heat too. By some coincidence, we happily found out that a longtime ex-teacher friend from Lakeside was working in Islamabad for some American government organization. He actually hunted me up and offered to help, having somehow heard that I was coming. There was also an ex-Lakeside student, who was teaching at a local international school. The ex-student was no help with our proposed trip though and thought it was kind of a silly idea. He couldn't figure out why we would want to go off in primitive, mountainous, wild and undeveloped surroundings in the brutal, almost unbearable heat.

I developed a theory some years ago that I call the Law of the Three Thousand. I noticed at a certain point in my travels, that nearly every place I've gone, even the most remote regions, I have run into someone that I know or that is somehow connected to someone I know. From restaurants in Rome and Singapore to villages in Nepal and Kenya, I've run into teachers, friends, and relatives of friends. My theory goes like this: there is a finite group of people that are part of your circle and that you have this connection with, and I somehow came up with a mathematical equation resulting in the number three thousand. So the fact that there were not one, but two Lakeside connections in Islamabad didn't surprise me, but did make me happy. My ex-teacher friend took me to a local van operator who organized trips north and into China, and he set up a van and a driver for us for us. That was a big help, because the temperature and humidity really takes away one's initiative.

Lucy: The driver's name, like almost everyone else's in Pakistan, was Khan. We chose this particular route because Bill had discovered that there was a newly opened road called the Karakoram Highway, built with great difficulty and expense by the governments of China and Pakistan, which actually followed one of the branches of the ancient Silk Road. It was a gravel road, hardly what you'd call a highway, which led from Islamabad north to the 15,000' Khunjerab Pass at the Chinese border. Although it was July, we had somehow not realized that temperatures would be a broiling 100 degrees or more. The heat considerably sapped our energies and we were all sweating profusely. Nurse Elen distributed pink electrolyte pills and gave us temperature readings along the way, the record being 108 degrees, and kept continually pouring water over our heads.

The primitive gravel road had cost the lives of some 2,000 workers because it was hacked through the Karakoram Mountain

Range, the western end of the Himalayas, home to several of the highest mountains in the world. It was beset by continual rockslides and avalanches and was without safety features of any kind, so the driving was rather exciting. The road, which threaded its way through the deep gorge of the Indus River, sometimes went narrowly close to the edge of a vertical drop of several hundred feet. At one point, the road had just broken off entirely, plunging an unlucky truck to its fate far below. There was no fence or sign to stop us from following suit, but luckily we saw the short spur road that had been improvised to avoid it. At one particularly rough place, we came upon the scene of a large, gaudily painted Pakistani truck trying to get up a steep incline. It completely blocked the road and several men were vainly trying to push it. Bill, Bill Hanson and Dick decided to get out and help push and that turned the tide, to the great hurrahs of all concerned.

Bill: In all of this trip and its arrangements, the most important place for me to actually see was in these mountains, the Pakistan Karakorums. Gilgit was its name. The town had appeared in many adventure and exploration stories I had read from childhood on—stories of periods in the 1800's and early 1900's. This was during the time of the British Raj, and I had read many stories where the English were apparently trying to keep the Russians out of northern India. There were constant battles and events in the border areas that had, for my young mind, a romantic ring. A great deal of the impressive prosperity of England in those years came from places like India. Afghanistan and China had Russia on the other side, also wanting access to that source of wealth. It was during that time when Winston Churchill managed to get himself involved in military border skirmishes, apparently as a way to become politically known. Since my boyhood days in Buffalo, I had hoped to one day actually see this romantic place called Gilgit.

Lucy: Our first day's van ride took 16 sweltering hours. We arrived in the dark at a hotel of sorts on the outskirts of Gilgit, with all of us looking forward eagerly to a shower and a good meal. First of all, everything was pitch dark; there was no electricity, no water and no food. We were told that it was much too late for food, but we could try walking into town. Our rooms were stiflingly hot and we were so drained of energy, Bill and I collapsed on our beds, as did Elen and Dixie. Dicky and Bill Hanson were determined to find food and set off into the village. The next day we all took a look around Gilgit and Bill bought the top half of the local costume, a loose cotton shirt that came down to his knees. He looked a bit like Peter O'Toole in Laurence of Arabia.

We then bundled into the van for another long hot day's drive through the deep Hunza valley, gradually gaining altitude through some pretty amazing scenery, and ending up in Karimabad. On the way, Bill pointed out the spectacular peaks of Rakaposhi and Nanga Parbat. The gray, bare rocks and unpaved road were dry and dusty, a genuine desert landscape except for sudden patches of bright green. These were caused by flumes cut into the mountain to catch the perpetual supply of water coming down from the glaciers above and then funnel it down through irrigation ditches into the valley below, thus creating a fruitful oasis. We stopped at the side of the road and Bill, Dick and Dixie and I climbed up the mountainside to examine the flumes and consider the ingenuity of such a simple solution. At Karimabad, the village in this oasis, we spent the night at a hotel where we were assured of hot and cold running water, described by Dicky when we tried it as "cold running silt." This was the first time we had ever seen gravel come out of a spigot.

Another day's drive, steadily gaining altitude, brought us to Gulmit of the apricot trees. There were large orchards and people along the road selling apricots and items made of the wood. I bought salad servers; elegant but much too fragile to use. The hotel, called The Silk Road Lodge, seemed like paradise when we arrived. It had a wonderful manager, running water, lights, and a view of Cathedral Mountain. We decided to spend an extra day there to rest up from driving. The hotel had a pretty spacious dining room where we sat down to dinner, at which point the lights promptly went off in the whole hotel. Then the five others completely surprised me with a birthday celebration, as it happened to be July 15th. The darkness did not dampen our celebration, and each brought out something—an artifact from Bill

& Elen, a memento from Bill, an old Band-Aid box of leaves and stones from Dixie, and from Dicky a funny poem. Bill Hanson produced a cake made of silt served on a Frisbee with "can't blow out" candles brought all the way from Seattle by Elen. It was all very jolly, and reminded me of other unusual places where my birthday had happened, like the middle of the Australian outback. Bill decided it would be fun and interesting to walk up a tributary glacial valley to the Pasu Glacier the following day. Four of us were very enthusiastic but Bill H. and Elen declined, perhaps sensibly for them, as it turned out to be more than a casual hike.

Bill: The mountains here were magical, not accessible to casual tourists, and by now everyone was starting to get accustomed to the altitude. The oppressive heat was over and energy and enthusiasm were reappearing. So the next day, Dick and Dixie and Lucy and I walked back along our high mountain road a ways to hike up a tributary glacial valley. I led the way from the road up a rough trail on the left side of this big runoff stream that we guessed was coming from the end of a glacier. It was a correct assumption. It was a vague trail, but soon led to an open, moderately steep area on the rocky side of the valley. We hiked quite a ways along it, north into the high mountains, along what was a mountain tributary glacier. The size of everything was staggering; the glacial boulders, the glacier, the view back towards the valley. Some photos were taken, but they don't do real justice to the enormousness of all the physical effects. There is one of Dick and Dixie below a massive glacial boulder the size of a house. There is also a photo of me in my new native garb, with a background of mountains behind me across the valley, and the mountains around me on both sides. The size and primitiveness of everything was astounding.

We crossed a steep, rocky slope and reached the glacier. The solid white, mountainous ice of the end of the glacier was before us and we made our way up and onto the flat glacial ice. All of this motion was taking time, and the day was getting on. We felt happy and successful with our big accomplishment and hiked (or slipped and slid) along the ice until it started to rain. At this point I decided we should head back. We got off the glacier and down onto the solid rocky terrain. These were rough glacial rocks, some small and others colossal, and we started across the slope towards the vague trail we had followed from the road. Dick and Dixie were getting a little winded by this time, and were stopping occasionally to catch their breath. We must have been close to ten or eleven thousand feet, and breath is hard to come by at that altitude. I was an old hand at being winded in the mountains and Lucy was moving along at my pace. As is usual practice, I was pushing to keep us going since mountains, especially ones as primitive in their development as these, were places to get out of before dark.

As we were crossing the rocky slope, a terrible clattering sound reached our ears, the sound of falling rock; first slowly, then gradually increasing in speed and size and noise. I have no idea what set it off. Small rocks started to come down, bouncing and shooting into the air. Then larger ones, huge boulders, came hurtling down the slope. That was enough to put the speed of light into Lucy and me and we hustled across the uneven slope, assuming Dick and Dixie were right behind us. When we reached the far side, I turned and saw that in fact, they were right in the middle of the avalanche! I immediately shouted out instructions to them as I could see the whole picture from where I was. *Get down behind a large rock—stay down—now run—get down again—duck!* Some of these boulders were big enough that I started to feel real concern that they might even break up the large boulders each of them were hiding behind. I was trying to get them off the slope, but staying in one spot didn't seem wise as the size of the boulders shooting down kept getting bigger. I could see Dixie crouching behind one big boulder, but only knew where Dick might be by the sound of his voice. The worst of the avalanche came when a boulder maybe 8 or 10 feet in size, the size of a bed that is, hit the boulder Dixie was behind. It bounced up into the air but did not break or dislodge Dixie's boulder.

This was one of those real life events that had turned into an actual life or death situation. From my safe spot, I could only watch and shout useful instructions, something I'd learned from mountaineering. It was a pretty sobering moment. I have to give credit to the quickness of Dick and Dixie following instructions and keeping their wits. Finally, after what was probably only a couple of minutes but seemed far longer, no stones were in motion. I kept on shouting, *Keep down,* just in case there were more rocks coming. After a few minutes I called, *Okay get up and run.* They both appeared like magic from behind a boulder, and raced across with the speed and grace of an antelope. To their credit, Dick and Dixie were not ashen nor terrified, but they didn't say a whole lot either. We still had quite a ways to go to get down to the road, and it helped to talk and walk off the nervous tension. We reached the road and our waiting van, where Khan the driver was napping, and then were driven back to the hotel.

Lucy: We stayed one more night in Gulmit, just to relax. Bill Hanson and I strolled down to look at an intriguing homemade rope suspension bridge stretched across the Indus River. There was absolutely no sign of anything on the other side that it could have been going to, so we called it "the bridge to nowhere." Bill insisted that I walk out on it so he could take a picture. I was dubious, being that there was a two hundred foot drop into the gorge and no sign of anyone actually using the bridge. But I thought, what the heck, and the picture is a good one because I happened to be wearing bright cherry colored pants and top, which show up nicely against the gray backdrop of rock and river.

The next day we reached Sust, the official border crossing between Pakistan and China. The following bamboola incident was later referred to by Dicky as, "Catch as catch-Kahn." Kahn, our wonderful and efficient driver, had been carrying, throughout the whole trip, a sealed envelope containing the money for the portion of our trip from the Chinese border to Kashgar. It was the Chinese equivalent of $400 per person (a gigantic rip-off but unavoidable). We went through the border formalities, met our agent with a new vehicle and used up our last rupees in a miniscule shop buying crackers and agate necklaces. Then we all got into the car and headed toward the Khunjerab Pass, when suddenly the agent started shouting excitedly to the driver to stop and turn around. It appeared that he had forgotten to get the crucial sealed envelope from Kahn. We zoomed back to the border check post and were aghast to see that our car had gone! Kahn had left, returning to Rawalpindi at top speed, impossible to catch. The six of us broke up in hysterical laughter. The alert agent however, leapt out of the car, raced across the border on foot, jumped into a white car and disappeared down the road in hot pursuit. We waited nervously for about 10 minutes, after which the agent returned waving the envelope triumphantly. He had caught Kahn, who had stopped very briefly for a snack.

With great relief, we were on our way again, passing through awe-inspiring scenery looking much like the bottom of the Grand Canyon. We were in a steep and narrow gorge with highly unstable slopes, rocks teetering precariously and shooting down in frequent rockslides. In some places, the rocks were so huge that the road was built right over them, only one lane wide. Last October, our agent told us, one huge slide blocked the river entirely so that cars were stopped and porters ferried luggage up and over the steep cliffs to be met by Chinese vehicles on the other side. The passengers, no doubt, had to proceed on foot, like the porters. Not surprisingly, the pass is closed for 6 months of each year. This road took 20 years to build and caused the deaths of 300 Pakistanis and 1500 Chinese, mostly through rockslides. Apparently, fighting sheep, high above the cliffs, sometimes causes slides. As the road started climbing steeply, we saw our first yaks and shepherds. Bill Hanson, checking his altimeter announced that we were at 13,400'. The landscape opened up with slopes now colored in ochre, burnt sienna and moss green. The river became a beautiful glacial green color with white froth, a lovely change from the gray silt of before. However, clouds were hanging low, concealing all the high peaks. The agent told us that in winter you can see many snow leopards and Marco Polo sheep. In summer, the animals go up as high as 20,000'.

The road was so steep it turned into switchbacks, and the scenery became bleak high alpine. It reminded me of Kosciusko, the highest mountain in Australia, one that you can drive all the way to the top of, as Dody, Dicky and I did back in 1953. We hit Khunjerab Pass (14,910' on Bill's altimeter), a spectacular spot where we got out to look at the small monument marking the pass.

It was windy, cloudy and starting to rain, so after taking photos we got back into the car and drove a short way down to the official border crossing and onto an unpaved road. Two smiling young Chinese men checked our passports and Bill Hanson proudly said, *Ding Hao*!

The countryside at 13,000' was a wide plain, rather an abrupt difference from the steep gorge on the Pakistani side. We arrived at Pitali, the Chinese entry check post, where officials were distinctly Han Chinese and not from western China. Here, we went through another passport check and customs and were transferred to a Chinese car and driver named Wong, with luggage in a separate car. Nearby was a small restaurant where we were offered a miraculous meal, many small dishes of freshly under-cooked green vegetables (the missing ingredient in the Pakistan diet), which we fell upon like wolves. Later, when we had reached the Pamir Plateau, we stopped at an inn by a large lake and ate another delicious lunch at an outdoor table. We were the only ones there to enjoy the spectacular view of the 20,000' mountains rising right above us.

Our new driver Wong drove us north to Tashkurgan, an ancient stop on the Silk Road where several caravan routes converged on the way to Kashgar. The countryside reminded us of Alaska—wide open, gravelly and bare—but the mountains were shrouded in clouds. The "best" hotel looked quite substantial but was unbelievably primitive—no water and no lights—and the plumbing was disastrous. We tossed a coin for the one double room that had a connecting bathroom. The Hansons thought they were lucky to have won until Bill noted that the toilet was a simple hole in the floor going down into the room below. So they ended up, like the rest of us, using the toilet (a hole in the ground) in an unlighted separate building down some stone steps and across a large courtyard. That night it was Dixie's turn to become violently ill. Too weak to get to the outdoor building, she threw up in a bucket in the corner of the room, which Dicky gallantly emptied.

The following day we drove north for eight hours to Kashgar, at the westernmost frontier of China, a key station on the Silk Road from Roman times. It still has the oldest continuous weekly market in the world, a lively center of trade for over a thousand years. We stayed in a reasonably modern hotel and went confidently to the CITS office to confirm our flight to Urumchi—on the north side of the desert—where we were to take a train east all the way across China to Beijing. We were calmly informed that our booking was cancelled because there was a large government meeting about to happen and it naturally took precedence over mere civilians. Bamboola again!

Bill: No one had any idea of how long this meeting would go on, nor seemed to take any responsibility for the fact that our plane reservations from Beijing back to Seattle couldn't be changed. Bill Hanson, being our interpreter, asked around for advice and someone suggested hiring another van and crossing between the mountains and the Taklamakan Desert, an area about the size of Germany. From there, Khotan, we might be able to find a plane to Urumchi. It was a gamble, because not only would we be backtracking but also, if there were no plane, we would have to drive for two and a half days all the way to Urumchi. Before leaving Kashgar we wanted to check out the famous market.

The next day was Sunday, which just happened to be the day of the weekly bazaar. People came from all the surrounding countryside on donkey carts or on foot, herding animals and carrying wares. The roads were jammed and not a car or truck to be seen. There were all kinds of fruits and vegetables, sheep, donkeys, horses, chickens and camels and stalls full of things like needles, clothing, daggers, halters, harnesses, wood and of course cooked food. Even though the temperature was now back around 100 degrees, the long-bearded Turks in wool caps and jackets seemed oblivious to it. The women were dressed in bright colored kerchiefs and wore gold spangles. It was all very exotic and left me with the feeling of having stepped back in time, except that these were modern times. It was a good feeling, to know that somewhere in the world things were just like they had been centuries earlier.

Lucy: The road to Khotan was supposed to be paved, but most was not so the ride was extremely rough. It took five hours to Yarkand through barren, gravelly desert marked only by telephone poles on either side, and punctuated by an occasional oasis, which always started and ended abruptly. These were watered by rivers coming from the glaciers in the Karakoram Range immediately above us. We were travelling along the route of the southern branch of the Silk Road, which went in a narrow ribbon between the immensely high mountains on our right hand side and the huge desert on our left. We had been told that the road would cross the Green Jade River, which was rumored to have real jade in it, so I insisted that we stop at the bridge and go underneath to have a look. We turned over stones in the shallow water, seeing nothing resembling jade, but suddenly out of nowhere an old crone appeared. She was carrying a dirty little bag, offering pieces of pale, translucent jade. I couldn't resist and bought a piece, as did Bill Hanson. When we got back to Seattle, Bill turned his in to a jeweler for money, but I kept mine as a reminder of the Green Jade River and the old crone.

We continued on our way and reached the oasis of Khotan at 9:30 pm. The three-year old hotel was already pretty derelict, with no visible signs of upkeep. However, though the bathrooms looked as if they dated from the 1930s, we didn't complain because there was running water, the beds were clean and there were lots of towels and even a fan. The manager was very smiley and in his weak English tried his best to take care of us. His first news was that there *was* a plane to Urumchi, but that it had been cancelled. Bamboola. We found out from two other stranded passengers that the plane had to make a forced landing in a rice paddy so all the planes were grounded for an engine check, but perhaps we'd get out the following day. To make up for it, the nice hotel manager suggested a visit to the Silk Factory. Before doing that, we told him that some of us had a yen to walk into the desert itself beyond the sight of anything but sand.

Driver Wong obligingly drove us through the richly fertile oasis watered by irrigation canals until it ended abruptly in the sand. We got out of the car and began walking, intrigued by the sight of sand dunes stretching endlessly into the distance. As soon as we started, we found ourselves followed by a little band of friendly and curious little urchins, the youngest looking about two years old. Dixie and I decided to teach them the Conga—one, two, three kick etc. They were of course delighted, and as we danced in a line along the top of some dunes, I was reminded immediately of the famous scene in the movie The Seventh Seal.

Bill: Bill Hanson was now in his glory, speaking Chinese and actually communicating with the locals. He led us to a small house on the edge of the great desert where he had heard that they made something a tourist might buy. I can't even remember what it was he wanted, only that the thing, and the small house or workshop where it was made, had a terribly unattractive smell and made my eyes water. This house was right on the edge of the Taklamakan, and we went on a short walk out into this genuine desert, which was full of large soft sand dunes. It was an incredible experience, realizing the desert ahead of us went on and on for hundreds, maybe even thousands of miles. Somewhere ahead of us to the east, the Chinese had realized how an atomic development project would be able to be kept secret, and how little damage it would do to its surroundings if some testing accident happened. The road across this section of desert was gated and barred. In addition no airplanes were allowed anywhere near that area.

After lunch at the hotel, we were taken to several interesting places, being told that Khotan was a very important station on the southern Silk Road. First we visited a jade factory, then a carpet factory, where we were served watermelon and finally, to a home based silk factory. This turned out to be a private house, with a family who did everything from growing the mulberry bushes to weaving the silk. It was like looking through a window into the ancient past, and as a matter of fact, the production of raw silk has been going on for the past 5,000 years in China. We watched the whole process in the courtyard. An old woman, the grandma I guess, was squatting on top of a clay stove, stirring a huge vat of boiling cocoons which were actually alive and jumping. The heat made the silk that was wound around the cocoons start to unravel in long threads, which the grandma then ladled up and hooked to a spindle. Below her, another woman sat on the floor turning a large wheel with a foot pedal, winding the thread around the spindle into one continuous thread. The old cocoons and cooked larvae were fed to the chickens. In another room, the silk threads were dyed and then woven on looms into various final products displayed in another room.

Lucy: The following day we went to the airport to see if there might be space on the plane to Urumchi. It was delayed but it did arrive. The airline was called CAAC, acronym for Chinese Airways Always Cancels (or Crashes), not very encouraging. We were all sitting on a long bench in the airport (the only bench) waiting anxiously for any confirmation, when a young American sat down next to me. During the long delay, I asked him what he was doing there and where he came from. He replied that he was on holiday from a small Pennsylvania college no one would ever have heard of but which turned out, amazingly, to be the Quaker college of Haverford near Philadelphia. When I told him that all six of us were Quakers or married to Quakers, he was duly astonished and quickly became our friend and ally in securing seats. He could speak Chinese and was adventuring out here in the middle of nowhere when he was turned back while hitchhiking on a truck filled with soldiers heading east beyond Khotan. Apparently the Chinese were conducting secret atomic tests at Lop Nor in the desert and it was strictly off limits to everyone not officially connected. This young man, Steven Kirrz, was going on the same plane across the desert to Urumchi, and instead of deserting us when we arrived, took us via public bus to our hotel. Urumchi, capital of Xinjiang province, is a large, industrial city and the first since Islamabad to feel modern. The next morning we got up at 8:30 and decided to go the travel agency to get the train seats we had booked, but the sour agent told us he needed four days advance notice. Bamboola again.

Bill: We wanted to be on the railroad line from Urumchi to Xian. From there we would then get a plane to Beijing. The travel agent said we would have to wait four days. Gloom. So we went down to the railroad station, which was a place of seeming chaos with screaming mobs of passengers waiting in long lines. The whole thing seemed kind of hopeless, but then our young Quaker friend swung into action, pushing his way through the mob right to the front of the lengthy line. I still have this wonderful image of him, actually having half his body stuck through the ticket window,

206

blocking all the other shouting people and getting our reservations and tickets for the actual next day. A great coup! Steven then went with Lucy and me to the CAAC office to book seats on the plane from Xian to Beijing. *Absolutely impossible*, we were told. Again, this young guy turned out to be a godsend, and somehow in Chinese explained our urgent need to get to Beijing to catch the plane to Seattle. He was so cheerful and persistent that the harassed agent agreed to call the airline in Xian. After an hour and a half of negotiation (Steven doing all the work, Lucy and I standing there trying to look important) we were told that the office was closed in Xian. We ended up spending most of the entire day at the train station with this young American, Steven, who I guess because he was a Quaker was the sort of person who wanted to be helpful and do the right thing. And by the end of the day, we had managed to get our tickets!

Lucy: We were the only foreigners to board the "soft sleeper," so-called because the Chinese had abolished classes and instead designated difference by calling them "soft sleeper," and "hard sleeper," meaning one compartment had mattresses and the other, hard wooden benches. Our compartment consisted of double-decker bunks on each side which, when pushed up, allowed room for us all to sit down. D & D and Bill and I slept in this one while the Hansons slept next door with two Chinese businessmen. Finally, the train lurched out of the station and we were on our way to cross China from west to east, a distance comparable to crossing the US. In those Communist days of the '80s, there was always a continual barrage of propaganda or loud music played from loudspeakers in every public place including trains, which were of course owned by the government. Since the noise was intolerable, Bill Hanson promptly wrenched the wires out of the wall so we could ride in peace.

We settled into our nests, broke out the fruit and cookies bought in Urumchi, and drank hot lemonade made from our lemon powder and the eternal thermos of hot water provided everywhere in China. Things even looked a bit civilized, with little lace doilies on the headrests, but the toilets were unspeakable. Then we embarked on one of our many long discussions. Bill D.

held forth on the meaningless lives of most Americans, especially the retired, rocking in their chairs by a swimming pool in Florida, the people he often referred to as "warm bodies," or "marshmallows." Dicky countered by saying that some people are happy to be able to relax and play golf after working hard all their lives at jobs they didn't like. The rest of us rolled our eyes, having heard some version of this discussion many times before.

Then we made our first visit to the dining car. The white tablecloths and pots of tea boded well for a relaxed and elegant Chinese meal. However, when the first course appeared it consisted of plate containing what looked alarmingly like a little pile of white worms or maggots in its center. They actually seemed to be moving. That was it for Dixie, Elen and me but Bill, Dick and Bill Hanson said they would try anything. The rest of the meal looked equally greasy and repulsive so the three women ended up leaving the dining car and from then on, bought jars of stewed fruit sold by women on the station platforms wherever we stopped. We also bought crackers or bread, and Dixie has a vague recollection of a cooked orange chicken suspended by its legs—tandoori? We spent three nights and four days on the train.

Bill: Bill Hanson was recovering, after feeling much deflated by the young Quaker man's day with us. Bill had been looking forward to being the China expert, guide and interpreter, and in fact basked in this for the first two days and was very helpful. Then this young American appeared—aggressive (for a Quaker), charming and fluent in Chinese and in ways of navigating their system. We all shifted our attention to Steven, who had arranged everything, and somehow this must have come across as competition for Bill. But to his credit, he cheerfully admitted that he was shown up and felt like a dragon dragging his tail. I couldn't blame him for feeling a bit downcast. I was the guy who had led all these beach hikes and mountain climbs, but here in China I was a know-nothing foreigner. I would probably have been waiting in that train station for days, not knowing what to do. Bill Hanson was very good-natured about this young Quaker guy showing him up, even joking about it later.

The train continued across the desert along the northern

branch of the Silk Road, which had been in use for about a thousand years by camel caravans. We traveled through the Gansu Corridor between Tibet and Mongolia, sometimes passing a small hamlet or shepherds with flocks of sheep but not much else. It was incredible to me, this huge unpopulated area of central China. I kept saying, "Where are all the people?" I had this image of China being one of the most heavily populated nations in the world, but here was all this empty space with not a person in sight. At each stop, some of the others rushed out to try and buy tea leaves, tea being one of the things China is known for. The train eventually went by a crumbling tower, the western end of The Great Wall, at Jiayuguang, which used to be considered the end of civilization. The Great Wall of China stretches over 6,000 miles across mountains and plains, protecting China's northern border from the barbarians of old. We saw fragments of mud walls 15 to 20 feet high and an occasional Watch Tower.

Lucy: Since the Hansons were leaving us at Xian, we had a little parting ceremony before our last day on the train. We realized this was the first foreign country we had traveled all the way across. It was especially interesting because we started at the most primitive part in the far west, where people were still living as they had for centuries, and moved east toward civilization and most of the huge population. We were now passing small, heavily cultivated fields, mud houses with tiled roofs and walled courtyards, alternating with very mountainous country and lots of tunnels. We had all been looking forward eagerly to our day in Xian when we would visit the extraordinary terracotta army of soldiers and horses buried underground with China's first emperor in the third century BC. However, we discovered the train would arrive in the evening, not early morning as we'd thought, eliminating any chance to see the terracottas, as well as any time to go to the airport to try for a booking. We only had time for an overnight in a hotel, and hope we could get a plane to Beijing in the morning.

In the meanwhile, we had all started coming down with coughs, sore throats and lassitude, but I was more severely affected than the others. We got to the airport early where we bid goodbye to the Hansons, who were flying directly to Shanghai, Bill's childhood home. At the airport, I collapsed on the pile of luggage and waited while Dixie and Bill Hanson tried to get tickets. There were no signs in English and they couldn't find anyone who spoke English. So Bill D. wrote in large print on a piece of paper our names, flight and destination, to give to the agent when they finally arrived at the head of the line. Bill handed the paper to the agent who couldn't read a word of it and threw it on the floor. Instead, he handed them a form in Chinese, which they couldn't read a word of either. Dixie then managed to dredge up some official, and after a long interval, a miracle happened and she handed us our tickets for the morning flight.

I remember nothing of the flight or of arriving at the hotel in Beijing, only that I felt sick as a dog and stayed in the hotel the rest of the day while the others went out to see the town. The next day, I woke with a headache, general aches and pains, a cough, sore throat and no energy, and stayed again in a darkened room in the dismal hotel while the others rented bikes and visited the Forbidden City and market. While they were gone, the light in the bathroom blew up which took two Chinese men five hours to fix, making the bathroom unusable. The next and last day was our planned for a visit to The Great Wall. I felt just as terrible and lethargic but could not bear the idea of missing what I was sure would be my one and only chance to see it, so I dragged myself out of bed and got into the taxi with the others. Beijing is a vast and sprawling city that took forever to cross on our 85 km drive to the Wall. On the way, I had to make an emergency stop to be sick in a ditch. Finally, the road started climbing into the mountains. A misty sky made the scene look like a Chinese painting.

Dicky had been to the Great Wall exactly 40 years before with the parents just before the Communists closed the country to foreigners. It was at that time that our father picked up a small fragment of the wall and brought it back to New Jersey to be placed in the wall of the newly built hangar. The Wall had since then become a major tourist attraction, both for Chinese and foreigners, and was swarming with people as far as you could see and crowded with souvenir shops selling T-shirts and postcards.

We walked up a long stone staircase to the top of the wall and then turned left, in order to reach the unreconstructed part. I tottered feebly up the steps and dragged myself slowly to the second watchtower where I had to lean over the side to be sick. At this point, having satisfied my urge to see one of the great wonders of the world, I decided to beat a dignified retreat. I was very glad to have seen it and collapsed in bed for the rest of the day.

Bill: The next morning we went to the airport where everything went remarkably smoothly. We were back in the modern world! Here, we ran into an American tour group clothed in polyester leisure suits displaying nametags. One particularly loud couple had the nametags of Herb and Bertha. This overweight couple, who couldn't stop talking about the souvenirs they had bought, were just the sort of people I associate with those who drive around for hours in the Sears parking lot trying to find a spot near the door. They were perfectly nice people, but seemed more interested in the souvenirs than where they had bought them, that being the Great Wall of China. And here is where I turned into that same sort of American, the type who has to buy something to prove they were there. While the others were in the security line, it came over me that I should buy a Mah Jong set, this being the quintessential Chinese game. I rushed over to an airport shop and purchased an elaborately carved Mah Jong set displayed in a wooden box. Somehow, this box slipped from my hands where all the tiles scattered across the marble floor. This provided much amusement from everyone standing nearby, including the Chinese customs officials.

On the plane ride home, it seemed like everyone on board was sick. I myself was coughing, and the rest of our group had various illnesses, Lucy being hit hardest of all. The flight attendant told us that every returning passenger from China she had talked to was sick. But we were happy to be onboard our flight home, and felt a great satisfaction at having actually made it. Considering all the bamboola of travel arrangements, unexpected delays, the language barrier, primitive hotels (especially bathrooms), bad food and sickness, we had survived this great adventure and were alive to tell the tale. I was sure that in a few years there would be reliable trains, good roads, updated hotels and modern communication and the Silk Road would become a popular tourist trip with air conditioned buses and tour guides. Happily, that era had not yet arrived and we were able to have a real adventure, one in which we ourselves did not know the outcome. Our little group of travelers, the Hansons, Peaslees, Lucy and myself, had traveled well together and overcome obstacles with good humor and no complaints. And so ended what I have come to call "An Accidental Circumnavigation of the Earth."

The world is mad with travel now—
no unknown place remains.
Perhaps Alfred North Whitehead was right,
adventure is a basic human longing.

Words on a page ensnare, stories entrap us.
Because of a poem, we go half way round the globe to ride
ramshackle boats down the Irrawaddy River.

from On the Road to Mandalay, **The Simple life**

The Race

A message burns the wires: he's had a heart attack.
My world goes black; blood plummets to my feet.
Just blocks away, the seven mile human ribbon ripples
lazily as thousands throng the streets of San Francisco
walking, jogging, joking, pushing prams. He made it
over Heartbreak Hill, past the Panhandle, into the Park
then fell. His heart stopped, full cardiac arrest, dead,
in any other time or place; but synchronicity, coincidence,
miracle or fate, whatever name we give to forces
that we cannot understand, gave him another chance.

If we lived back in ancient Greece where gods personify
those forces, ruling that one man should pay the price for pride,
another for neglect, perhaps Athena would have said
of him, It's not his time. There is something he has left undone.
In hours and days of waiting, I watch monitors and charts,
learning the foreign language of ischemia, infarction,
ventricle fibrillation, plaque and platelet—that stop
the flow of vital oxygen and blood. But other nouns

and verbs can block the pathways to the heart: moments
of our lives we let slip by through inattentive fingers,
smug confidence that makes us feel invincible.
I walk the park where flowers assail me like battalions
of wild color, hyperboles of purple, rose, magenta,
vermillion, violet and gold. Life takes me by the neck
and shakes me hard, wake up, it's right here all around you.
This time Monet and Rumi send their messages to me.

from **Migrations**

214

From Heartbreak Hill to Mandalay
by Bill

In the spring of 1995 I ran in the Bay To Breakers, a seven-mile marathon across San Francisco. I'd done this annually with Jonathan for the past few years, and it was an excuse for Lucy and me to come to the Bay Area to see Jonathan and Maryann and go to my favorite coffee shop, Café Trieste. This year I felt noticeably less energetic, but off we went when they released the hundred thousand of us across the starting line. I started off feeling I was having to work harder than usual, but made it over Heartbreak Hill, and somehow fell into jogging and talking with another runner who had also been a military pilot in a different war from me, a sort of compatriot. My next memory is waking up in a hospital bed.

I had had a cardiac arrest, and was only alive because two doctors, John Kane and Dean Ornish, were jogging a short ways behind me when I collapsed. I had apparently been clinically dead for about five minutes when these doctors got my heart beating again. In fact, Dean Ornish wrote about the episode in his next book and printed Lucy's poem in it. Two other runners also had heart attacks in this race and both died. I called the head of Lakeside School, Terry Macaluso, to let her know I wouldn't be back at my job the next week and also that by some strange coincidence a former math student of mine, Scott Merrick, would be doing my heart bypass surgery. She asked if he had been a good student and I replied, "I hope so." The heart attack effectively ended my teaching career, although Lakeside did create another job for me, giving me the title of Socratic Mentor, which I loved.

I gradually recovered over several months, but eventually got restless. The doctors had given me a number of restrictions in terms of diet and exercise, even driving, which I found onerous to follow. In fact, I don't think I did follow most of their restrictions, which seemed overly cautious. So in October, I suggested to Lucy that we go to Southeast Asia, an area we had never been to. She jumped at the idea and we came up with the idea of a two-month trip. We only had vague sorts of plans, and after spending a couple of days in Bangkok, we then headed north and spent a month staying in and around a small walled city in the north, Chiang Mai. Here, we happily met up with Janet Sturgeon, who we had shared an apartment with in Nepal, and who became a lifelong friend. She was doing some fieldwork for her thesis and was able to introduce us to various local areas and people. We had some small adventures, like taking a long wooden boat up a river, a boat that came equipped with a lounging guard with a submachine gun. After several happy weeks up in the north, Lucy said, "Let's go over to Burma and take a boat down the Irrawaddy River, like in the old Rudyard Kipling poem."

We both remembered all the songs and stories from the English colonial days in India and Burma, and could belt out the song, "On the Road to Mandalay," about British soldiers going north. Lucy's idea was a romantic one, to take the freight boat that went down the river from Mandalay to Rangoon. Incredibly enough, Mandalay is the only place on the whole of the Irrawaddy where there is an actual bridge, and this river runs 1,400 miles across Burma. Everywhere else you cross it by small boats. The Irrawaddy is a muddy brown river, maybe a hundred yards wide, with a strong north to south current of several miles an hour.

We flew to Mandalay from Chiang Mai in an elderly propeller passenger airplane. The airstrip at Mandalay was a concrete main runway, and then dirt and gravel. After landing, we were directed to a tent like shed, the border crossing into Burma. Inside was a military person, a soldier that is, who had a submachine gun laying on the table next to him. He didn't speak English but checked our passports for Burma visas. Lucy had made all the arrangements and everything seemed in order. In fact, a happy comforting event of our arrival was that there was also a woman holding up a sign that said, "Mr. William Dougall," who happened to be the tour guide that Lucy had drummed up. She took us to our hotel and asked how much money we wanted to change, and then got out large stacks of worn looking Burma paper money. We had no sense of what things were going to cost, so we changed a lot of our American dollars to be safe. It was a physically large amount of Burma paper money that we ended up owning.

We stayed in Mandalay for a couple of days, being tourists, wandering or being pedaled in rickshaws around the old walled city and down along the banks of the river to watch the bustling life all around us. As our first day got along towards evening, people started taking their shoes off and putting them in a sack on their back. I theorized that they were making them last longer due to less use. Suddenly it began to rain, and not the light drizzly rain we get in the Northwest. This rain came down in torrents, filling the streets almost knee deep in water. The cloudburst lasted for maybe an hour, and then stopped just as suddenly. The water in the streets went down, people put their shoes back on and went on about their business.

We were on a strict time frame because Burma was run by a military junta that allowed you to stay for no more than two weeks. We went to meet a man who arranged nautical affairs on the river, and who also spoke good English. We told him about our being familiar with the old Kipling writings about Burma, and Kipling's stories about the riverboat. He set up our passage for the journey on the river from Mandalay to Rangoon, and even came to see us off the next morning and wish us well. This first river boat took us to the remains of a walled city called Pagan, dated back to about 1100 AD, where we stayed a few days riding around the temples and ruins on rental bicycles. The next stage of our journey was on a commercial riverboat that was, as Lucy would say, a whole different kettle of fish.

We arrived at the riverbank at 4:30 a.m. and after walking up the plank onto the boat, we went to a tiny ticket office where the tickets were sold by candlelight. After looking at the primitive conditions on deck, we decided to buy a cabin for $60. There were sleeping bodies piled all over each other, including mothers and babies, some under a crude mosquito netting, with baskets and parcels of all kinds. On the main deck were the huddled masses, and we had to use flashlights to push through them and all their chickens and other things that squawked which we couldn't see in the dark. We were then ushered upstairs where the foreigners belong. The boat was completely run down—loose boards underfoot and paint almost totally peeled off. Our first class cabin consisted of two wooden bunks, with what I guess were supposed to be mattresses but felt like cloth covered boards, and a small dirty shelf. There was also an equally crude and basic eastern style toilet, a hole so foul-smelling that by the end of the trip we could barely enter it without literally gagging.

Lucy and I felt sort of deflated, having just spent what would be considered a fortune in Burma for our first class cabin. We decided to go look for food, which meant going back to the lower deck and through the hordes of people and chickens. At the end of the open deck was the food department, which consisted of a small counter where two open fires in large oil tins were burning, shooting sparks all over the wooden deck. Tea and bread were produced for us, and then a man ringing a bell literally chased us back upstairs where the foreigners belong.

As the boat went down river we passed two ancient capitals with pagodas and stupas, mainly white and one huge white domed stupa 300 meters high. We also passed numerous boats, mostly small gondola type ones with tall steering oar in the back, the steersman standing, and various types of passenger boats. At the first stop, the wharf was packed with a bustling crowd of people selling stalks of bananas, basket trays of samosas, pork rinds, oranges, bread, etc. All of those street sellers jumped on board to try to peddle their wares. Lucy and I bought bread and cake, those seeming to us to be the safest things to eat. The boat trip down the Irrawaddy was about as exotic as you can imagine, basically teeming with life and activity of all sorts, and the sense that nothing had changed here for a thousand years or more. There were also several monks on the boat and I actually saw one enjoying a cigar. That sort of poked a hole in my view of monks and my picture of them as living a very ascetic type of life with no worldly pleasures allowed.

We finally got off the boat in a small town where we would stay for a few days. Over the course of our several days going down the Irrawaddy, we had made friends with the people who ran the riverboat. They ended up walking with us along the bank of the river and Lucy and I were pleased that these river boat people had come to really like us, not seeing us as tourists but as interesting people. It seemed like a wonderful compliment. I think it was Lucy that really touched these people. She seems to reach people in no matter what country, probably because of her genuine Quaker respect towards strangers. She managed to make friends with these river boat people, in spite of the fact that she'd come down with a bad case of dysentery and had to spend most of her time in the awful toilet in our "first class" cabin.

We registered at the foreign tourist hotel on the bank of the river, said a great friendly farewell to the riverboat friends, and went up to our room. Lucy immediately took a shower and went to asleep. I sat around looking at guidebooks and, feeling restless and not ready for sleep, went out on the town. I walked around and soon saw that inland from the river, it was a modern small city, with paved streets and modern autos being driven around. I wanted to see some folklore kind of things, so I walked around and found a giant, maybe fifty-foot high, statue of the Buddha. This one was not illuminated by any lights, so it seemed really mysterious and appealing in the semi dark away, from streetlights. I then wandered around the modern, quite up to date parts of the city, and got myself in what you might call a bit of trouble a couple of times.

Military people who had overthrown democratically elected governments ran Burma, and they seemed to control things by having secret police out in the population in ordinary dress. One of my incidents was at a large modern roundabout with a big statue of a man on a horse waving a sword on the center island. I was standing on the walk outside the circular street admiring it, when an ordinary looking Burmese man came up to me and said in good English, but in sort of a pushy tone, "What are you doing looking at that statue?" He pulled out a badge showing he was a military person, so I had to think fast. I somehow knew the statue was of the local hero who had driven out the English, but also knew he was now in disfavor, so I came up with something about how I was impressed by the size of the statue. I told him that I didn't know who the statue represented, but was interested in the stonework. I even asked what kind of stone it was. I somehow sensed I was being checked up on so I decided to keep talking, and in fact talked for so long about mundane things that this secret military agent literally said, "I will let you go," and then told me where to walk to get to the train station. I think he was as relieved to be rid of me as I was him.

With some relief I thanked him and headed for the train station and my next incident. Naturally, I wasn't going to get on a train and leave, being that Lucy was asleep in the hotel with dysentery. But I really did want to find out when trains left for Rangoon, so I walked off without another look in the direction of the statue, and without any looks back at the secret agent. It was about 10 p.m. when I reached the train station. Lucy felt strongly that we should go to the actual town of Rangoon, being that the song lyrics say, *"Can't ya hear their paddles chunkin' from Rangoon to Mandalay?"* We had discovered that the song got it wrong and that the paddles can't chunk from Rangoon to Mandalay because the Irrawaddy River doesn't actually go through Rangoon, and instead flows out to the ocean some miles to the west. So I thought it would be a good idea to check out the times of the train and report back to Lucy. There didn't seem to be any windows or official looking personnel. Soon, with my aimless sort of motion around the train station, another secret agent who also had a pistol in his belt accosted me and wanted to know what I was doing.

I said as calmly as I could that I must go back to my hotel, and that my wife and I would come in the morning and take the train to Rangoon. This secret agent, like the other one, seemed to speak English comfortably. In retrospect I can see myself as being a loose cannon to them, a foreigner wandering around and not on a tour. I also didn't have any baggage, and that would have been another incriminating sign to a suspicious secret agent. So I started talking again, telling him about my wife's desire to take a riverboat trip from Mandalay to Rangoon and mentioning the song sung by

Sinatra. If I had been thinking clearly, that was the worst association I could make to a native Burmese man, being that Kipling, who wrote the words, was writing about how the British troops came to Mandalay to return it from Japanese to British rule. Fortunately for me, the secret agent didn't know the lyrics to the song, but did know and like Frank Sinatra. He asked me to sing the song but I told him I couldn't remember the words, and instead hummed it. Finally, happily, he said, "I will let you go," which seemed to be the thing these secret agents said to foreigners like me. I walked off as calmly and in as businesslike a way as I could muster.

The next morning we took the train to Rangoon and took a taxi to the old hotel on the waterfront whose name I remembered from reading about the English colonial days. I liked to stay in hotels that had a romantic association. When we first arrived in Nairobi Kenya, before I got the job up north we stayed at the Norfolk hotel where Ernest Hemingway had spent some time. I liked the idea of sitting somewhere that a person from history had also sat, and having a sense of what they might have seen and felt. So I was very depressed by the sight of the waterfront side of this multi-storied hotel, which had been modernized and charged a staggering amount for a room. We hunted around and discovered that the backside of this hotel, which was indeed from the good old days of colonialism, was enormously different in price from the front side, and we got a room that overlooked the city. Lucy relaxed and did some reading while I went out and wandered around. I saw the waterfront and ships, went into the streets and found a small sort of locals book shop where I struck up a conversation with the proprietor, who spoke English, and bought a small old book in English about the city.

The next day, we took a taxi and went to the famous Golden Temple, the Schwedagon Pagoda, a giant round stupa that was located on a hill on the far side of the city. This temple was believed to be anywhere from one to two thousand years old and supposedly contained relics of four previous Buddhas. The area was located on top of a small rise or hill, and the base level of the hill had covered tunnels with stores along the sides of the tunnel selling stuff aimed at the local population. The different tunnels all came out up on the higher level of the hill. We emerged into the open with this enormous graceful stupa, and small open air shops around the sides where Burmese tourists go to see the temple and buy local things to take home, like small statues of Buddha. The actual stupa itself was incredible, covered in gold plates and imbedded with thousands of diamonds and rubies. Kipling had visited the temple in the late 1800s and described it like this: *"Then, a golden mystery upheaved itself on the horizon, a beautiful winking wonder that blazed in the sun..."*

On our third day in Rangoon, since our tourist visas had run out, we went to the modern airport and took a plane back to Chiang Mai, Thailand. We took a taxi to our hotel, where we picked up our stored bags, and then went back the train station. Our next goal was an island off the coast of Thailand where we had heard you could rent grass shacks on beautiful undeveloped tropical sand beaches. We stored the majority of our luggage at the train station down south and took a train to the far eastern part of the coast. Just across the border were the famous ruins of Ankor Wat, but Cambodia was in violent turmoil and was too dangerous for casual tourist travel.

Lucy and I walked down to the commercial waterfront and got a ride on a boat, which was a cross between a tug and a supply boat for offshore islands. Free wheeling young tourists, mostly young American and Europeans bumming around, had given us tips on how to get out to these islands. The boat finally stopped at an island we had been told about, Koh Chang, and we got off and took a taxi over to the west side. There was a sort of colony aimed at stray tourists, and we rented a grass shack up on stilts on a beautiful sand beach. It was exotic and wonderful, and we sat in the ocean in chairs and felt like real tourists. The temperature was very hot and humid and the seawater was warm, not what you'd call refreshing. Nevertheless, it felt wonderful to be there on this tropical island.

One night, after Lucy got up to use the hole in the ground toilet, she woke me up with a sort of sibilantly hissing, "Bill! Bill!" I came awake slowly, being that it was hot and sultry, even in the middle of the night. I heard her voice hissing, "Bill! Come here!" until finally, I grumblingly did. There on the wall, in the light of her flashlight, was the biggest spider I have ever seen; at least as big as my hand, and there was Lucy saying, "Do something!" So I got my shoe and smashed the spider flat and brushed it off the wall, while Lucy made muffled shrieking types of sounds. And then I went back to bed, feeling a little like an important warrior.

At the end of our stay on Koh Chang, Lucy and I started feeling a little low, as though we'd gotten the local version of tourista. It took away our energy, and the stages of our trip back to Bangkok became increasingly uncomfortable. By the time we got on the 16-hour plane flight to Los Angeles, we were both pretty sick. This was something far worse than tourista because it involved a fever and aching joints, and was actually painful. Lucy was stricken in a pretty bad way, and in fact was so ill that when the plane arrived in L.A. they had to bring a wheelchair to get her off the plane. I called daughter Sorrel from the airport and she said, "Get her to the hospital!" in a commanding sort of way, so I did. It turned out that we had dengue fever, a pretty serious tropical disease, and one that you can actually die from. The other name is "break-bone fever" because it feels a little like your bones are being broken from inside.

Jonathan swung into action and told me to go ahead home to Seattle, and that he would fly down to L.A. and accompany Lucy back. Because I was pretty sick myself, I took him up on the offer. Lucy spent months getting over dengue fever, and it was a real shock to someone like her who naturally has so much energy and enthusiasm. Even so, neither of us regretted our magical trip to Thailand. Like most of our adventures, we made things up as we went along. I came up with the romantic notion that if it hadn't been for my heart attack ending my teaching career, and my innate restlessness and chafing at all these doctor restrictions, we might never have gone to Thailand and Burma. Our trip had been of the most exotic kind and our friendship with Janet, who had shared her flat with us in Kathmandu, was reinforced. Lucy was especially pleased to have taken the boat down the Irrawaddy River from Mandalay to Rangoon. Like me, she has a romantic streak.

Someone must always stay at home
to hold the center
like the hub of a wheel—
a pot of soup on the stove,
warm lights and a crackling fire
for the wanderers,
the dispersing family,
the unexpected guest.

The old are the memory keepers
who tell our stories over and over
so they last through the generations
and are carried on by the young
to be retold,
rewoven and reinforced
like the spider's web,
by unshakable links
that will always bind us
to our center
and to home.

from **Holding the Center**

Singin' songs of glory, don't you weep after me...

British Columbia
and
Home

The Simple Life

Amidst our many possessions, we dream of the simple life
without the time-consuming daily choices
without the wants that become needs
without constant noise and news.

We dream of time for nature and the spirit
for friends and family enjoyed at leisure
where life is purer, say,
in a little cabin in the woods.

But it turns out that the simple life
is a lot of trouble, almost a full time job—
what with chopping wood, hauling water,
battling insects and clearing brush.

And so, as I grow older, I look out my window
at the rushing creek and roughly mowed lawn,
reading Walden, comfortably ensconced
with a cup of hot tea and some buttered toast
on my eighteenth century chaise longue.

Our Cabin in BC
by Lucy

Back in the late sixties, we had a dream of having a little piece of wilderness where we could create something totally our own. Perhaps Bill always had the idea from a line in his favorite Yeats' poem, Innisfree; *And a small cabin build there, of clay and wattles made*...and I too yearned for a primitive place untouched by civilization. We settled on British Columbia, where true wilderness still existed but also seemed close enough to drive to from home. We loved our life in Woodinville, of course, but wanted an empty spot where we could do something our ancestors had—like build a log cabin on a wild river.

Our good friends the Stadlers and the Smiths had similar ideas and we thought that if three couples went in on it we'd be able to find a larger piece. So, in the spring and summer of 1970, we began to explore BC—first the area near Vancouver, and then farther north because wilderness was scarce near any big city. This gave us an excuse for many lively weekends, driving in our Carryall to explore areas east and west of the Fraser River. We always chose scenic picnic spots on rivers or lakes, or near waterfalls where we watched local Indians netting salmon as they swam north to spawn. We followed the Fraser River Canyon past Lytton, Lillouet, Spences Bridge and Williams Lake. On our final trip, Bill and I were alone and we decided to drive as far north as Prince George and then south to McBride, a small town between the Cariboo and Rocky Mountains, to see what was in that area.

We found a real estate agent who showed us various properties, none of them interesting, so we gave up and headed for home. Feeling rather dispirited, we were driving south along the Yellowhead Highway when we saw a small handwritten sign saying, *For Sale*, but were too tired to stop. A few miles later, we decided to take one more chance. We turned around and drove down the small and very primitive dirt road until it reached a diminutive trailer, the size of a shoebox. We knocked, and were welcomed by an eccentric oldish couple called Loy and Alberta Hanson. They were extremely garrulous, as though they had not seen another human being for years, and were crammed into the tiny space leaving just enough room for us to sit on a small bench. "They must really like each other," Bill remarked many times as we got to know them later on.

There was still plenty of light in this northern latitude so Loy insisted on taking us to survey the half section (320 acres) they wanted to sell, keeping one quarter of the section for themselves. They told us they were planning to build a house on their remaining quarter, but they never did in any of the 30 plus years we knew them. Besides, once we had bought the place, they found it very lively and entertaining to waylay our family and friends as they came through on their way down to the cabin, often trapping them for hours talking on and on. Pete has a vivid memory of himself and Lucy Anne arriving before the rest of the family and spending several hot and uncomfortable hours in the tiny trailer. When they finally managed to extricate themselves, Loy commented, "You city folk are always in a hurry."

Loy owned an antique tractor, which he called his "pusher." He had used it to clear the postage stamp area for the shoebox trailer and also to build an extremely rough, mile long track down to the Fraser River. It was clear when we got there that this was not the place to build a cabin. The river was wide and fast flowing and totally unsuitable for children. And so we were very happy to hear from Loy that he wanted to show us the nicest spot on the whole property, the one that he had originally picked to build their own house. It was perfect—on a bluff just above King Creek, a small tributary of the Fraser. It had a sensational view of three peaks in the Caribou range and the creek was glacial green and crystal clear; ideal for swimming, rafting or just playing in. Little did we know at the time, but this land was to become one of the most important places in our lives for the next nearly 40 years.

Loy and Alberta Hanson were as thrilled as we were to shake hands on the deal. This half section of land between the Cariboo and Rocky mountains was a dream come true. Mostly forested, with only one large clearing (an alfalfa field), the property teemed with wildlife; bear, moose, cougars, and any number of other creatures. The creek was filled with spawning salmon in late summer, and trout all year round. We were astounded at the asking price: $18,000 for 320 acres! It seemed too good to be true. We couldn't wait to share our discovery with the Stadlers and Smiths and drove home, brimming with our good fortune.

In July of 1970, the Dougalls, Stadlers, Smiths and Peaslees, with all our many children, drove the 600 miles up to McBride. We gathered in the alfalfa field and set up what we called "Tent City." Loy and Alberta had mentioned that July was a bad time for mosquitos and we had come prepared with mosquito spray and even head nets. Even so, we were totally unprepared for the swarms of whining insects that attacked so fiercely we were all driven to distraction. Although the temperature was the 80s, all of us had to resort to wearing long sleeve shirts, gloves and scarves. And since there weren't enough head nets to go round, we had to take turns.

The first order of business was to construct a mosquito proof tent with overlapping doors of netting, and build a large table and benches so that most of us could fit in as a temporary refuge. We also built a "biffy" behind the stacks of hay bales. Then we set off on an intense bushwhack down to the building site on King Creek, with 14 children and their parents being attacked on every side by armies of mosquitoes. This is what finally did in the Stadlers and Smiths, who came to the instant decision that Bill and I were welcome to buy the whole piece of land, which, with a loan made to us from my mother, we did. We were very happy with this outcome since we could then invite family and friends to visit at any time without consulting anyone else, which we did for many memorable years to come.

That first summer, we did a lot of exploring. The children discovered the remains of an old saw mill further up on King Creek. A huge pile of sawdust was slowly crumbling into the water, remnants of some logging operation in the past. The creek was a constant source of interest, especially for the young. It was also cooler, and relatively free from mosquitos, so they spent quite a lot of time splashing around there. Although the water ran fast, it wasn't deep (except in a few spots) and there were sandbars and small islands to explore. A great source of excitement were the animals tracks left in the sand. We often saw fresh bear prints and occasional cougar tracks. It was a thrill to be in the true wilderness, and we never grew tired of it. Another source of fascination for the young was the story of the horse runner's daughter.

Loy and Alberta shared this story with us one night when the came down for a visit to Tent City. Apparently, in 1915, a horse runner (as they were called back then) and his wife and young daughter settled on our land. They had swum 20 horses across the Fraser River and then laboriously built themselves a cabin, with no outside help at all. They built their cabin on an even smaller tributary that drained into King Creek. That winter was one of the coldest on record, with temperatures dropping to 60 below zero. One by one, the horses all froze to death. And then their 11-year-old daughter contracted one of the many diseases of the day and died. The husband hacked a shallow grave into the frozen ground and buried her, then built a picket fence around the grave. The horse runner and his wife were so broken hearted they left and never returned. Loy and Alberta told the children the approximate location of the grave and eventually they found it. The picket fence was still standing.

When we told Loy we wanted to build a log cabin, he said, "Then you must meet Heinrich Gunster, our German logger friend who lives up the road a couple of miles. He's just the man to talk to." Heinrich had built his own large and beautiful log house, so precisely that you could not fit even a knife in between the logs. He appeared in the alfalfa field a day or two later with his wife,

Terry, an ex-hairdresser from Los Angeles. She was dressed in a fluffy blouse and impeccable coiffure and to our astonishment had become, after moving to BC, an incredible wilderness wife. Her garden was huge and abundant and her energy boundless. She cooked and canned and froze for Heinrich, their three hearty sons, the farm hands and any guests, like us, who happened by. She milked the cow, made butter and cheese, ice cream and yogurt and when she had a spare moment, made soap. Her dinners were healthy and bountiful and Bill and I especially loved her rich desserts. Both Heinrich and Terry were non-stop talkers as well as do-ers and gave us a wonderful inside view of pioneer life.

Heinrich cut down the number of logs Bill wanted and transported them to the new site. He then taught us how to peel off the bark, cut a long groove down one side so we could fit them together like Lincoln Logs, how to turn them over with a peavey, how to split shakes from giant cedar stumps for the roof, and many other logger tricks. The process of building the cabin lasted for several summers. Having learned our lesson about mosquitos, we began going up in early August (when the weather dried out) and staying for the month until Bill had to get back for school. An endless procession of guests would appear, often staying for a week or more. All members of our immediate family, plus friends and relatives from around the country, participated in the slow process of putting up our log cabin.

We slept in tents, built a cook shack, and every summer, a new bridge across King Creek to the gravel bar that in later years we christened "Girl Island." This was a fond reference to the fact that while the men were slaving away at some project or another, the womenfolk would retire to Girl Island to escape mosquitos, read, chat, eat, and generally enjoy ourselves. After the cabin was completed, we then built a barn. The Schneiders and Dick Barkle gave one of their unforgettable Barkle-Schneider bashes in various spots on the property like the gravel bar, where Barkle dropped the steak he was going to grill (we ate it anyway) and left out the dessert (which our dogs found and devoured). This wild party lasted for hours and included playing round robin Ping-Pong in the upstairs of the new barn.

Over the years, many memorable events took place at our cabin in BC such as Jessica B. and John Cell becoming engaged on King Creek, and announcing the happy news to the family at dinner. One year, after we left for the summer, Jill and cousin Sharon, around 16 years old, decided to spend a few weeks alone at the cabin. They had their own set of adventures, including being chased by a moose down the driveway. The children (and some adults) often picked up inner tubes in McBride, and after being dropped off at a bridge on the main road, tubed down the creek until they reached the cabin. Evenings were spent eating lavish meals, playing games, singing, dancing, and all forms of general hilarity and laughter. The annual Perseid meteor showers (August 11th) always coincided with our time at the cabin, and a group of us invariably would troop up to the alfalfa field where we lay on blankets and tarps and marveled at shooting stars raining across the northern sky. There was something magical about being truly *away* from civilization—and this was even before the days of cell phones and other technology.

We also invited people up to the cabin in the winter, including groups of Lakeside students. Winters in BC are quite harsh; the temperature is routinely below zero with two or three feet of snow on the ground. It was usually impossible to drive down the driveway, which left us with the option of hiking or skiing down to the cabin with packs on our backs. On one memorable trip, the car a student was driving had it's windshield shattered, leaving Bill to drive the whole 600 miles back in the bitter cold with no windshield.

In later years, as the younger generation's lives became increasingly busy, Bill and I spent most of our month at the cabin alone. It was a new phase of our lives and we enjoyed the peace and solitude, often working on our own projects (me, poetry, Bill, puttering) and reveling in our wilderness retreat. The only thing standing in the way of paradise was Bill's ongoing war with the squirrels. The bench Bill built leaning against a tall tree with the view of the three peaks was our favorite sitting spot. For some reason, one particular squirrel had it in for Bill and began a guerrilla war specifically targeting him. It would drop cones on

Bill's head whenever he was sitting there, but never on me. The squirrel carried on his attack up into the big barn where Bill had installed a laptop computer on a home-built desk. There was no tree for the cones so the squirrel started nipping at Bill's ankles, to his mounting irritation. The war culminated one evening when somehow, the squirrel made his way into the cabin and literally dropped a stick of wood on Bill's head while he was lying in bed. Bill leapt up in a fury, grabbed a hammer, and began chasing the squirrel all around the cabin. I continued reading my Tolstoy book by candlelight, trying to ignore Bill's shouts and exclamations as he crashed around in the dark downstairs. Finally, I heard a large thunk and a crunch. "Got him," Bill said.

The last trip to our cabin in BC was a couple of years before Bill died. It became clear on that trip that the effort of primitive wilderness life, even in August, had become too much for us to handle. So, with great reluctance, we came to the conclusion that our main priority was to make sure the land was preserved in perpetuity. To that end, Bill and I sold the property to our nearest neighbor, Wes Keim, with the understanding that our family would have lifetime rights to use the cabin. But somehow, after Bill died, none of us had any interest in going up there, so important was his presence and buoyant energy that gave it life. But I will always treasure the memories of those blissful days on our little piece of wilderness, and in the small cabin we built there, nestled between the Cariboo and Rocky mountains.

What about rescuing our friends?
Forget that, Bill says, I'm going after the boat.
He races downstream and disappears.
I race after him, terrified.
It is now pitch dark. I call frantically
over and over until a disgruntled voice
comes out of the blackness—
The foldboat's gone.

We turn back, crawling
on hands and knees
through dense brush, slithering over logs,
sliding into the water, looking
for a place to cross to get to our car.
I can see nothing but Bill's white shirt,
hear nothing but his grunts and curses
and the roar of the river and finally,
hours later, a cry of triumph—
The bridge!

Thus ended his one and only practice
in a foldboat before running the rapids
of Hell's Canyon on the Snake River,
the first man ever to do so.

from Once in a Foldboat, **The Simple Life**

Losing the Chestnut on the Thompson River
by Lucy

While riding up on the train to our cabin in BC in the 1970s, we observed that the train followed the Thompson River for most of the way between Kamloops—where we left our car—all the way to Valemount. This intrigued Bill, who immediately conceived the plan of canoeing down it. We had no canoe, but did have time because it was summer vacation. Bill inquired around Lakeside and found that one of his good friends, Gary Maestretti, was the proud owner of a highly prized Chestnut canoe. We knew nothing about Chestnut canoes; neither that they were very beautiful and exceptionally well made, nor that Teddy Roosevelt had purchased several for a South American expedition in 1912. In any case, Bill persuaded Gary to lend us the Chestnut for our trip, failing to mention our canoeing skills (or lack thereof).

Bill picked a train station on the upper reaches of the Thompson as a good launching place, with Kamloops as the ultimate destination to the south. We enlisted another couple, Steve and Barbara Yarnall, who were always game for any adventure and who actually owned a canoe. We packed some supplies and boarded the train north, noticing as we looked out the windows that the river was exceedingly high, even over its banks, and running fast. Bill cheerfully pointed out that we would arrive at our destination that much sooner, and the rest of us dubiously agreed. We disembarked at the preplanned station and walked over to a little store with our gear to make some inquiries. When we told the locals where we were planning to put in they exclaimed, *Good heavens, not there or you'll go right over a waterfall!* They told us the place to put in was Mosquito Flats, a couple of miles downstream, and they would be glad to give us a ride. We were happy to avoid going over a waterfall, although the name Mosquito Flats implied it might not be an ideal spot for assembling all the gear and getting ready for the expedition. Unfortunately, it lived up to its name.

We launched the canoes and set off in the high water and fast current, delighted to be on an adventure. The main highway followed the course of the river, although quite high above it (as we found out later). Both canoes were catapulted down the river through several minor riffles, which gave us some needed practice. The Chestnut performed well in spite of Bill's and my own inexperience, and handled the rapids with ease, often pulling well ahead of the Yarnall's own canoe. The day was beautiful and we enjoyed every minute. Near dusk, we stopped to camp in a clearing next to the river where an old farm had once been. It had been a long and gratifying day.

As there were no guidebooks at the time, there were only two problems we knew of. The first via Duke Watson (who had canoed that section) was a series of whirlpools on the north side of Kamloops. The other was a waterfall a certain distance downriver from our current camping spot, where the Mad River flows into the Thompson. We knew about this waterfall because we had driven right by it a number of times, often stopping to look because it was quite dramatic. We were all fairly nervous about this dangerous spot and, having only a vague idea how far away it was, were constantly on the alert for the telltale roar. As we proceeded, Bill and Steve periodically stood up in the stern of each canoe, shading their eyes against the glare and searching for signs of the Mad River. As for myself, sitting in the bow of our Chestnut canoe and well ahead of the Yarnalls, I began to wish we had borrowed an old clinker instead of this streamlined vessel which was now shooting down some serious rapids.

By now, water was flying up and splashing over the bow and very quickly Bill and I found ourselves sitting up to our waists. I was getting extremely nervous (and cold) and therefore was immensely relieved when my ever-optimistic husband decided it was time to head for shore. The Mad River was now in sight, and the roar of the approaching waterfall could be heard over the rapids. However, our canoe—half full of water—was so heavy it was very hard to steer. In addition, we did not know any canoe strokes other than forward and backward. We paddled vigorously, both of us on the left side, hoping our efforts would get us over to the bank before the unthinkable happened and we plummeted over the waterfall. Had we known the draw stroke, it would have made a world of difference.

Eventually we got close enough to the bank for Bill to grab an overhanging branch, believing it would stop the canoe and we could get out. Instead, because the river was in full flood, the branch simply pulled Bill out like a cork, leaving me stranded in the swamped Chestnut. *Jump!* Bill shouted. I jumped, without a moment's delay and swam the short distance to shore. When I got there, Bill had already disappeared. The Yarnalls, who had watched this episode from the other shore, paddled across as fast as they could. We decided that Bill must have climbed up the steep bank to the road in some daring attempt to catch up with the canoe by hitching a ride, so we scrambled up the bank and did the same.

My adrenaline was running quite high at this point; we had escaped certain death going over the falls, yet we'd lost Gary Maestretti's prized Chestnut canoe. The Yarnalls and I hitchhiked down the highway in various stages, eventually crossing the river on the bridge at Vavenby. Much later, when we reconnected with Bill, we discovered that he had had an eventful time hitching rides down the highway, periodically rushing down to see if he could spot the Chestnut, then back to the road for another ride, all the while carrying his paddle because he had the rather insane idea of stopping in the middle of the Vavenby bridge and jumping down into the canoe as it went past. The bridge turned out to be at least forty feet above the river and I was extremely relieved that this ill-conceived idea had come to nothing.

We stopped at a little old-fashioned store in Vavenby and asked the storeowner if he had seen Bill. He answered laconically in a slow drawl, "You mean the guy carrying the paddle? Yes, I saw him go by a while back." We asked if there was any chance of a canoe washing up somewhere? He replied, "Oh yes, most things wash up on Martin Sands' sandbar downstream a bit." The Yarnalls went back for their canoe while I somehow made my way down to the sandbar. And there it was, stuck in the sand, the once beautiful Chestnut looking rather the worse for wear. Bill was there too, elated that we hadn't lost the canoe altogether. He concluded, by that measure, that the day had been a success and was already untying the supposedly waterproof storage bags that were still attached by lines to the Chestnut's gunnel. We spent the rest of the day, eventually joined by Barbara and Steve, spreading out the drenched contents on the nearby grass. This included the tent, which we pitched right then and there on Martin Sands' sandbar, and where we spent the night.

The final day we paddled down toward Kamloops with some foreboding, remembering the whirlpool warning. It just so happened that Duke Watson was going to be camping on an island just north of Kamloops and had told us he would keep an eye out for us in case our timing coincided. Bill and Steve, meanwhile, had been standing up in the sterns of our respective canoes scanning the now much wider river for the fateful whirlpools. On Bill's only previous canoe trip, down the Fraser River, Duke himself had been caught in a whirlpool. Bill often described the vivid image he had of Duke's canoe being sucked under vertically, while Duke held aloft the precious maps until all were completely submerged. Fortunately, Duke had survived that near-fatal encounter, and was now the figure we saw on a small island ahead, vigorously slapping his face and arms against mosquitoes. He waved us over.

We were reluctant to join the mosquitoes so only stopped for a moment.

"Where are the whirlpools?" Bill asked.

Duke smiled and calmly replied, "You've just come through them."

At Kamloops, we loaded the canoes onto our waiting cars and drove the six hours home, weary but somehow elated. Bill spent a considerable amount of time cleaning and washing the Chestnut canoe before returning it to Gary. To Bill and me, the dings and scratches told an exciting story, and we felt this made the canoe even more interesting and special with a real romantic appeal. Whether Gary shared our sentiments, we'll never know.

On Top

After the long, long walk
at last on the mountain top

where my pillow lies among
the craggy spikes of rock ,
where the stellar jay flaunts
its extravagant blue feathers

and I'm looking at the sky,
time falls away into blue space—
only this moment exists

as ephemeral as a dream.

from **Home & Away**

Three climbs and a Fire
by Lucy

Bill and I brought Lakeside students up to the cabin in British Columbia on several occasions. On one of these trips (which included Dick and Dixie) our closest neighbors, Loy and Alberta Hanson, introduced us to a family of Mennonites. They were extremely hospitable and invited all of us to come over and visit them. The visit itself was very interesting, and a revelation to the students to see the three daughters all sitting primly in a row on the couch in their long skirts and head kerchiefs. When they were asked why they dressed that way, they answered without embarrassment, "for modesty." Both parents were there also, of course, and when we told them where our cabin was, the father volunteered that the mother had climbed to the top of the highest of the three peaks across the Fraser River. Naturally, Bill regarded this as a challenge.

When we got back to the cabin that night, Bill proposed to Dick and Dixie and me that we climb the same peak the following day. Those three mountain peaks were not exceedingly high, nor covered in snow in the summer. But for Bill, the prospect of repeating a climb that had been done by a Mennonite woman in a long skirt was too much to resist. And so, when the rest of us declined for various reasons, off he went, and climbed up to the top of the peak alone. When he returned, he reported that there was a beautiful lake up there that you could not see from the cabin—a wonderful place to camp.

The following summer, Bill and I and Dick and Dixie, plus their two children and a friend, made the long drive to McBride once again. On a beautiful August evening, we were sitting on the bench we had built and gazing at the three peaks across the Fraser River. Bill had the habit of wanting to climb any mountains he could see, and when we had scouted a site on which to build our cabin, the dramatic view of these spectacular peaks had taken hold of his imagination. Now, thanks to the Mennonite woman who had been the inspiration for his first climb the previous summer, Bill proposed that our group should climb the highest peak again—and this time camp out on the lake he had discovered. On Bill's solo hike, he had found a vague sort of trail but wasn't sure he'd be able to find it again.

The next day, the seven of us piled into our truck and drove to Dunster, a nearby farming community. As there was no regular bridge, the only way to cross the Fraser River and reach the mountain was over a train trestle. Someone had told us it would be a good idea to make sure the morning train had gone by before starting to cross. We were all extremely apprehensive, as there was no definitive way to be sure the morning train had come through and no timetable to consult. And so we picked our nerve-wracking way along the single narrow track, navigating the cross ties, trying to ignore the huge and highly visible Fraser River roaring below and hoping we could make it to the other side before we met the next train head on.

We were deeply relieved to reach the far side safely but once there, it soon became apparent that Bill's vague sort of trail had disappeared altogether. We milled around, hoping to find some route up the mountain, and eventually resorted to climbing straight uphill. We thrashed our way through the trees and bushes, all of which seemed to lean down to create a nearly impenetrable wall, thwarting us at every step. A long time later the bushes gave out and the ground leveled off at a small and beautiful lake, just as we had been promised. Here, we set up camp and spent the night.

The next day Dixie and Jessica decided to stay and relax while the rest of us—Dick, Bill, Cutts, Danny and I continued down one slope and up another until we had set foot on all three peaks, fulfilling Bill's goal of climbing every mountain he could see from the cabin. But when we finally got back to Dunster (after another anxiety ridden walk across the train trestle) another mountain loomed into view. It reared up behind the gravel pit, a dark finger beckoning to Bill, yet another goal to reach. But this next mountain had to wait, for we were due to leave the cabin shortly and the Peaslees were headed home.

The next summer, Bill's first order of business upon our arrival in BC was to ask Loy and Alberta Hansen, from whom we'd bought our half section, about the mountain behind the gravel pit in Dunster. They told us that a nice young couple named Tom and Andrea had built a cabin up there. They were what people back then called hippies; very laid back and friendly, and who had made it clear that anyone who climbed up the mountain was welcome to use the cabin. Also, the owner of the old fashioned general store in Dunster told us that it was equipped with sleeping bags and a lantern. Bill was somewhat disappointed, as the hike did not sound particularly challenging. But Debbie Nicely (a teacher from Lakeside) and I were pleased that we wouldn't need to carry much equipment.

We started up the trail on a warm morning in August, confident and assured, with only daypacks to weigh us down. The trail quickly disintegrated into a rough track, and soon we were bushwhacking through dense brush, slapping at mosquitoes, our bare arms scratched and bleeding from brambles and sharp branches. At one point, near a dry lake, the trail disappeared altogether. After much traipsing around and beating through the brush, we finally stumbled on a small structure—the hippie couple's cabin. Debbie and I collapsed gratefully on the stoop while Bill went to scout around the area.

The very small cabin had a bunk on either side with a little shelf at the far end holding a lantern and a guest book for visitors to sign. We cooked supper outside on our camp stove and settled contentedly into the extremely thin cotton sleeping bags, leaving our packs outside leaning against the cabin. Debby slept in one bunk and Bill and I in the other. Bill turned off the lantern, but it would not go out and simply flickered unsteadily and made me nervous. After I had complained one too many times, Bill finally said, "Just open the valve and let the gas out." I obeyed, and instantly shooting flames erupted, jumping onto the cloth hangings on the cabin walls. I leaped out of bed, grabbed the flaming lantern and carried it frantically out of the cabin and flung it as far away as I could. My arm and hand were burned quite seriously and, as the nearby lake was dry, I slapped on cold dirt to cool them down. I then dragged our packs away from the structure and collapsed on the ground.

Meanwhile inside, Bill and Debby were trying vainly to beat down the flames, which were burning up the sleeping bags and other cloth insulating the walls. They finally gave up and ran outside, also barefoot, having not an instant left to carry out our boots. When we were all safely outside we pulled out of our packs something like rain pants to sit on— since we had no tent or mats or sleeping bags—and watched the cabin burn down to the ground.

We sat up all night, not speaking, each left to our own accompanying anxieties. We had burned down a stranger's cabin and there would be some reckoning for that. As well, we seemed to have an unfortunate history that involved burning other structures; our own family home (thanks to Bill) and a cabin on Vancouver Island. I had a deep foreboding, anticipating how we would explain yet another fire, another serious mishap with an element I myself had always had an innate fear of. How many times had I admonished my children to be careful with matches, with stovetops, with ovens, with lanterns? The burns on my arm and hand seared unmercifully as we sat, waiting for dawn and the charred remains of Tom and Andrea's cabin to be fully revealed.

At first light I saw three figures appear over the edge of the steep slope. They turned out to be Tom himself, and two friends, immensely relieved to see us alive. They had seen the fire from the valley below and were extremely concerned, not about the cabin, but about whoever had been in it. We were so happy to see them, and deeply relieved that our explanations and apologies could be dealt with immediately—and received with such grace and humility.

Bill managed to make us rough protection for our feet by cutting up one of the sleeping bags he had dragged out of the cabin and wrapping pieces around them with a bit of cord. We walked all the way down the mountain with our foot wrappings— much like Indian moccasins. I was in a sort of daze of pain and exhaustion, and when we reached the car, Bill drove me to the hospital in McBride. As soon as I sat on the table I promptly fainted from the burns and delayed shock. However, the doctor bandaged me up and all was well.

We had assured Tom that we would come back the next summer and help him build a new cabin, which we did. He told us we had actually done him a favor because he had found a much better location on a nearby lake that was permanent instead of seasonal. We built the new cabin in his driveway and sent it up the mountain in sections by helicopter, which took several trips. Bill and I, Debby, Tom and Andrea and several of their friends hiked all the way up the mountain and when we got to the site, immediately began to assemble the sections into a new cabin. Once completed, we had a joyful celebration with food and wine. Somehow, the guest book with a record of all who had stayed in the old cabin had survived. Beside our names, we added an addendum: *Accidentally burned the old cabin to the ground.*

Being Together

The getting it all out
the putting it all away
the wheel of life ever turning

for every ritual of the year
for every gathering with friends
for every day with the family.

The needed tasks
that make it happen,
have always happened

because we have always known
that in the end, what matters most
is being together.

from **Home and Away**

Thanksgiving in Woodinville
by Peter Berliner

I spent last Thanksgiving with 32 relatives, 14 family friends and seven ghosts. The place was packed. It wasn't at all like the Thanksgivings I had while growing up. There was no carefully set table, no cloth napkins in rings, fine china nor silver candleholders. Instead, we ate at tables built from plywood and metal legs. Each was 8' by 3'. Arranged end-to-end, they were enough to seat 50. There were all the traditional dishes—roast turkey with gravy and stuffing, mashed potatoes, green bean casserole, creamed onions, sweet potatoes, kale salads, and more laid out on more tables, from which the diners served themselves. There was no television in the basement broadcasting football. And no dozing off in the warmth of the living room after the pies were served. There were no awkward silences or family spats. There was no time for that.

Thanksgiving at the Dougalls is a busy affair—a succession of activities from afternoon to night, a ritual that has been cultivated and refined over more than half a century and passed on to four generations. The Dougall Thanksgiving tradition dates back to 1962 when three young married couples—Bill and Lucy Dougall, Anne and Dave Stadler, Bill and Elen Hanson—and their children (12 in all), gathered together at the Dougall's home in Woodinville, Washington. Bill and Lucy had bought the place in 1957, before the sprawl from Seattle began to encroach. At the time it was a remote, pastoral refuge with a white farmhouse set above the banks of a Little Bear Creek, a pristine waterway where salmon spawned and herons came to feed. There was a rope-swing that Robbie, at age eight, put up by shimmying out on an overhanging branch of an old willow tree. The rope was knotted about 20 feet over the creek and was long enough to allow those who dared to swing over the creek and jump to the other side. Mustering the courage to leap off the rope at the other side of the stream was a rite of passage for both young and old. It required a certain amount of agility to land without injury. Only one broken leg was recorded, but there were bumps and bruises too numerous to recall.

Most of the property—eleven acres in all—was in wetland or forest. But there was room for a pasture, which, over time, fed horses and ponies, an occasional cow, and sheep (including a ram named Bernard). The lawn was expansive enough for games of tag, kickball, croquet, and Capture the Flag. Adjacent to the old barn (now dilapidated beyond repair) was a murky pond. Moving to Woodinville may have seemed an odd choice for easterners like Bill and Lucy, who had migrated to Seattle from New Jersey after Bill was hired by Boeing. But both loved living amid the trees and beside the water's flow. Bill, an engineer at first and later a physics teacher at Lakeside School, was a doer. He had energy to burn. When he wasn't hiking, canoeing, or climbing, he was building or fixing things. In time, the chicken coop was torn down, and its foundation converted to a roughhewn tennis court. He built a garage and shop, and eventually, the green barn. Every spring he dug a garden and planted nine bean rows as homage to the Yeats poem, *The Lake Isle of Innisfree*.

Bill and Lucy had a facility for making friends, whom they invited to their home for spirited discussions about books, politics and the state of the world over good food and (many bottles of) wine. Their friends, Dave and Anne, Bill and Elen, Annick and David Smith, Dave Nash and others, had what Bill described as lots of enthusiasm about life. They were willing to try anything that was adventurous, silly or fun. This group became the core of the Thanksgiving gatherings replete with food and drink, fun and games, laughter and moments of reflection, sadness and joy. Over the years, as the children grew up, got married and had children of their own, and as new acquaintances and holiday orphans were encouraged to attend, the size of the group kept growing. I went to

248

my first Dougall Thanksgiving in 1971, two years after I married Bill and Lucy's eldest child, Lucy Anne. Then, as now, the order of activities was pretty much the same.

2:00 p.m. Cars roll down the gravel lane, crossing the wooden bridge to the Dougall property. Family and friends bearing appetizers, dinner dishes and desserts, crowd into the house, filling it with chatter and laughter. It quickly becomes crowded with people, particularly close to the long butcher-block counter where appetizers are set out. The participants (sometime as many as 50, or even 60 in total) range from babes in arms to nonagenarians. There is much whooping and exclaiming and hearty hugs (Dick Levin being, by all accounts, the leading hugger) as family and friends arrive.

3:00 p.m. The noisy chitchat is interrupted by an announcement of the imminent game of Baseball Golf. The captains and team rosters are named. In spite of nearly universal reluctance to leave the pleasant warmth of indoors, everyone dons coats, hats, scarves, raingear, and if fully prepared, rubber boots. Dean Ballard puts on his hip waders in anticipation of pond wading or creek crossing. Ready or not, everyone is herded outside. It is gray, and raining and cold—typical November weather. But at least it's not snowing.

3:20 p.m. By tradition, Bill Hanson was always the one to take the pre-game photo. Many of his group photos, which date back to the early 60s, are posted on the living room wall. This year, Rowan takes on that thankless but essential task. That done, the teams coalesce and the game begins.

Baseball Golf was invented by Lucy Dougall's father, Amos J. Peaslee (AJP), in the 1930's. It was often played at The Farm, the family's homestead in Clarksboro, New Jersey. AJP loved games of all kinds and was a continual source of energy and invention. He created Baseball Golf as a way to work up an appetite for Sunday dinners that followed Quaker meetings. It was played with as few as three people or as many cousins, aunts and uncles who were on hand. To play the game, goals were set up a couple of hundred yards apart. A member of each team began in turn by throwing a softball in the air and hitting it as far as possible toward the goal. Then, other members of each team took their turn at finding the ball and advancing it toward the target. It generally took between six and ten strokes to reach the goal. Then the process began again. In addition, AJP was sure to include some unusual routes that required the players to hit the ball over or through various outbuildings, which at times resulted in broken windows.

Bill Dougall thought it would be great to incorporate Baseball Golf as part of Thanksgiving in Woodinville. There was ample acreage, and any number of people could play. He particularly liked that it could be played in rain, snow, sleet or cold, or a combination of all three. Various wrinkles were added over the years. Targets (garbage can lids or buckets) were hung from tree branches, which meant at times that batters had to sit or even stand on a teammate's shoulders in order to attain the goal. Courses were drawn through standing water and across creeks. Rules were added. *A ball must travel at least the length of a bat. Backward hits do not count. You must hit the ball with a foot in the spot where the ball lay.* Even if where it lay was on the ice or deep in mud. It sounds quite simple. However, throwing a ball into the air and hitting it can lead to some erratic outcomes. As the games became competitive, there were relentless accusations of rule bending and questionable score keeping as teams vied for the shiny plastic trophy that Bill purchased at a yard sale.

But in truth, any drama stemmed less from the competition than from the real possibility that a small child would walk in the way of a bat or that the crowd of people who were blithely milling about in the midst of the game would be gob smacked by an errant softball. Indeed, there has been blood. Once, Rowan was hit in the face by Linnet's backswing. Sorrel hit herself in the mouth with her own bat. Elen Hanson took a blow to the ribs. Lucy Dougall swung a bat that was so slippery with ice that it flew out of her hands and hit Elly Kauffman on the head. Elly was not seen at a Dougall Thanksgiving again for twenty years. Other Thanksgiving injuries unrelated to Baseball Golf also occurred. Among them, Jill falling from the barn loft and bursting her kidney and Dave Stadler tripping on his way out the door and ending up at the ER. Still, as Bill Dougall often said, a Dougall Thanksgiving is statistically safer than driving down the freeway.

Thanksgiving weather in the Northwest can be hypothermic. Once in ten years, it lands on a perfectly lovely day. But more often, it rains or snows. Sometimes the pond freezes over, allowing a batter to walk onto the ice. As with most things, there is a correlation between the severity of the conditions and the endurance of memories. It is assumed by the Dougalls that anything that is hard to do and involves some measure of misery, is more likely to be remembered than things that are easy or comfortable and, therefore, is of greater value. It is not enough to venture outside on a wintry day when, given an option, we would gladly choose to stay inside. It's imperative to have to overcome any number of obstacles: a muddy pond, a running stream, a swampy field, or a briar patch, in order to locate an errant ball or find footing for the at bat. Often, instead of ending the game after the third target was reached, Bill had the teams race to the final goal, which happened to be a deteriorating old boat built by Bill and his brother. It turned a brisk walk through the fields into a lawless race in the dark.

5:30 p.m. The players return to the house full of energy and exhilaration from having survived the cold. There are last-minute food preparations amid the chaos. This year, we are greeted with Nick's hot mushroom soup, artfully made and served in small paper cups, *amuse bouche*, accompanied by Shelby's *gougeres*. After a bit, Sorrel, Cutts and Callie (or Dick Levin in years past) pick up guitars and begin singing. Others join in. It is a warm-up for the more extended session to come. In time a parade of people laden with bowls and platters of food, make their way to the green barn—a metal, utilitarian outbuilding about 100 yards from the kitchen. Nellie and Jonathan have artfully used bits of ribbon, candles and greenery to transform the large utility shed into a sparkling palace—or at least a suitable venue for dining. Plates and cutlery, bottles of wine and water await us. We fill our plates and find a place to sit. Then, without fanfare, we delve into our food and enjoy the people around us. The conversations are cheerful and there is more than enough for everyone.

As the meal progresses, I look up from time to time at the photos of those with whom we once shared Thanksgiving but who have since passed away. The ritual "Raising the Star" for anyone who died in the past year began after we lost the first of the elders. It seemed a fitting way to honor the generation that established the Thanksgiving tradition, by lifting a star to the heavens (or in this case, the rafters of the green barn). We have raised the stars of Amy Levin, Elen Hanson, Dave Stadler, Bill Hanson, Bill Dougall and Dick Peaslee. This ritual has the effect of making us feel that they are still with us, and somehow enjoying all of the merriment from above. In recent years, under the creative direction of Rowan and Callie, the honoring ceremony has been accompanied by tributes both sublime and ridiculous, music, light shows and skits. It is followed by an opportunity for anyone who wishes to share their thoughts. This year, a star is raised for Dick Peaslee to the accompaniment of *The Age of Aquarius,* highlighted by sharing the kinds of jokes that Dick loved to tell, including ones provoking laughter or groans, or a combination of both.

Dinner is generally interrupted by a series of toasts. Bill Hanson was known for his long rambling ones that often alluded to the wisdom of Lao Tsu, the Quran, the Bhagavad Gita or the Tao of Pooh. Even toasts by people less erudite, convey both comic and heartfelt gratitude and thanks-giving. After the toasts, some return to the house for coffee and the like. Others stay in the barn to break down the tables and clear out a space for a bit of exercise to ward off the lethargy that comes from feasting.

7 p.m. Round Robin Ping-Pong, as we call it, is a game in which each player serves a Ping-Pong ball or returns it, then moves in a circle around the table. It was first attempted at Lucy's childhood home, The Farm. Each player gets to have three misses before being eliminated. No matter what age, no one gets a break. Pretty soon people start dropping like flies and the circuit around the table becomes a race. The line gets shorter until a handful of players are madly dashing round the table, slamming paddles down, and volleying the ball amidst raucous cheers from the sidelines. The final two players have to take turns serving the ball, then running to the other side of the table and returning it to the other player. Whoever wins two of the three final points is the winner. Most often it is John or Nick, but sometimes it is Brighton, Linnet, Nate or somebody unexpected, like Caroline. Then there's a round of one miss and you're out (*One and Done*) which gives everyone another chance to win but doesn't last nearly as long.

In some years, the game is followed by the infamous Blow Ball. This game requires people to divide into two teams (up to 10 or 15 per side). Each team crouches on their knees on the long sides of the Ping-Pong table. A ball is placed in the middle of the table, and everyone begins to blow at the ball as hard as they can in an effort to push the ball off the other side. It is basically played until people begin to fall by the wayside due to hyperventilation or their knees giving out, whichever comes first. It is a game in which Dick Peaslee was the putative champion.

8:00 p.m. After the barn games, the crowd troops back down through the dark to the main house for dessert. The potluck desserts are always a hit, especially Lucy Anne and Linnet's chocolate wafer almond cheesecake, Pat Grave's chocolate mousse (except the year she brought a low-fat version after Bill' heart attack), Jill's pies, and lots more.

8:30 p.m. Another round of songs, led and played by Sorrel, Cutts and Callie. Gideon accompanies on his guitar. Sorrel is unabashed in leading the singing. Certain members of the group can really belt it out. Bill Dougall, Dick Levin, Anne Stadler, Lucy Dougall, Rowan, the Hansons and Dean Ballard especially. The rest of us follow along as best we can. This year, before the singing starts, we are treated to a semi-impromptu flute trio by Melinda, Wil and Cordelia. Any and all talent is celebrated.

We sing a sampling from what is called the "Good Old Songs," beginning perhaps with *This Little Light of Mine*, which brings to mind The Weavers. We might go on, depending on

Sorrel's inclination, to *Sixteen Tons* (a la Tennessee Ernie Ford), *Take me Home Country Roads*, or *Down by the Riverside*. Other favorites include *The City of New Orleans* (as sung by Arlo Guthrie) and Paul Simon's *The Boxer*. More playful songs include *O Bladi O blada*, *Happy Together*, *Charlie and the MTA* and *Those were the Days*, with people like Lucy Dougall, Lucy Anne, Jessica, Callie and Rowan shouting, stamping feet or doing the Can-Can. Bill Dougall was known to lead a train of people on top of the tables while singing *When the Saints Go Marching In*. We also sing one of Sorrel's originals, *Tubal Caine Mine*, based on a Thanksgiving trip to the Olympics up a treacherous logging road, in which Sorrel decides to ride with Bill Hanson *"to be on the safe side,"* and Bill Dougall leans out his window at the most precarious moment to shout *"Isn't this great!"*

9:30 p.m. By now the desserts have been laid to waste. The little ones are starting to fade. Some of the guests have begun their long trek back to the city. But often, there are many who are reluctant to leave. They might stay until the very last song, and sometimes we add a game or two. This time it is one in which two or more people act out an adverb "In the Manner Of." But for many years, we played a Dougall version of charades in which we divided into groups with the direction to come up with a theme—historical or literary—and pantomime it. Most often in three acts. Props and costumes were permitted, and all manner of treasures from the Dougall's travels abroad were repurposed for the plays, whether a WW2 gas mask, an African spear, a Scottish broadsword or a kangaroo skin. The actors weren't permitted to utter a sound, but the audience was more than welcome to hoot, holler and try to make sense out loud of the spectacle they were watching unfold. Some of the memorable skits performed over the years included *The Rise and Fall of the Roman Empire, The Seven Deadly Sins, Famous Assassinations in History* or *The Odyssey*, all mimed and performed in an assortment of theatrical head gear, to the great hilarity of all.

As I write this, it sounds incongruous. The idea of fifty or so friends and families spending a long day's Thanksgiving together in close quarters without eruptions of anger, remonstrations or resentment sounds practically un-American. Doing so for more than fifty years is incomprehensible. It wasn't as though these families were different than others. All of us at times, had suffered terrible or terrifying challenges, and the kind of misery that is bound to beset you if you live long enough. But these things do not readily surface on a day in which, by picking up a baseball bat or Ping-Pong paddle, a turkey drumstick or the melody of an old familiar tune, you can vanquish your cares, at least for a day.

The Thanksgiving that was hardest for me was in 1986. After 15 years of marriage, Lucy Anne and I decided to divorce, but we hadn't told anyone, neither our children nor our parents. We put off the announcement until the day after Thanksgiving. We would have one more Thanksgiving as a family. Throughout the day, the decision weighed heavily. I lasted through Baseball Golf, dinner and Ping-Pong. But I had to beg off before the desserts, and went home alone. Divorce can be a terrible thing, especially when children are involved. Tomorrow our lives would change forever. We would get through it. So would our children. But it hit me square in my heart that my loss would be compounded by severing ties to the Dougall family, along with the traditions of Thanksgiving, Christmas and other family events.

Fortunately for me, the Dougalls do not sever ties with people they care about. Even after the divorce was final, I continued to be embraced as part of their family—by Bill and Lucy, and by Lucy Anne and her siblings, Robbie, Jonathan, Jill and Sorrel. Not everyone knows this, but when a family is divided, it can also grow. I married Melinda two years later. The Dougalls all came to the ceremony. Melinda has become as much a part of Thanksgiving and other family traditions as any family member. And we are not the only ones. Others have continued to come, post-separations, and at times with new partners or spouses. It is further evidence to the power of tradition, even amid turmoil and change.

As rote as it may seem, the Thanksgiving tradition is also dynamic. Expect the unexpected. One year, Aaron Stadler brought a film crew from KING-5 TV, to do a feature on Baseball Golf. Several years ago, Rowan began engineering extended length music videos, shot entirely on Thanksgiving Day and enlisting everyone in the cast. Out of the workings of his inner genius, he created *Thanksgiving—Gangnam Style, That Turkey Talks Cray, Pedestal Pete* (my personal favorite) *and Westside Whip/Nae Nae* (starring Raina and Dean Ballard). All can be viewed at *You Tube/Rowan North/Thanksgiving.*

10 p.m. Before the day winds down, there is always time for two more songs. The first is Bill Dougall's favorite, *When I'm on my Journey.* Bill is no longer with us, but like the others for whom stars have been raised, is never far from our thoughts. We recall that he loved to sing and loved even more the idea of people singing together, and that without fail, when camped on a mountain slope or a wilderness beach, he pulled out a harmonica to play this mournful tune, and at parties or family gatherings, he busted out singing:

> *When I'm on my journey don't you weep after me*
> *When I'm on my journey don't you weep after me*
> *When I'm on my journey don't you weep after me*
> *I don't want you to weep after me.*

There have been times when we have sung it soulfully, like the hymn it was intended to be, or exuberantly, like an anthem. But since Bill died, it has become difficult to sing it at all without shedding some tears.

Before departing, we sing *Auld Lang Syne*, for ourselves, for loved ones who may be far away, and for the ghosts among us. We begin by standing in a circle, kids in the middle, and clasping hands. On each verse, we push in toward the center and out again, over and over, singing loudly and with great joy and enthusiasm. It is a fitting end to a day spent in the company of old friends and family. Only then, being on the verge of exhaustion, do we call it a night. Yet even as I head down the highway on the long drive home, I am looking forward to Thanksgiving at the Dougall's next year.

The Pond with Bill

I thought they would go on forever
those days of wild adventures and excitement
teeming with children, animals, friends and family,
gradually mellowing into evenings
sitting by the pond
sipping wine in slow delight
and gratitude for our rich life.

The benches now are empty, the table bare
but in the picture gallery of my mind
we sit there still and will,
as Burns wrote in our favorite song,
While the sands o' life shall run.

   from **Home and Away**